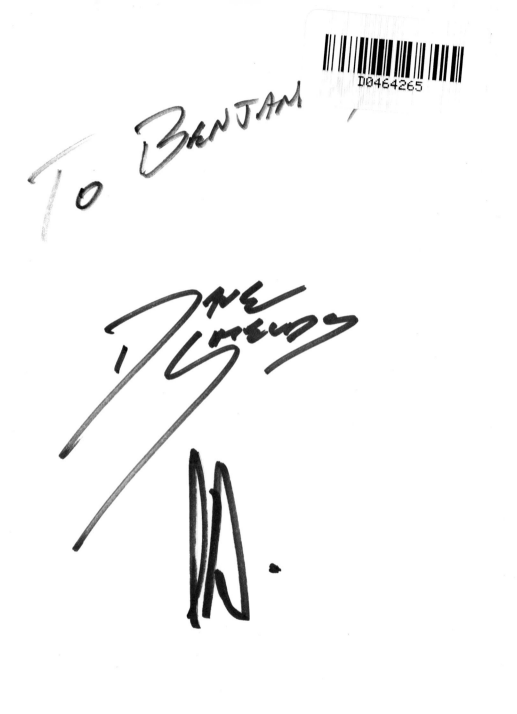

To BENJAM...

Tour de Life

From Coma to Competition

Tour de Life

From Coma to Competition

Saul Raisin

with

Dave Shields

Three Story Press

Salt Lake City
2007

Library of Congress Control Number: 2007901404
ISBN-13:   978-0-9748492-2-5
ISBN-10:   0-9748492-2-7

Published by **Three Story Press**
P.O. Box 17141
Salt Lake City, UT 84117

Manufactured in the United States of America

For Mom and Dad,
My best friends.
... Saul

Co-Author's Note

Often when I read a "true story," I find myself wondering how much poetic license the author took and why. I want the readers of this book to know up front that I did take limited license, and I want to explain my reasons. I hope you'll agree the purposes were legitimate and that my alterations don't diminish the remarkable nature of the story.

The most important change involves conversations in France between Saul's parents and his doctors. Language barriers made communication incredibly difficult for both parties. Their attempts to communicate about Saul's very complex situation were slow exchanges involving translators, diagrams, and lots of patience.

Instead of trying to re-create the challenging accents with techniques like phonetic spelling, I partially adapted the English translations of Saul's French medical records as dialogue. While the result isn't a completely accurate record of what was said, I believe it's the best method to convey the confusing nature of these exchanges while also providing the reader with a record of what the doctors were attempting to tell the Raisins.

Other alterations to the story are minor. For instance, the Raisins gave me information about all the events in this book, but I added details to fill out some scenes. Saul and his parents have shown intense determination throughout the writing of this book to tell their story as accurately as they possibly can. They worked very hard to reconstruct the timeline and recall the details of events that occurred while they were under great duress.

I'd like to thank the Raisin family once again for allowing me to help tell their inspirational story. Any inaccuracies in the final version are my fault, not theirs.

Sincerely,
Dave Shields
April 2007

Part I – Into the Fog

Day 1 – Tuesday, April 4, 2006

Yvonne Raisin stepped around her kitchen island and dropped into a chair at the table beside her husband. "I have the worst feeling inside, Jimmy, like something's trying to tell me it's a bad day." Uncomfortable premonitions were unusual for her. She tended to see the world from a sunny perspective.

Jim laid aside his Dalton Daily Citizen sports section. The headline celebrated the Atlanta Braves opening day victory in Los Angeles. He patted his wife's hand. "Worrying won't accomplish anything. Put your mind on something else for now." He spoke in his usual, calming drawl.

"You feel it too, don't you?" Yvonne heard even more desperation in her expressive Southern accent than she'd intended.

Jim patted her hand again.

She appreciated her husband's show of strength, but Yvonne knew him far too well not to see right through it. The calm, workmanlike approach he brought to everything from paying the bills to riding his bike was slightly off kilter. Today his sturdy frame had a bit of uncharacteristic sway. His mind was obviously racing.

Jim was so different from her in his approach to the world, though their vision was very much the same. Maybe that's what made them so strong together. To strangers his exterior could be deceiving. Where she was emotional, reactionary, and gregarious he was collected, introspective, and quiet. Jim tended to stand back from the crowd, arms folded or hands in his pockets, watching. Yvonne, on the other hand, was a small and agile woman, always in the middle of things, whipping others into a frenzy and livening up the party. At fifty years old his hair had grayed a bit, while hers was still jet black at forty-nine.

Reaching into her black, leather purse, she grabbed her cell phone. She flipped it open, hoping to discover the text message she'd been waiting for. Maybe her attention had been distracted for a moment and she'd missed the ring tone announcing its arrival.

She looked at the display, just the familiar photo of the two of them standing on either side of their son Saul with their arms comfortably draped about each other. Jim's face glowed with pride, while Saul looked striking in his Tour de Georgia "Best Young Rider" uniform. At the age of only twenty his time had been better than every rider in the competition younger than twenty-three. That day in April 2003 had been a watershed moment for Saul's burgeoning cycling career.

For one thing, it was the first time his extended family accepted what he was doing for a living. Many of them imagined him as a playboy who was simply avoiding college. He stunned them by proving himself at this major international event that just happened to travel through their own back yards. As Saul stood on the stage receiving his giant check along with kisses from the podium girls, even longtime acquaintances stood with mouths agape.

Saul's grandmother said, "All this time I thought he was just avoiding college. I didn't realize Saul was this good. I'm so proud of him."

It also earned him a spot on the USA Under 23 Development Team, the break that led to him being noticed by the elite Pro Tour teams. Saul's contract with Crédit Agricole, one of France's most prestigious cycling squads, had been the ultimate result.

Bicycle racing had opened up such a world of possibilities to him. Along the way he'd blossomed as a young man. But oh, the risks. At times like this Yvonne wondered if they were worth it.

Below the photo the time stamp rolled over to 4:00 PM. It was ten at night in France where Saul was racing in the Circuit de la Sarthe.

"It'll never ring if you sit there staring at it," Jim said.

Yvonne looked into her husband's deep brown eyes. "Saul should have texted us hours ago. He ought to be in bed by now. Why doesn't he return my messages?"

Jim put a comforting hand on her cheek. "He will, Mom. Obsessing won't make things happen sooner. Maybe he dropped his phone and it broke. Now quit worrying."

Yvonne nodded. Still, Saul had never been anywhere near this late before. After every race he always sent the two letter note: "OK." Only now did she recognize how much she'd come to depend on it.

She switched the ringer onto vibrate and wrapped her fingers around the phone. No way was she going to miss her son's call.

Jim sat beside her, now leafing absently through a real estate magazine. He tapped his finger on a floor plan. "I keep coming back to this one."

Yvonne glanced at the page. Her heart accelerated. He was pointing to the model she'd already fallen in love with. Last night she'd dreamed of watching sunsets from that wonderful balcony and of entertaining friends in the adjacent great room. She'd even imagined where all the furniture would go. She hadn't told Jim her feelings because she was hesitant to suggest spending more than they'd agreed.

The sale of the family business, Raisin Textiles, had been finalized December 31, 2005. That left them both unemployed, thrilled at the prospect, and enthusiastically adjusting to early retirement. They'd worked long hours for many years, and though they weren't quite as secure financially as they'd hoped to be, they were comfortable. Now they could travel when they wanted to, and they could choose to live wherever it suited them.

They'd already decided on the neighborhood. A condo on the Chattanooga River Walk would merge the best of all worlds. It would give them fantastic access to bike paths, shopping, and lively downtown events, plus they wouldn't be too far from either of their extended families in Dalton. Most of all, though, a condo meant freedom to visit Saul in Europe at the drop of a bicycle helmet. No lawn to mow, no pets to feed, no worries at all. Until tonight, it had only been a matter of finding the right property.

"I can tell you love this one. Want to make an offer?" Jim asked.

"Really! You're serious? Of course I do. It's my favori—" The cell phone's vibrating ring coursed up her arm like an electric shock.

Yvonne flipped the cover open and looked at the display. An incoming call from a number with a European exchange. Why wasn't Saul using his own cell phone like always? He knew as well as she did that the toll on this sort of call would be three times more expensive. "Hello?"

"*Bonsoir*, Yvonne."

The voice belonged to Saul's team manager, Roger Legeay, the top man at Crédit Agricole Cycling. He had only called Yvonne and Jim once in the two seasons their son had been on his team. That was two months ago to congratulate them when Saul won the toughest mountain stage in the Tour de Langkawi. Yvonne knew the team boss called only if the news was big. "How are you, Roger?"

"It is Saul I am calling about. He has crashed."

Yvonne felt a wave of nausea. "Oh no."

"Don't panic. It is maybe not as bad as you imagine," Roger said.

"I hope not." Yvonne trusted Roger because Saul had only good things to say about him. Still, Roger's English was weak, so communication could be tough. "What's he broken this time?"

"A collarbone, a rib, and a shoulder."

"Oh Lord." It surprised Yvonne that her first thoughts were of Saul's disappointment. She knew by now that broken bones heal, but he must be incredibly upset with the fitness he'd lose. He'd trained so hard through the winter and spring, and now all that effort would be wasted. Several weeks earlier Saul had called her to promise that the best was yet to come. He'd been putting out 410 watts sustained on climbs more than an hour long. He'd recently undergone fitness testing with remarkable results. A trainer measured his lactic threshold on the slopes of the Col de la Madone. Lactate is produced by every exercising muscle. The threshold is the point at which absorption can no longer keep up with production. Pain is the result, and this pain eventually forces the exercise to stop. Unlike VO2 Max which measures a person's ability to consume oxygen and is fairly stable over time, lactate threshold is highly trainable, though natural ability also plays a critical role. It's one of the best measures of physical fitness.

The drill was to climb a specific section of road at a set effort level, prick the finger, and measure lactate, then increase the effort by twenty-five watts and climb again. At 200 watts Saul measured only half a millimole of lactate per liter of blood, a reading far below average. At 250 watts his lactate climbed slightly but didn't rise in subsequent tests until he put in a 375 watt effort. That time he measured out at two point five millimoles. The tests continued with surprisingly little increase. With an amazing 525 watts of effort, Saul rose to only four millimoles. The trainer had never seen results like these. The lactate should have climbed more steeply and then peaked. He expected measurements in the teens at minimum by this point. Even setting lactate aside, few athletes could maintain such high wattages over a test of this length.

"Can you ride it at 550 watts?" the trainer asked.

Saul descended the road again and rested in preparation for the test; then he powered up the hill. When he finished, the trainer pricked his finger, ran the test and then looked at the results incredulously. "Impossible."

"What does it say?" Saul asked.

"Three point four millimoles of lactate per liter of blood. That's a lower number than the previous test. Lactate should always go up with effort, never down. Not only that, you're approaching one full horsepower. Men are not supposed to be as strong as horses."

Saul smiled.

"Ride it again. Full effort this time," the trainer said.

With no need to watch his power meter Saul put everything he had into the pedals. Not only did he set the best time for any athlete present, but he poured out over 550 watts sustained for almost six minutes.

The trainer ran the test. "Just four millimoles. I've never seen anything like this. You have no lactate threshold!"

"I feel strong," Saul said.

"You're too strong," the trainer said. "You've peaked too early. You have the fitness right now to win the Tour de France. You must take a week off the bike, maybe more."

Saul had followed the advice, but his fitness remained high. As a result, he was slated to start his first Grand Tour, the Giro d'Italia, in May. It was the first of pro cycling's trio of three-week races. Saul was optimistic he could produce a great result in Italy, possibly gaining an opportunity to race in cycling's most prestigious event, the Tour de France.

"Just a little bit more to tell," Roger said, bringing Yvonne back to the present. "Saul has cut on his forehead and he has much road rash."

Road rash referred to the skin abrasions that resulted from sliding on asphalt. Such an injury was always painful, but usually not serious. Roger had said something that concerned her, though. "Is the cut bad?"

"On his head?"

"Yes."

"I think it looks bad, but then they close it up. Staple everything shut. Maybe it is not so serious."

"Maybe?" It was so tough to gauge the level of injury listening to Roger.

"I think it is not serious. Sometimes I do not find the right words in English. Sorry. I can ask doctors to tell me more."

"So you're with him?" she asked. Normally Roger didn't attend the smaller races like this. She'd expected him to be in his offices outside Paris overseeing things.

"Yes. I drove here immediately when I got word of Saul's accident."

"Thank you Roger. We really appreciate the concern you've shown for him. Can I talk to Saul now?"

There was a long pause. "Just a precaution, but he is right now in Intensive Care. No cell phones allowed."

"Intensive care?"

Jim had been glancing casually about the room. Now his gaze locked on Yvonne. He pointed east in an arching gesture. Yvonne knew its meaning.

"Should one of us come to care for Saul? We could catch a flight tomorrow."

"No, no. I do not think that is necessary. Saul has been sitting up and talking with me. He is teasing the nurses. He will be better soon."

Yvonne nodded cautiously. "Thank you, but I'm worried. Please call if anything changes."

"Yes," Roger said. "I stay nearby. I will call again soon."

Day 2 – Wednesday, April 5, 2006

Yvonne lay in her dark bedroom with her eyes wide open. Shortly after speaking with Roger the previous evening, she'd called Saul's girlfriend Daniela at her apartment in Germany.

"Have you heard about Saul," Yvonne asked.

"No. Did he win today?" The pride in Daniela's tone was tangible. Her English was impeccable, right down to the British diction. Saul said she'd learned from a very proper and strict teacher. He'd also told them that her French was equally refined. German was her native tongue.

Yvonne took a deep breath and then explained the situation. "You speak the languages so well. Could you call Roger and make sure we've communicated correctly?"

"Of course," Daniela said.

Fifteen minutes later she called back and reconfirmed the information Yvonne already had. She also verified that a spur-of-the-moment trip to France was unnecessary.

Still, Yvonne's subconscious wouldn't rest. Finally, at 5:00 AM she couldn't stay in bed any longer. She eased herself from beneath the covers, being careful not to wake Jim, and tiptoed across the hardwood floor out of the bedroom and up the stairs to Saul's room.

Above her son's bed Lance Armstrong, clad in the mythic yellow jersey, charged down the Champs-Elysées at the 1999 Tour de France. Jim had given the huge mural to his son as a gift six years ago, and it had motivated Saul to train day after day. A jumbo-sized $5,000 check dated 4/27/2003 leaned against the far wall, Saul's reward for winning the Young Riders competition at the inaugural Tour de Georgia.

Trophies, cycling photographs, bib numbers, and all sorts of other race memorabilia decorated the remainder of the bedroom. There was a sign on one wall that read, "You're going to take my temperature where?" Could there be more plainspoken testimony to the number of times Saul had been injured?

Yvonne picked up one of the many memory books she'd put together for her son. This one had a Key to the City tied to the front cover. Moments before the cyclists headed out on the tough mountain stage from Dalton to Dahlonaga, Mayor Elrod had presented the token to Saul along with a proclamation deeming Friday, April 22, 2005, "Saul Raisin Day." From that day forward honors and articles started pouring in in such volume that she had to switch from memory books to plastic bins filled with keepsakes. They were stacked high in a guest room closet.

Dalton High School had overlooked Saul when they named their Athlete of the Year at the conclusion of his senior season. Only a couple of days before Saul left town to ride in the 2001 World Championships, the honor was given to yet another football player. But five years after high school Saul's athletic success had become difficult to overlook, and most of the city's population now knew something about Yvonne's son. It seemed particularly ironic when a school mate who had often teased Saul for shaving his legs—a ritual bicycle racers take as seriously as soldiers cleaning their weapons—asked for an autograph. Saul gave it gladly and then asked his former tormenter if he'd like to join him for a ride someday.

Yvonne sat on Saul's bed and thumbed through the mementos but stopped when she came to an enlargement of a photo Jim had taken. It had been shot in their living room prior to Saul's Senior Prom, the only school formal he'd ever attended. He had his arm around his date, and they both wore huge smiles. The image said so much about Saul.

He faced the camera directly. Such a posture might seem meaningless for most young boys, but Saul stood square and tall for a very important reason. He didn't want the image to record his "defect."

Around the time the boy turned twelve Jim had noticed Saul's back beginning to curve. They took him to see an Orthopaedic Surgeon who also specialized in Sports Medicine, Dr. J. Mitchell Frix.

"Your son is afflicted with Scheuermann's Disease, or kyphoscoliosis," the doctor said.

Jim and Yvonne looked at one another.

"Kyphosis is the more common name. It's presented as a forward curvature of the spine caused by wedging of three or more vertebrae," the doctor explained.

Yvonne pulled her son closer. Slight differences from the average didn't make Saul imperfect. This diagnosis seemed to suggest that he was somehow flawed. "Jim has a small curve in his back bones. His mother has one, too. It hasn't affected their ability to live full lives."

"Saul's back is developing a significant curve. If the condition progresses too far, or if he begins experiencing pain, we may have to operate."

"What do you mean by 'too far'?" Jim asked.

"We can take x-rays to measure the angle of the curve. If it goes over forty degrees surgical intervention may be unavoidable," Dr. Frix said.

"He's a very active boy," Yvonne said. "He plays little league football and baseball. He swims, plays soccer, rides his bicycle, and does karate. Would an operation affect those activities?"

"Yes. It might mean an end to them."

Yvonne gazed down at her son. Taking away athletics would rob him of the part of life he loved most. "We don't want that."

The doctor nodded. "I'd prefer to avoid it, too."

"Would a brace help?" Jim asked.

The doctor shook his head. "I don't think that would work in this instance."

"Besides, kids are so cruel. A brace could leave bigger scars than surgery," Yvonne said.

Dr. Frix made a note in his chart. "All right. Let's just monitor things for now. I want to be careful that we avoid complications."

"What sorts of complications?" Jim asked.

The doctor took a deep breath. "Every case is unique. Some patients experience diminished sensations in the lower extremities, lack of deep tendon reflexes, and even muscular atrophy. As he gets older he could be at greater risk for back injury, arthritis, and other conditions. He—"

"He also might live a completely normal life," Yvonne interrupted.

"Yes. Anything is possible. If the curve reaches forty degrees, though, it could have a significant impact on his life."

Dr. Frix couldn't possibly have imagined how prophetic his words would become.

Saul returned twice yearly for checkups. His back kept curving until the angle reached forty degrees when he was sixteen. Through two more years of checkups the curve increased by another five degrees, but that's where it stopped. The curve had gone beyond the preset threshold, but Saul had decided he didn't want the surgery, at least not until later in life. His back didn't seem to be causing him any physical problems, so Jim and Yvonne supported his decision.

Even if others saw Saul as deformed, Saul never would have. He'd been curious, determined, and fearless from the day he was born, and the diagnosis did nothing to change him. Once Saul set his mind to something he never gave up.

Eventually what he set his mind to was racing bikes, but officials of the sport discouraged him once they got a look at his back. Unfazed, Saul cleared the hurdle with a letter from his doctor:

November 22, 2000
RE: SAUL RAISIN
To Whom It May Concern:

Saul is a 17-year-old gentleman who has a diagnosis of Scheuermann's kyphoscoliosis. This should in no way impair his ability to ride bicycles or to race them competitively. From a medical standpoint, he is cleared for that type of activity. If you have any questions regarding this young man, please feel free to contact me.

Sincerely,
J. MITCHELL FRIX, MD

If Saul made up his mind not to do something he was equally impossible to sway. When Dalton High School administered the SAT tests Saul read only a couple of questions before deciding they were a waste of time. His focus was on becoming a pro bicycle racer, not on getting into college, so he laid his head down on the desk and took a nap.

Jim, Yvonne, teachers, councilors and others were horrified. He was a B student with a smattering of honors classes. He ought to do fine on the examination if he'd only take the time to answer the questions. They explained to him how important this test was to his future. Saul argued that spending time on such an exam didn't benefit him or his goals in any way, and furthermore, tests like these seemed like a lousy way to judge people's lives.

After much begging and prodding he showed up for a make-up examination, but by now he was entrenched in his decision not to take the test. He refused to pick up his pencil, and eventually walked out of the room.

Jim always said Saul got his tenacity from Yvonne, and Yvonne always said it came from Jim. In reality they both knew Saul had received a genetic double dose of bull-headedness. He never once allowed physical limitation or any other excuse to stand in his way.

Yvonne returned her gaze to the prom photo and memories of the intervening years flooded back. To her, the picture clearly showed the ways in which Saul's spinal condition had affected his life. She was both saddened and proud of the results. Saul's date was a shy Pakistani girl named Hira Rana. Cultural differences made her integration into their small Southern community challenging. Like the majority of Saul's close friends at the time, she was on the marginalized fringe of high-school society. Yet to Saul—and you could see this so clearly in his expression—she was perfect. Her smile proved that she was just as thrilled about the evening as he was.

When Saul came home that night he couldn't quit jabbering from excitement. He told Yvonne how Hira's favorite song came on as they entered the ballroom.

"C'mon, let's dance!" she said.

"It's too early. There's nobody else on the floor," Saul said.

Her eyes pleaded. "If you don't dance to this song with me you'll ruin my night."

Reluctantly he followed her onto the floor. He hadn't planned on showing off his dancing skills to everybody at Dalton High quite like this. He wasn't even sure he had any dance skills to show off with, but pretty soon he figured out that she did. He just stood there and let her make him look good with her incredible moves. The stunned student body watched in awe as Hira dazzled everybody. After the song ended the rest of the students joined in, and the prom went on to be a roaring success.

All Saul had ever really wanted was acceptance. At the 2001 Dalton High School Senior Prom he and Hira simply accepted one another for who they were. Afterward she was transformed, like a butterfly emerged from her cocoon. She bragged to the other girls how Saul had "treated her like a lady." Somehow the experience seemed to free her from shyness, and her confidence soared. Saul's reputation did, too.

A shadow at the door startled Yvonne. She looked up. Jim stood there staring fondly at her. "Oh, Mom. I wish you'd gotten more sleep. Roger said Saul is going to be fine."

"I know, but Jimmy, the Head Hoorah doesn't rush half way across France to visit a hospital for no reason. Roger's a busy man."

"It shows how much he cares."

"I agree, but it also proves there's reason to be scared. Besides, I'm Saul's mom. Worrying is in my job description. Any mother would be upset to learn their child had a list of injuries like that." She fell back on Saul's bed, looking up at the constellations of glow-in-the-dark stars her son had pasted on his ceiling a decade earlier.

Jim sat down beside her and moved her hair away from her eyes. "Yeah, but Saul's been banging himself up daily for twenty-three years now."

Yvonne couldn't help smiling. "Sometimes I think that boy was put on earth to give me a heart attack. What was it Roger said? Broken left clavicle—"

"That's his fifth collar bone break," Jim interrupted.

"Broken rib," Yvonne said.

"He's done that before, too."

"Broken left shoulder."

Jim scratched his temple. "I believe that's a first. He'll be proud."

"A big cut on his forehead."

"Lost count of the cuts a long time ago."

Yvonne glared chidingly. "And road rash everywhere."

"Skin abrasions don't count as an injury for a cyclist. That's like saying a mechanic got grease under his fingernails."

She waved a dismissive hand. "I never expected to give birth to Evel Knievel the Second."

Jim lay down beside her. "That's the spirit. You raised one tough kid. Roger said he was making friends with the medical staff as usual last night, acting like the injuries were no big deal. Saul's proven it many times before. He's a quick healer."

That was true. He'd recovered from so many injuries that she couldn't remember them all. The bad ones stuck out. In last May's Four Days of Dunkirk he was hit from behind by an inattentive motorcycle driver. He flew over his handlebars, and suffered several broken ribs, a fractured collar bone, a cracked hip, and a shattered bike. Saul couldn't get out of bed for days. The doctor told him not to touch his replacement bike for six weeks.

Not only did he touch the bike before then, he finished in the top forty of 160 starters at the Tour de Suisse. Saul passionately hated hospitals and just couldn't stay in bed recuperating. He needed to get on his bike and race.

The ringing cell phone startled Yvonne. Who would call this early?

Jim picked up the phone and handed it to her. He had a tough time both hearing and being understood on cell phones, particularly when a foreign accent was involved. As a result, Yvonne nearly always did the talking. She looked at the display before answering. It showed the same number as last night. Her stomach knotted.

"Hello Roger. How's Saul?"

"Good news today."

She tilted the phone away from her ear and motioned for Jim to listen in. Her husband leaned closer.

"Saul's condition has stabilized. I receive the doctor's slip for him to start riding in one month. Start racing in two months."

Jim patted Yvonne's leg. He'd been more anxious than he let on.

Yvonne's gut relaxed. "Wonderful. Can I speak to him?"

Roger paused. "Sorry. He is still in intensive care. They have to be cautious."

Yvonne put her hand atop Jim's to prevent him from patting any more. "You're sure we shouldn't catch a flight?"

"I think it is not necessary. Besides, what could you accomplish? I promise to watch after him. I feel obligation to stay near him because he has no family in France. I will make sure Saul is well."

"Thank you, Roger," Yvonne said. "He has nothing but praise for you."

"So we feel about one another the same. You see? Everybody likes Saul."

Jim nudged Yvonne happily. "Yeah, he's really blossomed in the last few years."

"If you have messages for him, I pass them along."

"Just tell him that we love him," Jim said.

"Of course. I call you if there are any changes."

"Thank you Roger. *Au revoir.*"

"*Au revoir.*"

Yvonne moved farther away to see her husband's expression. She still felt nervous, but the news was somewhat encouraging. "What do you think we should do?"

Jim thought for a moment. "Well, the airline would rob us for last-minute tickets, and like Roger says, what could we accomplish? Saul's condition is improving quickly. Let's post a message on his web site. His fans will want to know that everything's going to be all right. Then, I think we ought to head to Chattanooga and look at condos."

A day in the fresh Tennessee air breathed life into the Raisins. With their

thoughts and conversation constantly drifting to Saul, though, it wasn't the right time to make an offer on a new home. Instead, they spent most of their time strolling along the River Walk and imagining life in their new city. They returned to Dalton optimistic, excited, and exhausted.

After a lingering moment in Saul's room, Yvonne went to bed at ten o'clock.

*   *   *

The ringing phone pulled Yvonne from her early morning dreams. She fumbled with the handset for a moment and then put it to her ear. "Hello?" Sleep crackled her speech.

In the dark and silent room Roger's urgent response jolted her. "I have bad news, Yvonne. Saul has taken turn for worst."

"What's happened?"

"His brain has *blote*."

Yvonne implored Jim with her eyes. "What is *blote*?"

"You don't know *blote*?" Roger asked.

Yvonne switched on the desktop lamp and fumbled for her English to French dictionary.

"This *blote* squeezes his brain," Roger said.

There was a problem with Saul's brain? Yvonne started to cry. Moisture from her tear-covered hands made the dictionary pages stick together. Finally she gave up and returned her attention to the conversation. "Do you mean blood?"

Roger sounded frightened and stressed. "Yes. This is what I mean. The blood puts great pressure on his brain. There is no room for it in his skull. Saul has slipped to coma."

Coma? If there was a more frightening word in the English language, Yvonne couldn't imagine it. Somehow, in all the scenarios she'd been running through her head, nothing seemed nearly as terrifying as the reality of that single word.

Jim was now crying, too. "It will be okay, Yvonne. Everything will be okay."

She put her left arm around her husband and buried her face against his chest while still holding the phone to her ear. How could something like this happen to her son? It couldn't be real. It felt like maybe if she squeezed Jim tightly enough, if she kept the light out of her eyes, she could return to the way things had been only moments ago.

"The doctors need your permission for emergency brain operation. Can you give it?" Roger asked.

His question intruded on her efforts to fix the world and her thoughts became even more chaotic. Finally she asked, "Brain surgery?"

"That's what they need to do," Roger said.

Yvonne leaned back so that she could look at Jim's face. His eyes were in shock, like an antelope in a lion's grasp.

Finally he nodded.

Yvonne spoke into the phone. "Do whatever you believe is best for him, Roger."

"You should come to France now. Quickly."

"We will."

"I will stay with him until you get here."

She took in a shallow breath. "Please ask the doctors to be careful."

"Of course."

Jim climbed out of bed. "I'll find a flight. If we hurry we can catch the first plane out in the morning." He scrambled toward the kitchen to find the airline's phone number.

Yvonne watched him go and then mopped her tears with her sleeve before asking, "Can you do me a favor, Roger?"

"Anything."

"Please give Saul a kiss and tell him that his mom and dad love him."

"I will. I'll go kiss him right now, from you." His voice trembled with emotion. "Please come quickly. Saul needs his mama and papa more than anything."

"We're coming, Roger. We'll be there as soon as we can."

Day 3 – Thursday, April 6, 2006

Yvonne jumped from bed, grabbed her car keys, and headed for the garage. As she passed through the kitchen Jim stepped into her path. "Where are you going?"

"To Saul."

Jim shook his head. "You can't just get in the car and drive to France."

Yvonne stared at him, only gradually comprehending the problem. Good thing her husband was here to think straight. While she had no idea how to deal with this situation emotionally, she did know how to work with him. The years laboring at Raisin Textiles had taught them everything there was to know about one another. One of Jim's strengths had always been staying calm in the midst of chaos. Like the competent captain of a ship in stormy seas, he knew that no matter how hellacious things got, he needed to remain at the helm and maintain clear vision. Maybe his decade as a firefighter had taught him that. All that mattered right now was that he could be relied on to think clearly. "What should I do first?"

Jim's confused expression surprised her. "I don't know."

She'd never seen him so vulnerable. She thought about how invested Jim was in Saul's life. For almost a decade her husband had designed every family trip around their son's schedule. In fact, Saul's activities were often the central reason for traveling. Since his interest in cycling had developed they'd never gone anywhere that he wouldn't be able to ride his bike, and more often than not the vacation was to a bike race or cycling camp. Jim and Saul never parted company without a kiss. Yvonne always kissed her son goodbye as well, but that was typical for a mother. She knew the connection between this father and son was unusual, and she loved it. Finally she came up with a suggestion. "Can you find someone to drive us to the airport while I pack our suitcases?"

"Yeah, that's a good idea." Jim wiped away tears.

In that moment she saw her son in her husband, vulnerable and naïve. She realized that both of the men in her life needed immediate attention. "I love you, Jimmy. We'll get through this."

"I know we will. I love you, too."

Yvonne returned to the bedroom and noticed her cell phone. She ought to call Daniela! She searched the phone's memory for her number. Saul always bragged that he'd found his girlfriend on a mountaintop. He'd actually come upon her about six months ago while riding in the Alps on a trip with Jim, Yvonne, and several friends. At the end of one day's ride he told them about the special girl he'd met. He then added that since she was camping and it was going to be cold that evening, he'd invited her to spend the night in the lodge with them. Neither Jim

nor Yvonne was happy about the arrangements, but Saul was twenty-two years old at the time, so they dealt with it.

The relationship progressed. Saul's eyes sparkled each time he said Daniela's name, and when he was in Dalton he often blew kisses toward Europe for her to catch.

Yvonne pressed send.

"Hello." Daniela's voice was sweet and fluid.

"Hello, Daniela? This is Yvonne." She tossed several pairs of Jim's socks into a suitcase as she spoke.

"Is Saul all right?" Concern rose in Daniela's voice. She'd obviously already figured out the answer. Why else wouldn't the news be coming from him?

"He's having emergency brain surgery right now."

"Oh my God!"

"We're on our way to France, but it will take us until midday tomorrow to arrive. Can you go to him?"

"Of course. School is on holiday. I'll leave immediately."

Yvonne felt a wave of relief. "Thank you, Daniela. Saul needs you at his side. You're his angel. Please watch over him for us."

"I will."

"We'll see you tomorrow," Yvonne said.

"Yes. I've looked forward to seeing you again, but not like this."

Yvonne wiped a tear from her eye. "No. Not like this."

"Saul is strong. He's going to pull through quickly." Resolution had crept into Daniela's tone. It made Yvonne feel good. Saul needed such a positive spirit at his side.

"I sure hope so. Now, I've got a lot to do to get ready," Yvonne said as she loaded Jim's shaving kit with the necessary supplies.

"I understand. Travel safely."

Yvonne's thoughts remained on her son as she continued packing. Saul had always been so full of life. He'd jumped onto his first bicycle while wearing diapers at the age of two. He rode it away without training wheels. Athletics had always come easy for him. It was impossible to imagine him now lying nearly lifeless in a French hospital bed.

She closed the suitcases and looked around for the next job. When she noticed the bed she couldn't resist climbing back in. She didn't have the strength for this trial, and she felt utterly overwhelmed. She closed her eyes and began to pray. She wasn't a particularly religious woman, but God would certainly still be willing to help her son.

She didn't move a muscle, but she felt as if she was reaching out to the heavens with every fiber of her being. She pleaded with an intensity she'd never before felt capable of, yet she didn't utter an actual word. In that moment Yvonne

felt connected to higher powers. She believed that she was accomplishing something real—that she was reaching out with some indefinable life force toward her son on the other side of the planet. Her thoughts seemed to be rising and falling on tumultuous seas, driven by powers she neither understood, nor wanted to control.

The effort drained her. Her muscles ached and perspiration rose on her brow. She struggled to intensify her concentration even further.

And then, the connection was gone. It didn't end on a negative note at all, but on a feeling of completion, as if she'd done all she could do in that moment, and now she must gather her strength for the fight to come.

She opened her eyes. Jim had returned to the bedroom. He took her hand. "I wish I knew what's going to happen with Saul. I don't know what tragedy or triumph we'll experience next, but I do know that I'm the luckiest man on earth to have you by my side."

Their relationship had always been very close, but Yvonne knew these words came from especially deep within. She kissed him.

Jim shivered. "I guess I ought to get back in bed, too."

Yvonne held the covers, and he climbed beneath them. Jim kept shaking, and soon chills ran down Yvonne's spine, as well.

When her husband closed his eyes Yvonne knew he was saying a silent prayer. After he finished she hugged him. She needed his physical contact to strengthen her. In their embrace she thought about how fortunate she was to have found her soul mate and built her life with him. Jim returned her embrace tightly, as if defying fate to separate them.

The Raisins had married young, not long after high school. They labored as a team, the first ten years to gather capital to create a business, he as a full-time firefighter and part-time house painter, and she working for one of the giant floor covering companies that gave Dalton its nick-name: Carpet Capital of the World. When Jim's brother and sister came up with a business plan to create a discount clothing company they invited Jim to join them. He and his brother already had entrepreneurial experience having founded and then sold the town's first bike shop, Dalton Bicycles in 1975. The Raisins gathered their cash and invested it. They spent the next twenty years working elbow to elbow to build their business.

Six years into Jim and Yvonne's union Saul had arrived, and he fused them together even more strongly. Having a second child was never a serious consideration. Their workdays were long and money was tight. High blood pressure had been a concern during Yvonne's first pregnancy, and the doctor believed a second pregnancy might require up to six months of bed rest. Stepping away from the work force for that sort of time wasn't an option. Besides, how could a second child be an improvement upon the one they already had?

After a long time lying motionless in one another's arms Jim whispered. "I

booked us a flight. We're single-handedly bringing Delta out of bankruptcy."

"At least we can get to where Saul is. I'd gladly pay anything they asked," Yvonne said.

"I know. Me too."

"So, what do we do now?"

"We're flying out of Chattanooga at 9:00 AM. Then we have a long layover in Atlanta since our flight to Paris doesn't leave until 5:00 PM. That's because morning flights from here would reach Europe in the middle of the night. We'll get in early tomorrow morning."

"It's nearly 5:00 AM now."

Jim sighed. "Yeah. We'd better get moving. We have some hard work ahead of us, and then a long, tough day of travel."

"I guess I ought to post an update to Saul's blog," Yvonne said.

Jim nodded. "Good idea."

Yvonne went to the computer and logged onto Saul's site. She read her entry from the day before:

Accident
Contributed by Saul's Parents
Wednesday, 05 April 2006
Saul is resting in a hospital in France with a broken collar bone and a broken rib … He has bruising and road rash that includes his face … They have him on pain medicine so he can rest … The cat scan shows everything is good … Hopefully he will be back racing in July the doctors have told us … Saul's parents

Then she typed:

Thoughts
Contributed by Saul's Parents
Thursday, 06 April 2006
Saul has had an unexpected turn for the worse … Please keep him in your thoughts … we are on our way to France to be with him … we will try to keep you updated … Saul's parents

The doorbell rang, and Yvonne went to answer it. Jim's younger brother Phil stood on the porch. His look of compassion reminded her how fragile she felt, but crying in public was not her way so she fought back the tears.

"Everything's going to be fine, Yvonne. I'm driving you to the airport. You'll be with him soon."

"Thank you." She didn't know what else to say.

It wasn't long before they were in the car. They discussed what ifs, and they chastised themselves for not having headed to Europe when Roger first called, but mostly they felt lost.

"You two are in no condition to travel," Phil said. "I should go with you."

Jim looked at him helplessly. "It's too expensive. We'll be all right."

"I sure hope so," Phil said. "It would be tough to go at the last moment like this, but I just know I should. Teresa said I ought to when I left the house."

Jim put his hand on his brother's shoulder. "We'll be all right. You can help us from here."

Phil nodded. "Please stay safe."

Somehow they found their way, hand in hand, through the airport and into a plane and then through a much larger airport and into the waiting area for a much larger plane. All around them the hustle and bustle of travelers seemed oddly routine. The devastating news about Saul obviously had no impact on the world at large, and that made the Raisins feel all the more isolated.

On the CNN monitor Yvonne watched the story of a U.S. Hummer which had been blown to smithereens that morning in western Iraq. The number of dead wasn't yet known.

"Think of the families," Yvonne said. "Somewhere, people are paying an unimaginable price."

Jim pulled her closer.

On the television an Iraqi woman wailed, pounding her fists on the hood of a rusted sedan. Had she lost a child? Yvonne also thought of the parents of U.S. Marines. Their worlds were about to come unhinged as the result of the news she was watching. Their tragedies felt overwhelmingly real, and somehow more personal than similar stories had the day before. The devastation saddened her, but the awareness of so many other sufferers didn't make Saul's situation any more bearable.

After hours of waiting the boarding calls began. Jim led her by the hand into the plane. They found their seats far back in coach, an aisle and a window. Yvonne felt thankful for the relative privacy. She and her husband could whisper with little risk of being overheard.

The wait to pull back from the gate seemed interminable. Finally the flight departed. The mountains of northern Georgia where Saul fell in love with the bike were momentarily visible on the horizon. Then the aircraft banked and pointed its nose toward Europe. Soon the only visible scenery was sky and water.

Yvonne's thoughts drifted to her first intercontinental flight in October 2001, less than a month after the World Trade Center towers came crashing down. The family was on their way to the World Cycling Championships in Lisbon, Portugal. A universe of possibilities seemed to lie at Saul's feet. They'd all been so excited. How different that flight had felt from this one.

Jim and Yvonne held hands and often looked at one another, but they hardly spoke. Now and then cold chills would descend Yvonne's spine. She noticed that Jimmy was experiencing the same thing. He found blankets and wrapped her in them. She made him use some, too.

"Remember how I used to ride my bike to work as a fireman?" Jim spoke in a dreamlike whisper.

Yvonne nodded.

"And when I got off work, I'd pedal over to Saul's day care. One day when he was about eighteen months old I put him in the carrier seat and took of pedaling. He pulled the tail of my shirt over his head and fell asleep, so content. I rode for miles, not wanting to change my cadence or do anything else that might disturb him." A tear trickled down Jim's face.

Yvonne dabbed at his cheek with the corner of her blanket.

"What great times we had together," Jim said.

The plane took a sharp dive. An overhead luggage bin popped open and something fell out. Women gasped, and a baby started wailing. Anxious chatter swept through the aircraft. The seat belt sign came on, and the pilot made an apology over the PA. The Raisins remained totally silent, unable to devote attention to a less serious emergency than their son's condition.

They cuddled together as the turbulence continued. Even as newlyweds they'd never held hands so much in one day. They had never been so silent in one another's presence, either. Yvonne knew Jim was as lost in thought and prayer as she was.

Finally she whispered, "Maybe there will be good news when we arrive."

"I hope. It's so hard to be on this side of things."

"What are you saying?" Yvonne asked.

Jim looked at her. "When I was a firefighter tragedy became clinical. I guess we had to treat it that way in order to cope. If we became emotionally involved we couldn't do our jobs. There were days I saw terrible things, but somehow they didn't seem terrible in the normal way. They were just things, challenges that needed to be handled in the best way possible. I learned that if I planned for the worst, or at least accepted it as a possibility, that even bad news could have an encouraging side." He paused. "But I can't do that now that the tragedy involves my son."

Yvonne swallowed hard. She squeezed his hand tighter.

Jim looked directly into the reading lamp, but his gaze seemed to settle on something much farther away. "Oh Saul, please fight!"

Day 4 – Friday, April 7, 2006

The fuselage quivered when the wheels touched asphalt, and then with a mighty roar the huge Pratt & Whitney engines reversed their thrust and the plane shuddered to a stop. It was such a relief to finally be connected by land to where Saul lay.

Jim got the flight attendant's attention. "Can we hang on to these blankets? We're in desperate need of sleep."

"Of course," the flight attendant said. "Please take care of yourselves."

Yvonne imagined herself curled up on the floor of the ICU. That would be fine with her. As long as she was near Saul nothing else would matter.

Fortunately they had no checked luggage, so they bypassed the crowds at the baggage carrousel. Still, it took a long time to get through customs and begin searching for the Crédit Agricole employee who would drive them the 300 remaining kilometers to be with Saul.

Their initial plan had been to take the high speed TGV train to Angers, but Roger realized that too many things could go wrong with a pair of ultra-stressed travelers trying to navigate their way through a foreign land. Yvonne and Jim had been grateful for the help, but now they worried that they might never find their driver. They had no idea what he looked like or where he would be waiting.

Yvonne searched the sea of strangers for somebody holding their name on a placard, but her mind seemed to have lost the ability to take in details. She felt fortunate that she already knew the airport because her inability to communicate with most people, or to even read the signs, made the place feel chaotic.

"Yvonne? Jim?"

She spun toward a familiar voice. There stood their good friend Lionel Marie. What a welcome surprise! Yvonne threw her arms around Saul's former team directeur's neck. "Oh, I'm so happy you're here. Please, Lionel, tell me Saul is still okay." The question slipped out almost before she realized she'd asked it. She braced herself for the answer.

Lionel nodded. "Yes. He is still alive."

Yvonne had been so fearful of the answer to this question. The relief Lionel's answer brought with it overwhelmed her. "Oh, thank you. Thank you!"

Lionel hushed her with a calm finger to the lips. "But now is a time to be quiet and think."

Yvonne nodded. That sounded like good advice. Lionel had earned the right to tell her how to deal with this situation. About two and a half years previous he'd saved Saul's life. At the time he was directeur sportif of Crédit Agricole's Espoir Team, roughly equivalent to the role of head college football coach in America.

They were racing at the 2003 Trans-Alsace where Saul was competing as a member of the USA Under 23 Developmental Team. The morning of Stage Two, Lionel approached Saul about the possibility of joining Crédit Agricole. This was the moment Saul had been aiming at for years: the opportunity to turn pro.

Lionel said he'd had his eye on Saul ever since the Ronde de l'Izard Under 23 World Cup. In that race Saul single-handedly pulled the peloton, or tightly packed group of cyclists, for a large portion of the route. Aerodynamics dictate that on level ground the lead rider in the peloton expends thirty or even forty percent more energy than the men trailing him, so saving a teammate's energy by sheltering him from the wind can make an enormous difference in the outcome of a race. At the Ronde de l'Izard, for instance, Saul successfully helped teammate Patrick McCarty capture the win.

Not only that, but despite all the extra work he put in, Saul somehow mustered the strength to finish third. Lionel had been interested in recruiting an American for his squad to mix things up a bit, so he checked around and heard more good things about Saul.

Now that he knew of Lionel's interest, Saul was anxious to prove he could deliver results. Shortly after the race began, though, the lead rider nicked a roadside barrier. It flipped into Saul's path and he crashed into it at full speed. He cartwheeled down the pavement and smashed face first into a cement post. There he lay with dislodged teeth jammed back into his mouth. He wasn't breathing.

Seeing the blood running out of Saul's mouth the quick thinking Lionel jumped from his team car. His vehicle continued rolling and crashed into another stopped car. Lionel forced a finger into Saul's mouth to clear his airway. Saul instinctually bit down on Lionel's finger so hard that he couldn't remove it from Saul's mouth without help.

An ambulance rushed Saul to the hospital where they soon stabilized him. He returned to America to have his teeth fixed and remained there for three weeks while the swelling in his face subsided. A note arrived from Lionel telling Saul that he'd never regained the feeling in the tip of his finger, but also praising him for his toughness and asking if he still wanted to join the Crédit Agricole's Espoir Squad.

Espoir in French means *hope*, an interesting description of how the French view developing cyclists. To Yvonne it eloquently expressed the passion these fans have for the future of cycling. She loved the word, and held a soft spot for Lionel because of his hope for her son. It warmed her heart to know he'd seen Saul in those terms, and over time she'd come to see Lionel as *hope* personified. It was the emotion she needed most now, and it gratified her to have Lionel's gentle presence nearby.

Saul signed onto the team as soon as he returned to Europe. Lionel watched over his protégé like a little brother, helping Saul to establish a home base near his on the border of Monaco. The two men became best friends in the process.

A tall, thin man in a Crédit Agricole shirt stepped forward beside Lionel. This must be the driver Roger had sent. She looked at Lionel again. "I hope you'll be traveling to Angers with us."

Lionel nodded. "I have to see Saul. I need to touch him. Your boy is among the strongest I've ever known. I love him very much. He is special."

"Thank you, Lionel," Yvonne said. "He loves you too, and so do we. Now, let's go to him. Quickly."

*   *   *

The French countryside rolled anonymously past Yvonne's rear passenger-side window as they sped down the Autoroute. These high-speed toll roads were extremely efficient, but they isolated travelers from the world they were passing through even more completely than American Interstates. The periodic rest stops were entirely lacking in French charm. It was a trade off that Yvonne usually didn't like, but she was more than willing to make it today. All that mattered was reaching Saul's side.

Half way through the three-hour drive they pulled into one of the rest stops. "Roger will take us the rest of the way," Lionel said.

As they parked in front of a convenience store Yvonne noticed Roger talking to another man beside a car. The lines in his fifty-something-year-old face seemed deeper than she remembered, and his receding brown hair was not as well combed as usual. His expression brightened when he noticed they had arrived, and he hurried toward them. The other man followed.

"Ah. I'm so glad you have made it." He hugged Yvonne and then Jim, with the appropriate sort of *bise* for each.

Saul once tried to instruct Yvonne in the protocol for the polite French kisses, but she couldn't recall his advice at this moment.

"It's such a relief to finally be here," Yvonne said.

"Dr. Ménard and I," Roger indicated the other man, "have just been talking about you. Let's not delay. Please get in my car and we'll talk on the way."

Dr. Ménard shook hands with each of the Raisins.

Their previous driver who spoke no English but whose heart was obviously with them said some solemn words in French and then gave Yvonne and Jim each a *bise*. The gesture showed they'd been accepted into his world as friends. As he climbed into his car to leave, Yvonne felt grateful for his support.

Everybody else got into Roger's car. Yvonne recalled Saul mentioning that Dr. Ménard was a competent but quiet man who was very dedicated to the cyclists under his care. He was the Crédit Agricole team physician. He was only slightly taller than Yvonne and a couple of years older. His once dark hair had grayed at the temples and somehow seemed to accentuate his kind smile.

Roger cleared his throat. "Dr. Ménard can help me with medical questions if you have any, but he speaks little English so I will translate. We still do not know as much as we wish we did. Lots of questions. Have you seen any newspapers since you landed?"

"No," Yvonne said. "We can't read French anyway."

He nodded, a concerned look on his face. "Well, there are reports that Saul crashed due to epileptic seizure. They have written that he has been a known epileptic since crash in 2003 Trans-Alsace."

"That's not true," Yvonne said. "Why would anybody say that?"

Roger nodded. "If he had been diagnosed as epileptic neither our team nor Union Cycliste International would have cleared him to race. Unfortunately, a theory of seizures spread among reporters. Within hours it appeared on hundreds of cycling sites in dozens of languages. The idea was based on some thin evidence, if you can call it that. First, Saul had seizure after he hit ground on Tuesday—"

"Good Lord! I didn't know that?" Yvonne's heart raced.

Roger asked Dr. Ménard a series of questions in French. Finally he translated. "A hard impact to the head will often cause a seizure. It probably happened as a result of the crash, not before it."

"What's the other evidence," Jim asked.

"Another cyclist who was nearby claims Saul was riding in 'a trance-like state' before the crash. He says Saul swerved into the man beside him and then went down. He also says Saul did not outstretch his arm or do anything else to break his fall."

"He's implying Saul was unconscious before he hit the ground? Do you believe that's what happened?" Jim asked.

Roger shrugged. "When you see Saul's left hand you can tell me if you believe he didn't try to use it to break his fall. I think that the memory of a cyclist swerving to avoid a crash in the midst of a charging peloton is not reliable. There is too much happening too fast. Each man's concentration must be on his own survival."

"What else does the story say?" Jim asked.

"It claims Saul had previous seizure when he crashed at Trans-Alsace. This is not true, though Saul did lose consciousness on that day. The doctors see no connection between the crashes, and they believe Saul is not epileptic. Jean-Jacques Henry, the Crédit Agricole directeur in charge of the race, tells me Saul had been on the front riding full speed. He captured the breakaway moments before his crash. It seems unlikely that Saul's first seizure ever would come while riding at full power like this, but who can say?"

Jim nodded. "What do you think caused the accident?"

"Maybe a flat tire, maybe a dropped chain, maybe bad road. Many things are possible."

"Do they know why he went into a coma?" Jim asked.

Roger consulted with Dr. Ménard for a moment. "Saul was bleeding into his brain cavity, increasing the pressure inside."

Dr. Ménard nodded several times, as if to add weight to the translation.

"This is when I call you," Roger said. "Because of the blood, the pressure on Saul's brain became very high, forcing him into coma. He was on verge of death. There was only one solution. Open the skull and relieve pressure, so this is what they did."

"Open the skull," Jim repeated. "Wow."

"Yes. It is frightening," Roger said. "In all my years I've never been through anything so rough."

"Yeah, this is definitely the toughest thing we've ever dealt with," Yvonne said. "No matter how it comes out, I don't ever want Saul to ride a bike again."

*   *   *

Three hours of driving, mostly in silence, put them at the doorstep of Centre Hospitalier Universitaire d'Angers, or CHU d'Angers as it was commonly called. It was a very old building with an ornate, church-like entrance. Inside Yvonne noticed dirty walls and peeling paint, but it smelled clean.

Yvonne's tears and tension increased at every turn. Her exhausted mind couldn't comprehend lots of things, but as she hurried through the twisting and turning halls escorted urgently by the men, the irony of a hospital with "dAngers" printed all over the place was one she didn't miss. It took her a moment to realize that A N G E R S spelled the name of the city they were in. When Roger and other Frenchmen said the name it sounded like, On-zshay. The French pronunciation was so beautiful, she never would have guessed the spelling was the same as such a coarse English word.

They reached an elevator and took it to another floor. Finally, they entered a waiting room.

Daniela stood up, her hair now in short blonde dreadlocks, her slate blue eyes sharp and clear. Her expression seemed to contain equal parts hope and fear. "Yvonne?"

"Daniela!" They embraced, squeezing tightly as if each of them contained something the other couldn't do without.

"He's got a huge fight ahead of him," Daniela said, "but he's so damn tough. If anybody can make it, Saul can."

"It's nice of you to say that," Yvonne whispered.

As Jim hugged Daniela, Yvonne inspected her more closely. She had an athlete's physique and a confident carriage. She seemed to exude female strength. No wonder Saul was crazy about her.

"When will we get to see Saul?" Jim asked.

"The rules are strict, but they will break them for us today. This is one of Saul's doctors." Daniela indicated a woman in a white coat standing nearby. "She will update us on his condition before we go to his room."

The woman Daniela pointed out had short black hair and looked to be in her mid-fifties, but her most notable feature was her down turned lips. Her facial wrinkles seemed to indicate her frown was a somewhat permanent expression. Maybe it was the result of working in such a sad place. She opened the door to a small conference room, indicating that everybody should enter.

Yvonne, Jim, Daniela, Dr. Ménard, Lionel, Roger, and the lady doctor all stepped into the room. As Yvonne took her seat Daniela put a comforting hand on hers. Lionel looked upset.

The doctor appeared concerned. "Hello Mr. and Mrs. Raisin," she said in a thick accent.

Yvonne nodded. She had to concentrate hard to understand her words.

The doctor spoke again. "Your son is not doing well. Presently he is living hour to hour and could die at any moment."

Yvonne and Jim, whose hands were already practically fused, held onto each other even tighter when this bombshell dropped. The statement seemed so blunt.

Lionel asked her something in French.

The doctor flipped through a few sheets on her clipboard. "Mr. Raisin has many injuries including broken bones, but his head is our primary concern. A CT scan showed right frontal contusion and small subdural hemorrhage with no sign of cerebral edema and no traumatic lesion at the level of the skull or neck."

Yvonne could tell that the doctor was doing her best to make the situation understandable, but the language barrier was an extreme challenge, especially under these circumstances. The gravity of the conversation was almost too much to bear.

"What caused his condition to get so much worse after the first day?" Jim asked.

The lady doctor crinkled her brow. "This patient suffered a severe impact to the head. He complained of headache and had slight temperature of 38 degrees centigrade. He began showing increased somnolence. On night of April five he suffered important neurological worsening, which, by 4:00 AM resulted in dilated, nonreactive right pupil, deep coma with Glasgow score of four, with decerebrate movement on the left and attitude of opisthotonos."

"That was when he went to surgery?" Jim asked.

The doctor nodded. "The patient was intubated and sedated. Emergency CT scan showed severe deterioration of hemorrhagic contusion in frontal temporal area on right with mid-line shift. Also right temporal lobe herniation and hypo-density in brain stem."

Yvonne felt dizzy.

The doctor glanced back at the medical chart. "The patient was placed under sedation with Pentothal, Depakine and Mannitol and left pupil became responsive, but pupil on right remained dilated. An intra-cranial pressure monitor was placed and indicated moderately elevated level at fifteen millimeters of mercury initially. He was taken from surgery back to intensive care."

"Was he conscious?" Yvonne asked.

She shook her head. "No. He had fallen into coma."

"She just described his surgery," Jim whispered. Then he looked at the doctor and asked a new question. "Why didn't they operate earlier, before the problem became so bad?"

The doctor looked confused. "The surgeon has great expertise and handled this correctly."

"Yes," Jim said. "I'm just trying to understand what happened."

The lady doctor cleared her throat. "Often these things cure themselves. It is normal to monitor such situations and hope for best. Good neurosurgeons are cautious artists, reluctant to use scalpel. Saul did well until night of fifth, so strategy was sound, even though it did not work out as we had hoped."

Jim nodded. "Your explanation helps."

Yvonne battled nausea.

"By beginning of afternoon intracranial pressure had tendency to increase in spite of sedation, with cerebral perfusion pressure at the limit of sixty to sixty-five millimeters of mercury. A decision of partial right temporal lobectomy was made by—"

"Lobectomy? This is a second operation?" Jim asked. "They removed part of his brain?"

"They what?" Yvonne whispered.

Jim put an arm around her.

Yvonne looked at him wild eyed. The news was too difficult to digest. What had they done to her son? Until this moment she'd held out hope, but if part of his brain was missing how could the Saul she knew and loved ever return? She felt her face puckering as if she'd sucked a lemon. This time she couldn't hold back her tears in public no matter how hard she tried. Jim pulled her closer as everyone searched their belongings for handkerchiefs and tissues. Soon she had a larger collection than she knew what to do with.

"I'm sorry," she sobbed to no one in particular. "It's just been so hard."

Everybody made compassionate gestures and spoke comforting words, but Yvonne couldn't control her emotions. Jim rescued her in his arms. Under the influence of his comforting words, slowly but surely, she regained her composure.

The breakdown seemed to have affected the doctor. She spoke slower now. "This portion of brain removed was nonfunctional part. The tissue was damaged,

and its removal necessary to control bleeding and allow room for swelling. The rest of brain could not have been saved otherwise. In addition to this piece of temporal lobe, voluminous clots were evacuated after opening the dura."

Yvonne felt overwhelmed. Beside her Jim somehow seemed in control.

"What part of the brain was it?" he asked.

"Second and third Gyri of temporal lobe, T2 and T3."

Yvonne didn't understand the answer. She didn't understand anything at the moment. She just wanted to see her son. What was left of him, at least.

"A CT scan in immediate post-operative period showed hemorrhagic contusion on right frontal and decrease in mass effect in right temporal lobe as well as post-op changes in brain." The doctor looked at Yvonne and Jim, still frowning.

Yvonne's world had been rocked long before stepping into this room, but now it had come off its axis. Due to communication challenges she hardly understood anything the doctor had told her, but the few nuggets she could comprehend were exceedingly bad. She finally thought of a question she dared to ask. "How is he doing, right now?"

The doctor looked at her compassionately. "From neurological standpoint, he suffered an increase of intracranial pressure throughout day today, even though he is still sedated with Hipnovel and Morphine, necessitating a continuous Pentathol coma. This is allowing normalization of intra-cranial pressure with preservation of adequate cerebral profusion pressure. On clinical side he is in deep coma because of his sedation and a small anisocoria."

Jim cautiously phrased another question. "So the coma was drug induced?"

"No. He went into coma on his own, but drugs are keeping him in unconscious state now."

"When will he wake up?" Jim asked.

"I cannot give you false hope," the doctor said. "You should not expect for him to live. If he somehow does he'll be in a bed, or at best a wheelchair, for rest of his life."

Yvonne closed her eyes.

Jim drew in a long, slow breath. "How long until we'll know?"

"I doubt he will come out of coma for thirty days," the doctor said. "Maybe sixty days … if at all."

Yvonne couldn't take any more devastating news. She looked at her watch. It was just after two o'clock. "Can we see our son now?"

The doctor looked at her own watch. "Normally the first visit is from 1500 to 1630, and second from 1830 to 2000, but today we can make exception."

Yvonne converted the times in her head. It was 1400 right now, so they were being allowed in an hour early.

The doctor opened the conference room door and motioned for the others to exit.

"This is best hospital in all of France for brain injury," Roger said. "We are fortunate it was so nearby his accident."

Yvonne hoped he was right. At the moment she just wished she could understand what was going on.

"Health care in Europe is different from America," Daniela said. "First, it's socialized. Doctors here are not so highly paid. They practice medicine for love, not money. Also, they are very specialized. A surgeon operates but doesn't make rounds or meet with patients. Those sorts of jobs are handled by ICU doctors and others."

The lady doctor must have heard them speaking. "Mr. Raisin's surgeon is one of the best in world for this type of surgery. You can trust his decisions." Then she put a finger to her lips as they reached the ICU door. She pointed out the sterile clothing they must wear. She showed them the lockers where they could store their belongings. "Normally only two visitors at a time, but we will allow four today because of urgency."

Jim looked at the other four. "Dr. Ménard and Roger first, I guess. Then we'll be able to ask questions and Roger can translate the doctor's answers." Lionel, and Daniela stepped aside as Jim, Yvonne, Roger, and Dr. Ménard dressed.

"We request that you remain quiet for comfort of other patients," the lady doctor said.

Yvonne nodded, frightened at her recent lack of control. "I understand."

"As I said before, your son is on death's doorstep. He will not be able to hear you or feel your touch. Maybe things will eventually be a little bit better. Maybe not. We do not know."

Yvonne nodded numbly as she stepped through the door. Her eyes took a moment to adjust to the dim light. Behind the nurses' station a panel of monitors recorded vital signs for a roomful of patients. A nurse whisked quietly past them. Around the periphery were individual patient rooms, each with a huge glass window for a wall. Inside each she could see a patient and his or her personal array of sterile looking monitors and complex life-support equipment.

Somehow, Yvonne sensed Saul immediately. She tiptoed across the room toward the space she believed he occupied, Jim's hand still firmly in her own. The man in the bed she neared didn't look anything like Saul, yet she could feel his presence in a powerful way. She stepped into his enclosure. The rhythmic throb of a ventilator filled the room.

The man's face was unrecognizable, swollen and covered with cuts. The top half of his head was completely wrapped in bandages so no hair was visible. She didn't recognize the pale body, either. Where was her deeply tanned and bright-eyed boy? Maybe this wasn't her son, after all.

She looked closer. The left hand was damaged beyond recognition. It was twice the normal size and completely black and blue. The bones inside must be

shattered. But the right hand was unmistakable. She'd never before realized Saul's hands were so recognizable to her.

Then she noticed the feet. They looked just like his father's. This was definitely Saul. Oh, God.

He looked so swollen and bruised that Yvonne was afraid to touch him, but she couldn't stay away, either. Various portions of his shoulders and arms were black, purple, blue, and yellow. His skin looked awful. The head of Saul's bed was elevated. His neck was arched back and to the right in an uncomfortable looking position.

Jim barely made it into the chair beside the bed. The sight of Saul knocked the wind out of him and he couldn't even stand up. When Saul was a baby he was extremely sick one week with stomach virus. Jim took the time off work and cared for him like a mother would. Jim was always taking care of Saul as a baby, many times better than Yvonne could. These days Jim knew when Saul was sick, tired, or upset in the same way the most in-tune mother might, but he obviously hadn't been prepared for this. Seeing his son, his pride and joy, in such a condition had overwhelmed all frequencies.

A black-haired nurse stepped into the enclosure behind them and shut the door.

Yvonne returned her attention to Saul. Each time she asked a question, Roger consulted with Dr. Ménard and then explained things in a soft whisper. Dr. Ménard watched their reactions closely, his own eyes glistening with tears.

Yvonne stepped to the bed and kissed her son's cheek. As she neared him she caught a pungent aroma. Only once her nose and lips were in contact with his skin could she smell the unmistakable scent of her own son over the other odor. "Mama's here, Saul. Everything is going to be okay."

Saul made no response.

Instinctually, she reached out to rearrange his uncomfortable looking neck, but the nurse gently stopped her. "*Non, non.*" She pointed to the tube down his throat and then indicated a straight line.

Yvonne understood, but it was very hard to stand there doing nothing with her son's neck crooked like that.

The nurse gave some instructions and Roger translated. "You may touch only the tips of the fingers on his right hand, and his right cheek."

Yvonne's heart ached. She'd crossed an ocean. There must be more she could do for her son than touch his fingertips. "What is that smell?"

"It comes from the medication," Roger said after talking it over with Dr. Ménard.

"Why is he so stiff?" Yvonne asked.

Roger and the doctor conferenced again before he answered, "It is a physiological reaction to the brain trauma. Opisthotonos is the clinical name."

"He looks …" Jim couldn't finish his sentence, but Yvonne knew the word her husband hadn't been able to say.

Dead.

They stared at him for a long time before asking more questions.

Through Roger Dr. Ménard explained the respirator tube down Saul's throat and the readouts on the machine it led to. Saul's skull was thickly wrapped, or maybe it was swollen and wrapped thinly. Dr. Ménard pointed out where the wires monitoring skull pressure led out of the head to a box that displayed the readout. Currently it was twenty-seven millimeters of mercury.

Saul's left forehead and upper lip had road rash were he'd slid across the ground. There was a big cut visible on his neck and lots more scabbing on his body. Another tube ran into Saul's nose to drain stomach acid. Dr. Ménard told them it could also be used for feeding. Lots of additional wires and tubes ran between Saul and machines around the room. Heart rate, oxygenation, heart rhythm, and many other functions were being recorded.

Saul's temperature was frighteningly high. To help control it the IVs running into his body were iced. He also had an ice pack on his groin and another on his head. They'd built a sheet tent over his body using the bed railings as support. A fan blew air beneath the structure to cool his torso.

Jim touched the fingers of Saul's right hand and kissed them. Then he gingerly stood and kissed his son's cheek as well. "Oh Saul, what have you done to yourself this time?" Tears glistened on his cheeks.

Yvonne tasted the salt water that must have been sheening her own face. Her emotions had been rubbed completely raw.

"They sure have a lot of IV's running into you, Son," Jim said.

Yvonne shivered. "You're a fighter, Saul, and now you're in the fight of your life. Don't you dare give up! These doctors and nurses have worked hard to save you. It's time to show them how strong you are." Even as she spoke she wondered if her son would live, and if he lived, would he be in a nursing home? Would he know his parents again? Would he ever talk or walk? So many questions.

They kissed him again and again until the right side of his face was as tear covered as theirs.

"We'll stay at your side every moment we can," Yvonne said. "Every time the hospital will let us in we'll come back. We'll be here. Your Dad and I love you more than life, Saul. We're going to get you well."

"The brain pressure reading just went down to twenty-six. That's good, right?" Roger asked. Then he asked the question to Dr. Ménard.

Dr. Ménard explained things with an expression that looked slightly pleased.

"The lower the number goes the better," Roger said. "In a healthy brain the pressure is about ten. Saul's pressure got as high as sixty-five. That is way too high. Many people would not have lived through that. Even if it stays at level it is now, eventually it would be too much to survive."

Yvonne kept her eyes on the monitor as she spoke. "You can't leave us, Saul. We couldn't live without you." The monitor seemed very sensitive, and it went down another increment. Was Saul responding to her voice?

She kept talking to him, feeling immense satisfaction that the pressure on Saul's brain was improving. It felt empowering to accomplish something positive.

Lionel touched Yvonne on the shoulder and she noticed that Dr. Ménard had left. Daniela had taken Roger's place. The nurse was no longer there, either.

"Phew," Lionel said under his breath. "This is very hard."

Yvonne put an arm around him, as much to support herself as to support him.

Lionel pointed to the brain pressure monitor. "The doctor told me if that gauge had gone any higher Saul wouldn't have survived."

"Then we've got to get it down to normal," Yvonne said. "Talk to Saul. He needs to know you're here. It will make him feel better."

Lionel nodded and then stepped forward gingerly. "Hello my friend. Fate has dealt you a tough blow. Your injuries have shaken me to my core." He looked back at Yvonne and Jim and continued. "Everybody in cycling is praying for you. Stuart O'Grady told me that if he could transfer his energy he'd give every ounce of it to you. I would too. As we so often say, you are our favorite *raisin*."

Yvonne smiled at the comment. In French "*raisin*" meant "grape," and there weren't many things more beloved than the grape in this land.

They silently watched Saul for a long moment.

Then Lionel leaned close and whispered, "I'm a better man for having known you, my friend. Bon courage."

Yvonne looked at Lionel's face. His eyes were red and his cheeks were swollen. What a terrible day this was.

Lionel straightened, and then gave a polite nod to Yvonne then Jim, before turning and walking sadly from the room.

Yvonne motioned to Daniela. "He needs to hear from you, too."

Daniela stepped forward. "Saul, I'm here. I love you so much."

The monitor went down to twenty-five.

"Keep talking to him," Jim said.

Yvonne was impressed by Daniela's composure under such trying circumstances. She had a magnetic sort of confidence, and a smile that made it feel like eventually everything would be right.

Daniela whispered to Saul for a long time. Yvonne didn't try to listen in. She just watched the monitor, and felt grateful that her son obviously loved hearing Daniela's voice so much. The gauge had dropped to twenty-four.

Eventually Daniela excused herself from the room and left Jim and Yvonne to be alone with their son for the last half hour. Yvonne found herself thinking about how clean this portion of the hospital was, though the building as a whole was old and dirty. She was so glad Saul was in a well-kept place. Like every parent, Yvonne wanted the best for her child, and she wanted him to be happy. A clean bed would make him as happy as he could be for now. She wondered what else she could do to help her son get well.

Before she knew it the black-haired nurse was guiding them out of the room. When they reached the door to the hallway the nurse pointed to the clock and held up two fingers. Her meaning was clear. They could return for another visit in two hours. "*Merci*. Thank you for taking care of my son," Yvonne said.

The nurse smiled and looked fondly toward Saul's bed, letting them know with her eyes that she would watch out for him.

Jim and Yvonne stumbled toward the waiting room. Roger intercepted them and led them to a small bar. They shared a sandwich and a Coke Lite, and then spent the rest of their time making calls to their family in Georgia on their cell phones. Yvonne tried not to think about the roaming charges they must be ringing up because finding a better phone plan was out of the question at the moment.

At 1830 they pressed the button next to the ICU door. The black-haired nurse reappeared and led them back into the ICU. They followed like zombies.

Seeing Saul, even though they'd already done it before, shocked them anew. His complexion had such a sickly tone. Yvonne steeled herself and stepped forward. She laid her cheek gently on her son's forehead and talked in a soft tone. "What a day it's been, Saul. We flew halfway around the world at the spur of the moment. Grandma's at our house right now, probably trying to figure out how to pay our bills."

Jim held Saul's hand and kissed it from time to time.

Yvonne kissed Saul's forehead. "Not everything is sad, though. I have some exciting news. Noah rode his bike without training wheels this week. He dreams of being just like his cousin. We're going to survive this, you know. Daddy and I will be by your side, fighting for as long as it takes."

"Saul. I love you," Jim said. "I love you with all my heart. The doctor might not think you can hear me, but I know you can. You were in a bad accident, so now you need to fight. You can get better. You can recover from this. I know you can."

Then he began singing a song he'd sung many times to Saul as an infant:

You are my Sunshine
My only Sunshine.
You make me happy
When skies are grey.
You'll never know, dear,
How much I love you.
Please don't take my Sunshine away.

Yvonne joined in. By the end of the song she was crying like a baby, and her eyes were on Jim. When the nurse tapped her on the shoulder and pointed to the clock Yvonne couldn't believe it was already time to go. She gave Saul another kiss, reluctantly stood, and took Jim's hand in hers again as they left the room.

Day 5 – Saturday April 8, 2006

Yvonne gasped for air in ragged puffs while terrible visions swirled in her head. She lay in a bed, she wasn't sure where, trying to separate reality from illusion and put each in its place. She recalled that this was how Saul sometimes used to wake.

Starting at age three, he suffered night terrors two to three times a year. They lasted into his mid-teens and were a hideous experience for the whole family. Usually Jim and Yvonne would find him walking through the house in the middle of the night, talking to himself. They would try to wake him gently using soft speech or cold rags. He'd scream and struggle from their arms. Often he'd say things that seemed to come from recent experiences. Once, he though he was Mario from the video game and said he was stuck in a dungeon. He kept leaping, as if over imaginary barrels. Another time he was the Karate Kid, pinching Jim's nose and going "Honk, honk," but there was nothing funny about it because he was enduring a nightmare he couldn't wake from.

He'd frequently make mean monster faces like he was trying to scare something away. Often he'd come down sick within the next few days, and they began to wonder if the early symptoms of a virus were causing the problem. They videoed one episode and took it to a doctor. He wasn't able to prescribe much except sympathy.

Usually, once Saul woke up he didn't know what had happened, but the older he got the more aware he became. Eventually he learned to wake himself and interrupt the episodes. Today in this darkened room Yvonne found herself hoping that she'd begun having them too. Her best hope for sanity was to rise this morning and discover that the events she thought she'd experienced over the last several days were really only a dream.

She looked to her left. Jim lay beside her in the dim light. This was no dream. They definitely weren't in their home, though she had no idea where they actually were. It looked like a hotel room. Maybe a Holiday Inn. That's when she realized she wasn't sleeping beneath the Delta blanket as she'd half expected.

Jim's eyes were shut. She doubted she'd slept more than a couple of hours the entire night, and if she had to guess she'd say he slept even less. Once when she'd awakened she discovered him sitting at the foot of the bed.

If he was sleeping now, she didn't want to wake him, but where were they? Slowly vague details returned. Last night, after they left Saul, Roger had driven them through a maze of streets. He deposited them in a hotel room. When he left, they'd gone straight to bed. This might be a problem.

She touched Jim's shoulder. "Honey?"

His eyes opened. He hadn't been asleep. "What is it?"

"Remember the time we visited Saul and got lost in Paris?"

"Yeah. Of course."

"We might as well have been on another planet." They had hardly been able to ask questions, and even when they succeeded they couldn't understand the answers. They couldn't read street signs or simple directions, and they didn't understand the most basic customs.

"Eventually we got everything straightened out," he said.

"Yeah. But this is a lot worse. Where are we?"

"Somewhere in France."

Her nerves were fried, and he was kidding around. "Could you tell me how to get from here to Saul?"

"No."

"That's all you can say?" She sat up in bed. "When we step out that door we'll be lost, Jimmy. I've never felt so helpless in my life."

Jim looked at his watch. "We've got hours to figure out how to see Saul during visiting hours. Right now we need sleep.

"Jimmy!" She switched on the light.

"Don't you remember? Daniela, Roger, and Lionel are all here. So is Noël Dejonckheere."

She recalled a few more details. Saul's coach from the Under-23 US National Team had arrived late the previous evening. He was the man who'd given Saul the opportunity to develop and display his talent in Europe. Saul's time on that team had been one of many crucial steps in reaching the pro level. "Oh, yes," Yvonne said.

"All of these people said they'd help take care of us." He picked up a piece of paper from the nightstand. "Here are their room numbers."

"Call one of them. They'll be up."

He dialed something into the phone on the nightstand. "Hi."

A moment later he said, "Thanks," then hung up.

Yvonne's mind raced. "What happened?"

"Daniela's coming," Jim said.

There was a knock at the door.

Yvonne pulled her nightgown tight around her, checked to make sure the security chain was in place, and opened the door a crack.

"How did you sleep?" Daniela asked.

Yvonne shut the door, removed the chain, and reopened the door. "Oh, are we ever glad to see you. We didn't know how we were going to manage."

"Good morning, Daniela," Jim said. "Thanks for looking out for us."

"No problem." Daniela said. "Are you ready to go to the breakfast buffet?"

"We'd like to clean up first," Jim said.

"Can I bring either of you a cup of coffee?"

Yvonne's heartbeat started to come under control. She and Jim's impressions of Daniela hadn't been good when they first met half a year ago in the Alps. They felt she was out of line coming to stay with a family she didn't know. But then she showed up at Saul's a few days later and they came to appreciate her because of how happy she made their son. They were also impressed with how quickly she'd been willing to come to his side now, when he needed her most. As a result, Yvonne found herself falling in love with Daniela as well. "You're so sweet! No coffee for either of us. Thanks. Saul drinks enough for the entire family."

Daniela laughed. The sound had a pure quality, like a mountain stream tumbling over polished stones. "One thing I've learned since being around Saul is that pro cyclists drink more coffee than anybody else on the planet."

"That's our boy," Jim said.

"I'll be waiting for you at the breakfast buffet. This afternoon Roger will drive us to the hospital." They agreed to the plan, and Daniela left with a friendly smile.

As soon as the door shut Yvonne said, "She reminds me of how vibrant Saul has always been. She's so young and optimistic."

"Yeah. I know what you mean." Jim searched through his suitcase for clothing. "People like that don't belong in hospitals. Saul wouldn't want to live the remainder of his life in a place like that."

"I know, Jimmy. I know." Yvonne held her toothbrush in one hand as she searched through their toiletries for the toothpaste tube with the other.

"So, we're agreed?"

Yvonne looked at him, suddenly recognizing the weight of his statement. Finally she nodded, but neither of them dared voice what they'd agreed about: no life support.

*   *   *

As they ate lunch Roger said, "Unfortunately it will soon be time for me to return to Crédit Agricole headquarters. I'm sorry, but I must get back to my office. Your hotel room will be covered by Crédit Agricole for as long as you need it."

"Thank you for everything, Roger," Yvonne said.

"I only wish it was possible for me to stay and watch over you," he said.

Yvonne understood why he had to go, but she wished he could stay, as well. As they talked she learned that by the next morning Lionel and Noël were going to have to leave, too. That meant the Raisins would have to rely entirely on Daniela for translating and a whole lot more. Could she handle everything?

Daniela explained to Yvonne how she'd already figured out the bus routes necessary to get them back and forth from the hotel, as well as lots of other logistics. Meanwhile, Noël and Lionel were making plans to get a cell phone SIM card so the Raisins' telephone charges would be reduced while they were in Europe. They'd found Saul's phone in his luggage but it was password protected and their efforts to break the code locked the phone instead. Once they solved the problem Yvonne would carry two phones, one for calls to home, the other to Europe.

Yvonne listened to all the planning without entirely comprehending it. She looked at Jim and could tell he wasn't fully absorbing what the others were talking about, either. She felt so grateful for these angels who were willing to take care of so many details for her and her husband. She couldn't possibly have dealt with this sort of stuff at the moment.

By 1:00 PM, or 1300 hours as Yvonne was trying to transition into thinking of it, Daniela led the Raisins into the hospital and up to the ICU waiting room. Roger, Lionel, and Noël were also with them. Yvonne prepared herself for another briefing with the lady doctor, but instead a kind looking gentleman, about forty-five years old with a paunchy stomach and a lot of white speckles in his black hair walked toward Jim and extended a hand.

"I'm Doctor Fesard," he said.

"Jim Raisin," Jim said, shaking the doctor's hand. Then he introduced the others.

"Let's step into the conference room," the doctor said. His accent was thick but his English wasn't bad.

As soon as they'd taken their seats the doctor began speaking.

"Saul's condition remains hour to hour. Probably he will not make it," Dr. Fesard said.

A lump seized Yvonne's throat. She had often appreciated the direct way Europeans tended to communicate, but the lack of sugar coating made this topic tough.

After a moment Jim spoke. "Are you the lead doctor on his case?"

Dr. Fesard looked confused. "All of the ICU doctors, we are a team. We make our decisions together as a team. Before we act we must come to a consensus."

Jim nodded. "Thank you for the explanation. If Saul does survive the coma, what do you think will happen next?"

"It is too early to say. Expect the coma to continue for fourteen days at least. Thirty is more likely. Maybe much longer."

Yvonne wondered how she could possibly survive a month of days like this.

"Can you tell us more about the surgery?" Jim asked. "They removed a piece of his brain. What does that part do?"

"It was a portion of motor strip. Right side of brain controls left side of body. As I've said, Saul's chances of survival are still very low, but without surgery he would be dead for sure."

Jim nodded. "We understand. But are you saying that if he does come out of his coma he won't be able to use his left side?"

The doctor nodded. "*Oui*. Paralyzed."

Yvonne felt betrayed. Yesterday when the first doctor told them that the portion that had been removed was unnecessary she felt skeptical, but she allowed herself to believe. Now that hope seemed lost.

Jim held Yvonne as if worried she'd overreact. Saul's life was in these people's hands. They both wished they could understand more about their son's situation and even the backgrounds of the doctors treating him, but questioning the medical team or processes wouldn't be culturally acceptable. As much as they wanted to know more, biasing Saul's physicians against him was way too high a price to pay.

"Besides problems on his left side, do you expect Saul to be functional if he recovers?" Jim asked.

The doctor looked him in the eye. "It does not look promising."

Jim tightened his grip slightly on Yvonne's hand. "If Saul … if he was to get worse again … he wouldn't want to live his life that way. It will be bad enough if he can't use his left arm or leg. Can't ride a bike. Can't play sports. Besides, he's left handed. A life hooked to machines? No. No way. Not for Saul."

The doctor nodded. "I understand. We also do not believe in keeping patients alive without quality of life. It is too early for such a decision, though. Let's see if he can live through each hour today, and then if he can continue tomorrow."

"Thank you. Can we go see our son now?" Yvonne asked.

"Yes," Dr. Fesard answered. "You know the procedure."

Yvonne walked down the hallway holding her husband's hand, a hollow feeling in the pit of her stomach. As they neared the ICU doors Jim stopped in his tracks. Yvonne turned to him.

"If Saul doesn't make it, do we donate his organs?" Jim appeared as blindsided by his own question as she felt. They'd just dealt with what seemed to be such a momentous decision only to have another one emerge in its place.

"I don't have the strength to think about that right now," Yvonne said.

Yvonne, Jim, and Daniela went to the locker area. They put on the blue shoe covers and yellow sterile gowns and sanitized their hands.

Daniela depressed the intercom button. "*Merci*, Saul Raisin."

"*Oui. Entrez*," a metallic sounding voice answered.

"Two only, I think," Daniela said. She waved the Raisins through the door.

Yvonne looked for the black-haired nurse as she stepped into the ICU, but then she realized this was an entirely new crew. Of course it made sense that all of the doctors and staff had to take time off, but she craved a shred of familiarity. Why couldn't the black-haired nurse have been there today?

As they approached Saul's room Yvonne's heart sank again. It wasn't that her son looked worse. That probably wasn't possible. It was that he didn't look better. Even his bruises looked the same. Somehow she'd convinced herself that she was going to see at least a small improvement. She swallowed hard and tried to hide her disappointment. No way was Saul going to get bad vibes from her and Jim.

Dr. Fesard happened to walk nearby.

"Why is his head elevated like that?" Yvonne asked.

The doctor looked at her with a puzzled expression. "Because that's where his head needs to be. You can trust us to treat him correctly."

She nodded, not satisfied with the answer but sensing she shouldn't push for more.

She stepped to the bed and gently laid her head on her son's shoulder. Then she started talking about their day. Jim told Saul about some recent bike rides in Georgia, about work he'd done helping to clear trails at a new Dalton community mountain-biking park, and about rides he'd recently taken with mutual friends.

All too soon visiting hours were nearing a close. Yvonne wanted so desperately to somehow help her son. Then she recalled a time when Saul had a high fever as an infant, and she remembered the calming influence one nursery song always had on him. She leaned close, touching her cheek to his, and brushing her lips against his ear as she sang:

> Twinkle, twinkle, little star,
> How I wonder what you are.
> Up above the world so high,
> Like a diamond in the sky,
> Twinkle, twinkle, little star,
> How I wonder what you are.

After leaving Saul's room the Raisins wandered to the cafeteria and pointed out food they thought they might be able to digest. Yvonne chose a croissant and Jim picked out a chocolate tart. He handed the cashier money and she gave him back an assortment of change. Yvonne could tell that her husband had no more idea what he'd paid than she did, nor did he care. His mind was filled to the brim with more important concerns. She followed him across the room to a table far away from other diners.

Jim kept poking at his tart with a fork, but didn't pick it up. "Who should I call to ask what we should do if Saul doesn't make it?"

She shrugged.

"There's so much I don't know," Jim said. "How do we get him home? What documents have to be processed? What arrangements ought to be made?"

Yvonne was trying to come up with a response when she looked up to find Daniela standing beside the table.

"This is another of Saul's doctors," Daniela said.

Yvonne looked at the tall, skinny man. "Thank you for helping our son."

"He doesn't speak English well, but he has some ideas that might be helpful." Daniela took a seat and motioned for the doctor to do the same. The doctor, who must have been about forty years old, folded his lanky frame into a chair. A pair of black rimmed glasses rested on his pointed nose. He ran his palm along his slicked-back, black hair.

"We're listening," Jim said.

"This gentleman is not only a doctor of medicine. He's a doctor of philosophy. He sees this as a time of reflection, a time of potential growth for both of you and for Saul. Life is an uncertain game. Most of the players spend their energy trying to convince themselves it ought to be predictable and fair. It's neither."

The words struck Yvonne in a powerful way. Maybe it was because her mind was constantly on Saul, but she realized that certainty had never been important to him, and she also realized that was one of the qualities she loved about him most. "What does The Philosopher think we should do differently?"

Daniela spoke to the doctor in French and then translated. "He suggests you start walking."

The simplicity of the suggestion struck Yvonne perfectly. As obvious as it seemed now, she wondered if she ever would have thought of it herself. Already, their ordeal seemed to have been going on forever, yet they were only a few days into it. She'd never survive if she didn't start taking care of herself. She was even more concerned about Jim. "Go walking. That's good advice."

"Maybe it will help clear our minds," Jim said.

A clear mind sounded like such a lofty goal. Could walking put them in the mental state to make the decisions they faced? The future would be easier once they could think straight, and they couldn't possibly achieve that within these walls.

Jim looked at Daniela earnestly. "Can he give us a medical opinion?"

"I'll ask," Daniela said. "What do you want to know?"

"We've been getting mixed information on this. We need to know the answer. If Saul comes out of the coma, what sort of problems can we expect to be permanent?"

Daniela asked the doctor in her flowing French. She had such an unconscious grace. He answered in staccato sentences, and she translated each time he paused.

"*Votre fils ne pourra jamais être le même.*"

Daniela's normally stoic expression sank. Of everyone, she had been the strongest so far. It frightened Yvonne to see her look so worried. "He says it isn't possible for Saul to ever be the same."

"*Il est impossible de dire dans quelle mesure son cerveau pourra récupérer.*"

"It's impossible to say how well his mind can recover."

"*Mais nous savons qu'il restera paralysé du côté gauche.*"

"But we know the left side of his body will be paralyzed," Daniela translated.

Yvonne swallowed hard. Not "we think," but "we know." Her son would never have the use of half his body again. She gritted her teeth and tried to digest this information. Could she help Saul figure out ways to make his life meaningful even without the use of his left arm and leg? She wasn't sure.

Day 6 - Sunday, April 9, 2006

Church bells peeled through the town, but despite the Sabbath the pace on the streets in this city of a quarter million people had hardly abated. Jim and Yvonne stood beside Daniela at a busy Angers intersection. Unlike at a traffic light, the cars in a roundabout rarely cleared for pedestrians to cross. Finally, Daniela saw a gap. "Let's go!"

Yvonne ran across the street dragging her luggage behind her. This morning they were moving to Logis Ozanam. It was an accommodation set up for the families of critically ill patients. The major advantage was that it was only a five-minute walk from the front door of CHU d'Angers. They'd decided that the double bus transfer and long walk to get from hotel to hospital and back each day was just too complicated. It would be nice to have a home base so much closer to Saul.

Yvonne and Jim followed Daniela toward the hospital. At least, that's the direction Yvonne hoped they were going. The ground they covered now didn't seem even slightly familiar.

"It never occurred to me that the weather here would be this cold," Yvonne said.

The sun peeked through patchy clouds today, but the air was brisk. Both Jim and Yvonne wore short-sleeved shirts with a blue Delta Air Lines blanket wrapped around their shoulders. They were holding hands as usual and walking as close together as possible to preserve heat.

"We'll find a place where you can buy some warm clothes later this afternoon," Daniela said. "I noticed that neither of you ate much. Do we need to find something you like better?"

Yvonne shook her head. "It's not that. We just can't eat."

"We're a mess, Daniela. I hope you don't get tired of us," Jim said.

Yvonne noticed he'd forgotten to remove the little pieces of toilet paper stuck to his face where he'd nicked himself shaving in three places that morning. She gently picked them off. "It's almost like we're your little ducklings, Daniela. I feel dependent on you for everything; like the toothpaste you lent us yesterday morning."

Daniela giggled. "I like helping you. Don't worry about it."

"I can't believe I mistook a tube of anti-fungal cream for Colgate when I was packing. We've also got to find a way to replace the medication I forgot. I don't know where my mind has gone."

"I do," Jim said. "You left it in Dalton along with mine."

Yvonne couldn't suppress a slight smile. That's certainly how it felt. Then she pointed to a soaring Catholic cathedral across street where the bell ringing originated. Ornate stone spires scraped the cloudy sky. "Do we have time to stop in there? I'd like to pray."

"Of course," Daniela said, "But that's the Cathédrale St-Maurice. You're not Catholic."

Jim strode toward the church. "No, but we'll take all the help we can get."

The impossibly high vaulted interior of the cathedral felt serene. Even in running shoes, Yvonne felt her footfalls reverberating from the mosaic tile floor to the thick, gray walls. Magical light filtered down to their level from stained glass windows high on the walls. Yvonne soaked in all of the tranquility she could.

After prayers they resumed their trek. Yvonne breathed a sigh of relief when she finally recognized the distinctive marble and copper dome of the hospital. Their first order of business, though, was getting settled in their new accommodations. They dragged their luggage past the front entrance of the hospital and then up a winding road until they reached a small building labeled "Logis Ozanam."

An elderly nun greeted them at the door. "*Américains?*"

Yvonne nodded.

"*Parlez-vous français?*"

"*Non.* Sorry," Yvonne said.

"I no speak English," the nun said.

Yvonne pointed to Daniela, approaching up the cobbled road. "She can help."

The nun spoke in compassionate tones to Daniela who translated to the Raisins. Then she walked them through the common areas: a kitchen for all to share, a communal washer and dryer, a sitting room with a television, a library, and a lovely little patio with a garden. Finally she showed them to their room: three cots instead of a bed, a tiny shower, a private toilet. They could use the extra cot as a makeshift dresser. The accommodations were very simple, but clean. It was perfect.

Yvonne decided to unpack for the first time. It felt comforting to fold her belongings and organize them on the spare cot. As she worked Daniela and the nun talked. Yvonne understood that Daniela would be upstairs where three families shared a single bath. Having her nearby calmed Yvonne even further. Daniela had become her life raft in uncertain seas.

When the unpacking was done Yvonne, Jim, and Daniela headed off through the streets of Angers just as the Philosopher had suggested. For the first few miles they were silent. Yvonne found herself thinking about the doctor's prognosis for Saul's left side. She thought Jim might be, too.

When Daniela stepped into a store to buy some fruit Jim spoke up. "I'm not suggesting in any way that we give up on Saul's recovery, but we have to plan for what might happen."

Yvonne realized she'd been wrong about his thoughts.

Jim continued. "If we can build something from the tragedy, maybe that's better than doing nothing at all."

"What are you getting at?" Yvonne asked.

"There might not be a bigger heart than Saul's on this planet. It shouldn't go to waste. He'd live on in a sense."

"We tried to talk about this with Saul once, remember? He didn't want it."

Jim looked down at her. He'd aged a lot in the past few days. "Maybe that's because to Saul dying seemed impossible. That's what I thought when I was his age. I was rappelling off dangerous cliffs and spelunking through flooded caves. I rode my bike fast down hills, and I drove my car even faster up them. It wasn't because I had a death wish; it was because I thought I was immortal. Since then I've learned differently."

"But Saul's heart might not even fit into a regular-sized chest. His lungs either," Yvonne said. During his first year with Crédit Agricole's Espoir Team their doctors had done extensive tests on him. Many people with a curved spine have a stooped posture and a caved chest, but as a consequence of Saul's purposefully straight posture, his chest was normal. Coupled with his kyphosis, the result was that Saul's chest cavity was much larger than average. The doctors concluded that if his chest had been caved, despite the shape of his back, he wouldn't have been an exceptional endurance athlete.

Next they tested his physiological parameters. That's when they discovered that Saul's lung capacity was double that of the average person. His heart size hadn't yet been accurately measured, but it was definitely big as well. During the mandatory physicals prior to a recent team camp he'd undergone an ultrasound. When the doctor saw Saul's heart on the monitor he couldn't believe it. He told a nearby reporter that Saul's heart was more than twice the average size. The reporter scoffed, and the doctor challenged him to climb onto an examination table for a comparison.

Others gathered around. They gasped in amazement as they watched side-by-side ultrasounds. Some observers estimated that Saul's heart was triple the size of the journalists. Several joked that the test actually proved a different suspicion—that this particular reporter was heartless.

Doctors would never know for certain whether Saul's lung and heart were larger than normal because of the greater space in his chest, or if their size was the result of the massive amounts of training he did, though the latter explanation seemed more likely. The important point was that, without realizing it, Saul had uniquely sculpted his body to excel at cycling. He'd turned a cosmetic weakness into an enormous physical strength. The uniquely shaped back that classmates used to tease Saul about now housed a super-sized engine room.

Jim put a hand on Yvonne's. His eyes glistened beneath a sheen of tears.

"Saul also avoided talking about organ donation because he always believed that to reach his goals he had to focus on Plan A, never acknowledge Plan B. But there are times in life you have to make adjustments. Also, back when we talked to him about this stuff I don't think he was mature enough to understand what it really meant. Remember, he worried that if he became an organ donor an overanxious doctor might take some of his vital parts away before he was actually dead."

Yvonne thought about the statement. Jim was right that Saul had dismissed the idea partly based on belligerent misperceptions. Her opinion about donating her own organs had always been strong. If a person can give the gift of life after their own life is no more, what a beautiful way to live on. If it was her decision to make, and if Saul's situation came to that, she now knew she'd do it. She would honor her son by donating his organs. For now, though, she wanted to hang onto him more than anything, and she planned to fight alongside him with everything she had. "I agree with you, Jimmy. But let's not tell the doctors yet. I don't want anybody assuming that we're giving up the fight."

Jim nodded. "Good thinking. It's just between us."

Daniela rejoined them and handed out nectarines. They walked along slowly until they found an Internet Café. Jim stepped inside and paid for access. He typed in www.SaulRaisin.com. He got a message that appeared to be the French equivalent of "This page cannot be displayed." He rechecked the address he'd typed in. It was pure gibberish. This time he typed more carefully and discovered that some of the keys were in different places than the keyboards he was used to. He hunted and pecked until he had entered the correct address. When the site came up he clicked on the guestbook.

Thousands of entries appeared, all wishing Saul well and offering prayers. Yvonne's eyes welled with tears again. Some of the notes were from friends of the family; others were from people who apparently knew their son, but the vast majority were from people who simply wanted to say that their thoughts were with Saul and they were devastated by what they'd heard. The messages overflowed with admiration, encouragement, inspiration, prayers, and hope. Reading these thoughts, Yvonne felt less alone in the world.

Jim and Yvonne knew how to add posts to Saul's blog from their home computer where everything had already been configured, but they had no idea how to do it from this public machine. They needed to say something to all the well-wishers, though, so they added an entry to the guestbook:

We want to thank everyone for their love and prayers. Please keep sending them to Saul. Saul is stable but still in a deep coma. Hopefully soon we will have good news. Love, Jim and Yvonne and Daniela

*   *   *

That afternoon two of Saul's best friends showed up. Kilian Patour, a current Crédit Agricole teammate, and Geoffroy LeQuatre, who left Crédit Agricole for Cofidis last year, had both been like brothers to Saul. They wanted to visit his bedside and encourage him to get well.

"We can't take you to see him," Jim said. "You don't realize how bad it is."

"We can handle it," Kilian said.

Yvonne put her hand on Kilian's. "Saul's in a very bad way. You don't need to see that. It's too frightening and depressing."

Saul's friends left, disappointed but understanding.

Prior to the days first visit with Saul the Raisins and Daniela spoke again with the lady doctor they'd met on their first day in the same conference room. Yvonne steeled herself for the harsh delivery to come.

The doctor's expression was as clinical as before as she flipped open the medical chart. "Saul's intra-cranial pressure has normalized and remained constant for past forty-eight hours. Consequently, we have decided to discontinue Pentathol."

"Is that the medication that's keeping him in the coma?" Jim asked.

The doctor nodded.

"Does this mean he's improving?" Jim asked.

The doctor shook her head. "It means he is stable, but by no means out of danger."

"How soon will he wake up?"

The doctor thought for a moment. "Don't be sure yet that he will wake up. If he does, maybe fourteen days is a good estimate, but it might take three months or more."

Yvonne nodded reluctantly. "When will we be able to speak with the surgeon who performed Saul's operation?"

The doctor looked confused. "That won't be necessary. You can speak to me."

"We'd just like to hear his opinion of how things went," Yvonne said.

"The surgeon is very busy man," the doctor explained. "He's one of world's top neurologists. Saul is under my care and that of other ICU doctors now."

In America talking with the surgeon would be standard procedure. Yvonne realized that it didn't matter how things were done at home, though. This was France, and they were proud of doing things in their own ways. "Yes. We understand. Please thank him for saving Saul's life."

The doctor nodded, still wearing her permanent frown.

"Is there anything else we need to discuss before we visit with our son?" Yvonne asked.

The doctor took a prescription pad from her pocket. She scribbled as she spoke. "Fill this at pharmacy. You mentioned your anxiety to your friend, Roger. He told Dr. Ménard who asked me to give you something to help. These are pills for nerves. They are for both of you. Your health is as important as Saul's."

*   *   *

The two visits with Saul went much like the previous ones. They told their son about their day, talked to him about home, kissed him again and again, and repeated how much they loved him. They sang songs from his childhood: "Lavender Blue," the "ABC Song," "Mockingbird Song," and anything else they could think of. They reviewed birthdays, the names of family members and acquaintances, and mailing addresses. They tried everything they possibly could to stimulate his mind.

That evening, shortly after they retired for the night, one of Yvonne's cell phones rang. It showed a phone number she didn't recognize.

"Hello?" she said.

"Hi, Mrs. Raisin. This is Lance Armstrong. I'm calling to offer you help in any way I can."

Yvonne smiled. "Lance! You can't imagine what it will mean to Saul simply to know that you called. I can't wait to tell him."

"Good. Then tell him this. He's a punk." There was laughter in Lance's tone, but Yvonne was confused.

"Will that mean something to him?" she asked.

"Yeah. He'll remember. We met up on a training ride last year along with Axel Merckx. We rode really hard for five hours. Saul and I dropped Axel several times. On the slopes of the day's last climb, the Col de Braus, it was just Saul and me. Then he attacked!"

In cycling an "attack" is a vicious acceleration intended to leave the competition behind, or at least put them into serious pain. Yvonne grinned wider than she had for days. She'd heard Saul's version of this same story the evening after it happened.

"Once I caught my breath at the top I asked him, 'What kind of a punk are you, Raisin? Nobody attacks me. I make them pay.' But I couldn't drop Saul. We laughed so hard." Lance chuckled again at the memory and then added, "Saul has got to get better because I need to ride with him again. That boy of yours is crazy strong."

Yvonne laughed. Wasn't it just like her Saul to ignore convention and attack the man the rest of the peloton feared? It felt so good to come upon a bright spot in the midst of such a dark time. "Thank you, Lance," she said. "I just hope he lives. I'm going to tell him about your call when we visit him tomorrow. He hears our words. We know he does."

"I'm sure you're right," Lance said. "Stay strong, okay. Call anytime, and if you need anything in America—help with doctors, hospitals, anything at all—I'll be honored to do whatever I can."

Day 7 - Monday, April 10, 2006

At a bakery in the heart of Angers, Yvonne and Jim pointed to the pastries they wanted for breakfast. Daniela gave their order to the cashier in flowing French and then paid while Jim and Yvonne took their food to a corner table like well-behaved children.

On previous visits to France, breakfast had been Yvonne's favorite part of the day. She'd loved the easy cadence of a fresh morning getting underway in ancient corridors where similar routines had been replayed for centuries. She'd savored the smells of fresh-baked bread wafting from stone ovens. She'd salivated over pastries that put American-made counterparts to shame. That was on previous trips, though. This time everything had changed. She could tell the same old-world magic existed in this town, but barriers in her mind prevented her from experiencing it in the same carefree way as before.

The center of the town was made up of small shops on cobbled, pedestrian-only streets. Down the lane, Yvonne watched as a shopkeeper filled an oaken bucket from a communal well. He added soap to the water and then used a long brush to polish the cobbled walk in front of his hat store. Instead of marveling at his charm the way she would have liked to, she felt jealous of the man's simple concerns. She needed an unimportant task for herself. "How far are we going to walk today?" she asked.

"Ten miles, I'd guess," Jim said. "Maybe more."

Daniela squeezed Yvonne's forearm as she pulled up a chair and sat down. "That's a long way, but it won't be a problem because if either of us falls behind, Jim's neon coat will be visible for blocks."

A burst of laughter escaped Yvonne's lips before she even thought to hold it back. Thank God Daniela was here to lighten the mood every now and then. Her comment about Jim's clothing hit the mark, even though they all knew there was no chance he'd be blocks ahead of either of them. Jim needed to hold Yvonne's hand just as much as she needed to hold his.

Still, she couldn't get used to seeing her husband in the loud blue and green fleece parka he'd purchased the day before. He'd selected it because it happened to be for sale in a grocery store in the modern part of town. Yvonne had tried to talk him out of it but he'd been too bullheaded to spend an extra moment shopping for something he liked. She'd taken the time to find a gray sweater that at least matched her tastes.

Yvonne looked at the slate sky. "Maybe we should buy umbrellas."

Jim shook his head. "I doubt we'll need them."

Yvonne's cell phone rang. "Hi Roger."

"Hello, Yvonne. I have update on Saul." Roger understood how confused the Raisins were by their face-to-face doctors meetings, so he'd come up with a way to help them better understand Saul's status. Dr. Ménard would get updated information from the hospital and relay it to Roger who would pass it on to Yvonne. He planned to do this once or twice a day, depending on the situation. It wasn't very efficient, but it really ought to help to fill in the blanks. "You know about the reduction in Pentathol?"

"Yes. Has he begun waking?" Yvonne asked hopefully.

"That is still maybe weeks away, but this is step in right direction," Roger said.

They talked about other minor developments. It was mainly a rehash of things she already knew, but it was comforting to speak.

"I appreciate all the help you're giving us Roger," Yvonne said.

"I am doing this for me, as well." Roger answered.

Yvonne knew he was hurting almost as badly as she and Jim were. She'd seen it in his face while he'd been with them, and she could hear it in his voice now. He wanted to do anything he could to help. She felt so grateful for his support. Roger was such a gentle man and a true friend.

After Roger's call the three of them walked along the Maine River to where it emptied into the Loire. The city occupied the opposite bank as well. From there they headed east, wandering along in a half daze. Along the way they stepped into each church they passed, regardless of denomination, for a moment of prayer. At about the five-mile mark it began drizzling.

Yvonne almost made a comment about umbrellas, but she glanced at her husband and held herself back. He was hurting so badly and she loved him far too much to cause more pain over a petty issue. She knew he was equally sensitive to her feelings. In their entire married life they'd never had a major argument, but since the accident occurred they hadn't even had a mild disagreement.

Jim took off his parka and held it over the women's heads. "No use for all of us to get wet."

The parka wasn't very effective protection, though, and they were all soaked to the bone by the time they found a place to buy umbrellas. They hurried into the shelter of Logis Ozanam, shivering cold, at two in the afternoon. That left barely enough time to warm up and dry off before going to see Saul.

*   *   *

Yvonne wished she could take something into her son's room to brighten the place up, but flowers and balloons weren't allowed. The doctors wanted to keep the environment as sterile as possible. Decorations would just get in the way, and Saul probably wouldn't have been aware of them, anyway.

Yvonne approached her son's bedside. The bulky bandaging on his head had been replaced with a much simpler version. She could now see his hair for the first time. Some tufts were still full length, but wide swaths had been shaved for the surgery and to sew up the wound. She touched the stubbly growth near a jagged scar that ran almost to the crown of his head. "It's raining today, Saul. That's why I can't open your window." The room's only natural light came from an opening high above his head. It was impossible to see anything through it except for a rectangular chunk of gray sky.

She lifted his right hand and stroked it. "I love you, Saul."

Jim told Saul he loved him, too. Then he told his son about the cycling accident that had put him into the coma, going over all the details. He'd done this before, and he'd do it again. They didn't want Saul to wake up and immediately become scared and confused.

"Lance called last night," Yvonne said. "He told me to tell you you're a punk."

Saul lay motionless. The gray pallor of his skin made him feel very distant.

Yvonne kept stroking his hand. "You wouldn't believe how many people are praying for you."

Saul's right bicep twitched.

Yvonne's heart skipped a beat.

"Did you see that, Honey?" Jim asked.

She nodded, hardly able to contain the excitement. "You can hear us, can't you Saul."

His right calf twitched.

She took a deep breath. "Your dad and I love you so much. We know you're fighting with everything you have. We're here to help you get better."

Saul's fingers twitched ever so slightly against her palm. She looked at her husband and then pointed at the fingers. "Jimmy, he's trying to move!"

"The brain pressure is decreasing, too," Jim said, pointing at the monitor. "I'll tell the doctor." He hurried to the nurses' station.

Yvonne kept speaking to Saul while she watched Jim talk to that day's on-duty doctor, the Philosopher. Jim explained what they'd seen in a charade-like manner. The Philosopher followed him back to Saul's room and watched for a moment.

Saul's left bicep twitched.

"That's his paralyzed side!" Jim said.

The Philosopher nodded. He seemed deep in thought, searching for the words in English to explain what was going on. "This is … normal."

Yvonne's spirits deflated. "But he hasn't moved before."

"He has for us." The doctor indicated Saul's fingers and toes. "We pinch to test pain response. He twitches to pull away, much like you are seeing. No pain reaction on the left, though. It is paralyzed. Sorry."

Yvonne looked at the doctor with pleading eyes, but there was nothing more to be said. These movements were apparently tiny and random muscle spasms. Nothing more. After awhile the Philosopher nodded politely and then returned to the nurses' station.

Jim put an arm around Yvonne. God, it was difficult to have their bubbles burst daily. The doctor seemed determined to paint their world in gloomy shades.

After the visit they dragged themselves to the waiting room to talk and sip Coke Lites. They were becoming familiar, at least by sight, with the friends and families of other critically ill patients. The language barrier and the personal nature of the situations made it hard to learn much, but it was obvious that most of the prognoses were bleak. A polite "*bonjour*" and later "*au revoir*" was often the only conversation. The bloodshot eyes and drawn faces told the Raisins their fellow mourners were generally receiving bad news. This day was particularly gloomy in the waiting room as a little girl across the hall from Saul clung to life after crashing on a scooter. Death always lurked nearby at the CHU d'Angers ICU.

It didn't help that there was no natural light in the waiting room. Two of the walls were banks of industrial looking lockers where visitors could store their personal items. The chairs were old and worn. A vase of fresh flowers set out daily by the hospital staff was the only bright spot in the bleak space.

The Raisins returned to Saul's bedside for a second visit from 6:30 to 8:00 PM. The bed across the hall the little girl had occupied was now vacant.

Yvonne grieved for the lost child, but there was nothing she could do. She had to devote her energy to Saul. She and Jim talked and wept and sang with their son, but as always, the time felt too short. It would have been nice if the hospital staff allowed morning visits, but it wasn't their way.

Yvonne tried not to overlook the good things. They were keeping Saul clean. The nurses and doctors spoke to him often in French, and even used English when they could. Yvonne felt such efforts were going the extra mile on their part. Saul had ended up in the best place possible, considering the circumstances. The staff here clearly cared about her son's comfort, and they were doing everything possible to help him recover.

After the second visit ended Jim and Yvonne wandered back to Logis Ozanam and made a salad. While they ate in the garden a pleasant old lady showed up and tried to teach them French. Yvonne loved the sound of the language and wished she could learn it. She knew that Jim did too, but their minds were so frazzled they couldn't retain much.

They went to bed early, both mentally and physically exhausted. Yvonne knew sleep would be fitful and morning would come soon. She had to recuperate as much as possible before it did. She was here for one purpose only: Saul. Learning French would have been nice, but for the moment she had to focus her limited energy on her son. After all, each painful visit was potentially the last one she'd ever get to make.

Day 8 – Tuesday, April 11, 2006

Yvonne looked at the bottle of stress pills the lady doctor had prescribed for her and Jim. "I don't want to take these any more. I don't like the way they make me feel, and I don't think they work anyway."

"Yeah," Jim said. "The only thing that would relieve my stress is good news about Saul."

Yvonne tossed the pills into a trash can, simultaneously uncertain how much more bad news she could take, and certain that the pills didn't make the news seem any better. Her cell phone rang. She looked at the display before answering. "Bonjour, Roger."

He spoke urgently. "Yvonne, Dr. Ménard is at the hospital waiting on you. Can you go there now?"

The Crédit Agricole team physician was in town again? "Of course. What's going on?"

"He will fill you in," Roger said.

Along with Daniela, the Raisins hurried to the ICU waiting room. They pressed the intercom and asked for Dr. Ménard. A nurse told them there would be a delay, so Jim went to the restroom while the women took seats on the couch.

Soon Dr. Ménard stepped out of the ICU.

"This is a surprise. What are you doing here?" Yvonne asked.

Dr. Ménard hugged her and then kissed her cheek. "Where goes Jim?"

"In the restroom."

The doctor said something in French to Daniela and then she said, "Go get him, quick. Dr. Ménard says he has important news."

Yvonne didn't know what to think. In the short time they'd been acquainted she'd come to know Dr. Ménard as a gentle and dignified man, certainly not the sort to interrupt someone's privacy under any circumstance, but now his attitude was urgent. She hurried to the restroom door and knocked. "Jimmy, what are you doing in there? Hurry up!"

Jim stepped into the hallway. "What is it?"

Dr. Ménard already had the door to the private conference room open. Daniela was seated inside. The doctor gestured for the Raisins to join them. When they did he closed the door and turned toward them. Now Yvonne noticed tears in his eyes, but he seemed to be grinning.

As Dr. Ménard spoke rapidly a brilliant smile spread across his face.

Daniela translated. "Saul is coming out of his coma."

Yvonne couldn't believe her ears. It was the best news imaginable. She sprang to her feet. "He's what? How can they tell? What's Saul doing?"

Beside her Jim was asking the same sorts of questions, but Daniela wasn't paying attention to either of them as she urgently interrogated the doctor. Yvonne caught Daniela's eye and somehow ended up in her arms. Jim hugged both of them. The women started bouncing in anticipation. Jim joined them and they also pulled Dr. Ménard into their hugs

"Let's hear what else the doctor has to tell us," Jim said.

Dr. Ménard looked on the verge of bursting with joy. Tears of happiness streaked his face. He spoke rapidly.

"He says Saul can't speak because of the tube down his throat," Daniela said, "but he is slightly coherent."

"Can he communicate?" Yvonne asked.

"Not exactly," Daniela translated. "His eyes are closed and he's probably pretty confused, but that's to be expected. This is a very important step. These are extremely encouraging signs."

"What body parts has he moved?" Jim asked.

"His arms and legs, and his fingers and toes. Most of his movement is just caused by agitation, not an effort to communicate or anything like that, but any movement at all is very meaningful."

Yvonne looked at Jim. Her husband practically glowed with relief. "The left side?"

Daniela asked Dr. Ménard. He nodded as he spoke.

Daniela looked proud as she delivered the translation. "Both hands. Both feet. His movement on the left is much less than the right, and he has facial paralysis on the left as well, but he's doing better than the doctors expected in every respect."

"Thank you God," Jim silently said. "Oh, thank you. Thank you. Thank you for giving me my boy back."

Tension drained from Jim so rapidly Yvonne could feel it flowing from the room. She leaned down and hugged her husband. "Saul's a fighter. I knew he'd make it!"

"What a glorious day," Jim said. "This is the best day of my life!"

Dr. Ménard and Daniela had embraced. Everybody was covered with tears, even stoic Daniela. Her joy was unmistakable.

"I can hardly wait to see him. I'm tingling from head to toe," Yvonne said.

"That's why it's good we have a moment to compose ourselves," Daniela said. "I feel the same. The reason Dr. Ménard brought us into this private room to share the news was out of respect for the other patient's families. It wouldn't be proper to celebrate in the midst of their suffering. We should hide our joy until we are with Saul."

Yvonne had come to accept that French ways were different from hers. If they believed she should keep her joy private, she'd do her best to abide by that standard. She didn't want to offend anybody. She just wanted her son back. Saul was returning to life and that's all that mattered.

Finally the nurse came to invite them into the ICU. Yvonne did her best to hide her smile, but she wasn't entirely successful. She could hardly refrain from running to her son. At this moment she felt such joy there was no way she could keep it from overflowing.

As they approached Saul's bed, two more nurses stood watching him in what seemed to be a mixture of amazement and anticipation. Yvonne peered at her son's eyes as she neared him, but they were closed. She saw no movement at all. Had he slipped back into the coma again? She gently took his right hand in hers. "I love you, Saul."

He squeezed her hand. Once. Twice. Three times.

Yvonne looked up at Daniela in amazement. "He said he loves me."

"He spoke?" Daniela asked.

Yvonne shook her head. Her fingers were still pulsating with the incredible message Saul had delivered through them. "When he was four years old Saul decided he was too big for hugs and kisses in public. Jim showed him that three squeezes means 'I love you.' Saul still uses his silent code with me often, and he did it just now."

Jim took hold of Saul's left hand lightly. "I love you, Saul."

Yvonne watched the left hand contract slightly, three times.

Color rushed into Jim's face. Tears ran down his cheeks. "I don't care what the doctors said. There's more here than they thought there would be."

A nurse asked Daniela something in French, and Daniela spoke with her. Then translated to English. "She thinks maybe you are mistaken. This is too quick for such things to happen."

Yvonne signaled the nurse to come over. She put the woman's hand into Saul's, and then said, "I love you with all my heart, Saul Raisin."

The nurse's expression became concentrated for a moment, and then her jaw dropped open. "Il serre!"

The nurse cried and spoke to Saul in French. Then she politely stepped aside, thanking Yvonne as she hurried to tell the doctor.

Watching Saul at this moment was déjà vu. She recalled waking him from his crib two decades ago one day when she'd been in a hurry to get to some appointment. He'd obviously been in a very deep sleep, yet he was pleasant and determined to cooperate even though he was by no means all there. Saul's expression was dull, particularly around the closed eyes. He drooled. He looked incredibly weak.

Yvonne stepped away from the bed. "Come talk to him, Daniela."

Daniela stepped forward and took Saul's hand in a finger to finger grip. "I'm here, Saul. I love you. You're strong. You will get through this."

Saul, his eyes still closed, used his thumb to pin Daniela's thumb against his index finger.

"You dirty cheater," Daniela said. "You didn't warn me we were going to have a thumb war."

Saul's expression didn't change. Eyes closed. Face placid.

Daniela kissed him and then began a rhythmic chant. "One, two, three, four, let's, have, a thumb, war." At each word she touched her thumb alternately to the fleshy part of the first knuckle of Saul's hand and then hers. He moved his thumb in the opposite direction.

Before she knew it Saul had pinned her thumb again. Daniela giggled. It sounded even more refreshing than her laughter from previous days.

"Best three out of five," Daniela said.

Jim leaned down to Saul's ear. "Let her win this time. She's been so good to us. She deserves it."

"One, two, three, four, let's, have, a thumb, war."

Daniela faked left, then right, then left again—and suddenly she was pinned. Even freshly emerged from a coma, Saul played to win.

The Philosopher, who in many ways had been the gloomiest of all their doctors, stood at the foot of the bed. Yvonne didn't know how long he'd been watching, but guessed the nurse sent him in. He watched Daniela playing with her boyfriend for awhile, and then a smile broke across his face. "This is wonderful."

Day 9 – Wednesday April 12, 2006

As the Raisins headed out for their walk the nun who ran Logis Ozanam approached them. She wore a warm smile as usual. Then she tapped her ear and pointed in the direction of the hospital to indicate she'd heard the news. Yvonne and Jim nodded happily.

The nun laid both hands on her heart in a loving gesture. Then she steepled them in front of her face as if praying. When Yvonne nodded again the nun spread her arms in the general direction of Saul's hospital bed, seeming to pantomime that she'd been sending prayers his way.

"Oh, thank you so much." Yvonne hugged the nun. So many people, so many wonderful souls, the majority of whom she didn't even know, had prayed for her son to heal. Saul's miracle yesterday was the result. How could she ever repay all of this kindness?

Yvonne's spirit felt elevated as she stepped into the bright sunlight. For the first time she actually noticed the large, diverse campus. CHU d'Angers was an older building, rundown both outside and inside, except for the ICU which was new and clean. The stonework was eroded and many of the decorative sconces were broken. Other beautiful buildings surrounded it. French architects seemed to have a particular knack for creating incredible spaces.

"Look, there are flower boxes beneath nearly every window on nearly every building," Jim said, as though noticing his surroundings for the first time.

"Angers is sometimes called the most flowered city in Europe," Daniela said.

All along their walk they pointed out other pretty things to one another: old buildings, ornate fountains, gnarled trees, and graceful archways. They walked to the beautiful gothic Cathédrale St-Maurice where Yvonne had already prayed many times, but for the first time she noticed the façade of ornate stonework. Full sized historic figures were sculpted into the stone pillars at the entrance. Yvonne wondered what significance these people had to the town's history.

Later in their walk they passed an imposing fortress that seemed to glower over the city from behind turreted walls. It looked to be a thirteenth century structure, not at all ornate like the fairytale castles of later eras. High on the ramparts there were a few cross shaped battlements for shooting arrows through, but despite its utilitarian nature, the castle did have a decorative touch. The builders had constructed most of it using dark rock similar to the outcroppings in the immediate vicinity, but they'd accented the walls by inserting narrow horizontal lines of white stone at regular intervals. The moat, which probably contained crocodiles at one point in the castle's history, now housed an intricate garden where perfectly manicured plants and vibrantly colored flowers made up an ornate, living tapestry.

"It's called the Château d'Angers," Daniela said. "The Nazis used this castle as an ammunitions dump. The Allies were forced to bomb it. Much of this town was destroyed in World War II, but as you can see, they've done a remarkable job restoring it."

The road to Logis Ozanam was tight and cobbled. Men worked on rebuilding a wall. Jim and Yvonne watched as the craftsmen hand chiseled the perfectly new wall, flat and clean, to make it look old. The French invested a lot of money and effort in maintaining the aged texture of their cities.

Speaking of money, the Raisins were running low on cash. They contacted Gérard, a Crédit Agricole banker and a good friend of Saul's.

He arranged for them to go by one of the branches and get what they needed. Then he said, "I don't think of Americans in the way I once did. Do you know what changed me?"

"No," Yvonne said.

"Saul. Because of him, I see things differently than before. He always thinks of others first. That took me by surprise. It did not match my preconceptions of your country. He has helped me see that all Americans are individuals, and that some of them are very good people. I think this understanding will have great importance in my life."

Yvonne smiled. "There are many good people in France, too."

"Yes, there are." Gérard's tone conveyed his pleasure. "Saul will always be loved by them. France will forever have a place in its heart for him."

"Thank you, Gérard," Yvonne said.

They returned to Logis Ozanam just in time to greet Jim's younger brother Phil and his wife Teresa. They'd called that morning from Charles de Gaulle airport in Paris, and again while rushing along at 300 kilometers per hour on the TGV train from Paris to Angers. Now they'd completed their big day of travel, carrying with them long sleeve t-shirts, medicine, and other supplies Jim and Yvonne had forgotten when they sprinted out of Dalton a week earlier.

Phil wore the same compassionate expression that had put Yvonne on the verge of tears when she saw him more than a week earlier on their doorstep. That morning she held back tears of misery. Today, just a week later, she was blinking back tears of joy.

"This is killing Phil and me," Teresa said. "I can't imagine what the two of you are going through."

Yvonne hugged her in-laws and then introduced Daniela. More hugs were shared.

"I already love this girl," Teresa said.

As soon as the hellos were complete Jim said, "I'll bet you thought we forgot to get a present for Phil." His birthday had been the day before.

Phil looked at Jim with a confused expression. "You didn't need to—"

"We have a present and you'd better not take it back," Jim said. "Saul is awake!"

Teresa burst into tears. She'd long had a reputation as waterworks city, but now she was a mess. Soon Jim and Phil couldn't resist crying, and that caused Yvonne to start sobbing too, but this was a happy cry. It invigorated her to share good news with loved ones, and it comforted her to hear people speak with familiar Southern accents.

"You can't imagine how hard this has been," Yvonne said, "and partly for reasons we never expected."

"Like what?" Teresa asked.

"Cultural differences. The biggest problem is that language isolates us almost completely. We can't make the simplest requests without a translator."

"I thought most of the world spoke English as a second language," Phil said.

"That's an attitude the French resent. Even those who do speak English are sometimes unhappy that we would show up in their country without making the effort to learn their language."

"The French are very proud," Jim said. "Many of them love American culture, but others resent our influence. It aggravates them to see vineyards disappear and Golden Arches spring up in their place."

"I don't blame them for that," Phil said. "Keep the Golden Arches out of my neighborhood, too."

Jim nodded in agreement. "So when an American shows up and expects everybody to speak English it can anger them. They feel disrespected. But if language was the only challenge it might be easy to overcome."

"What are the others?" Phil asked.

"Everything is done differently here," Yvonne said. "The letters on a computer keyboard aren't in the same places, a doctor's relationship with his patient is different, distances and temperature are measured on unfamiliar scales, common courtesies are far more important, the health-care system is confusing in a different way than ours. We were in such shock when we arrived that for the first several days it didn't occur to us that we were insulting people critical to Saul's health at nearly every turn. When we asked simple questions like, 'Why is the head of Saul's bed elevated today?' it came out sounding like a criticism, as if we were doubting the doctor's wisdom."

Jim nodded. "Now we try to make sure our comments show respect. It's the same sort of respect we'd try to show to an American doctor, except we need to be more careful of our words here in France."

"So you don't ask questions?" Teresa asked.

Yvonne shook her head. "We still ask questions, and they do their best to give us answers, but we can tell they are sometimes as confused by our ways as we are by theirs. We pretty much understand the main thing we can do here is offer support to Saul and to make things better for him. Frustrating his doctors wouldn't benefit him. It really doesn't make a difference whether we understand why they've elevated Saul's head or not, but it makes a big difference whether the medical staff feels respected or not, so that's our focus."

That afternoon Jim and Yvonne were very excited to see their son alongside Phil and Teresa. For the first time, Yvonne made an effort to memorize the route through the hospital to Saul's room as Daniela led them along. It wasn't difficult to get there, but until now she'd been incapable of devoting attention to unnecessary details. Her mind had been fixed only on Saul in his tiny, antiseptic room.

They arrived a bit too early. Everybody took seats in the bleak little waiting room and waited.

"Only two at a time are allowed, so we'll have to rotate through," Jim said. "Yvonne and I will briefly go first if it's okay with everyone."

"Of course," Teresa said.

Phil nodded his agreement. "Remember that time, before Teresa and I were dating, when you drove me to Florida?"

Yvonne chuckled. "The ice storm. We were stuck in the car for twelve hours and Saul played that little hand-held video game the whole time. I can still remember the obnoxious music. I thought you were going to kill him."

"I almost did. He was such a little pain in the butt." Phil chuckled. "Now I'd do anything to return to those days."

"Do you remember the mountain bike ride where he couldn't keep up and then we all got lost?" Jim asked.

Phil grinned. "Yeah. That was the last time I could go faster than him. What was he? Twelve years old?"

"That sounds about right," Yvonne said.

"Then there was the time he knocked himself out during that BMX race in Calhoun. They hauled him to the hospital, and he practically drove that cute little doctor insane with his incessant 'Who's your Daddy?' routine. What a kid you got yourselves."

"Yeah," Jim said. "What a kid."

Yvonne experienced an unusual contentment. It was like relatives had dropped by for a visit in their Dalton living room. "This is so nice," she said.

"What is?" Jim asked.

"Talking normal about old times. I wish Saul could be here in the middle of it. It's the sort of stuff he needs to hear, listening to us jabber about life. I'll bet that would be good for him."

"I'm sure you're right," Jim said.

When the Raisins were finally allowed into the ICU Saul's eyes were open. He winked at Jim. Jim stood there for awhile, and then turned away. Yvonne watched him wipe a tear from his eye.

Despite the wink, Saul looked so scared. His eyes were watery and red. He looked to be deep in a fog and utterly confused. Fatigue emanated from every pore. Then his left side began shuddering.

"What's wrong with him?" Yvonne asked.

The tremor became more violent.

Jim got a nurse's attention and showed her what Saul was going through. "Normal?"

The nurse watched Saul for a moment as the shaking subsided. "*Oui. Normal,*" she said.

As comforting as it was to hear that things were all right, it frightened Yvonne to have such incomplete access to information. She wanted to know why he had the tremor in the first place, whether he was expected to have more, and how long they would last.

The others rotated through the room for brief visits. Saul gave a weak thumbs-up to his Uncle Phil and held onto his Aunt Teresa's hand. As visiting hours wound down Yvonne and Daniela were at Saul's side.

Yvonne decided to repeat a story from the day before. "Lance called."

Saul looked at her, mustering all the concentration he could.

"He says you're a punk."

Saul stared at her.

"Lance thinks you're a tough kid," Yvonne said.

Saul blinked.

"Lance is right," Daniela said.

Yvonne turned to Daniela. "Did Saul ever tell you about when he used to play football?"

"No."

"When he was fourteen he hurt his thumb in the first game of the year. The coach told him he ought to go see the doctor, but Saul said he'd be all right and that he wanted to play. He taped himself up with bubble wrap and duct tape, went back out, and made a game-saving tackle. Afterwards the thumb got swollen up so we went to the doctors. Turned out he'd broken a bone in his hand and torn a ligament. The doctor couldn't believe Saul had been able to play through the pain."

"Doesn't surprise me," Daniela said.

Yvonne smiled. "There's more. Saul taped himself back up for the next game, and the next game, and the next. He played the whole season with that bad thumb. That's a big deal in Dalton because it's the most football crazy town you'll ever find."

Daniela laughed. "I've heard Americans love football."

"Americans do love football, but Southerners live for it. After the season ended, the coach of Saul's team took him to the high school and introduced him to the varsity coach. He said, 'I want you to meet your best player for next season. This boy is tougher than tough.' Well the high school coach got excited about Saul joining his team, but that summer Saul fell in love with bicycle racing and the rest is history. Saul decided he wasn't interested in playing football, even though everybody begged him to. Some people were downright angry that he didn't play, as if he was somehow obligated. But that's how Saul is. Once he makes up his mind about something nobody's going to change it."

"Is that true, Saul?" Daniela asked.

He looked at her blankly. She leaned down and kissed him and then took his hand. "Thumb war?" she asked.

Saul's thumb started moving around, trying to pin hers down.

After a minute or so Saul suddenly began to tire. His foggy eyes closed but then opened again with a start. He looked around anxiously. He appeared to be frightened, like a small child separated from his mother. Yvonne wanted to take him in her arms and carry him from the hospital. She wanted to hold him to her and keep him safe. Of course that wasn't possible. She could still barely touch him because of the risk of complicating one injury or another. An honest to goodness hug would have been way too painful and dangerous to risk.

Saul was clearly exhausted. Soon, even fear wasn't motivating enough to keep him awake, and his eyelids drooped. He fought several more times for consciousness, but it was a losing battle. His eyes remained closed for longer and longer periods of time.

Yvonne caressed Saul's cheek, trying to ease him into sleep. "He's still got a long way to go, but he's going to make it, Daniela."

With a shiver, Saul dropped into REM sleep.

A nurse tapped Yvonne on the shoulder and pointed toward the door. After another brief moment of silently watching her son, Yvonne gathered her things and headed from the room. She rejoined the others in the waiting room. Teresa's eyes were filled with tears.

"He has a long, long way to go," Phil said, "but his progress is encouraging."

Jim nodded. "He's way ahead of what the doctors told us to expect. That's a good sign … a really good sign. The doctors are stunned. I love seeing their amazement, in a crazy sort of way."

"Yeah. We're lucky, Jimmy. We got a special little boy," Yvonne said.

Jim smiled. "The best part is, we still have him. I see flashes that tell me Saul's still in there. His mind, I mean. Things might be kind of hazy, but every once in awhile I catch a glimpse of the old Saul behind those eyes."

"Like when he winked at you?" Yvonne asked.

"Yeah," Jim smiled, "that wink. To me, it was worth more than all the money in the world."

Day 10 – Thursday, April 13, 2006

Jim, Yvonne, and Daniela strolled with Phil and Teresa through an open street market watching the locals barter for fruit, fish, crafts, and other supplies.

Daniela was speaking with Roger on the phone, getting the morning update. She listened for awhile and then translated. "The ICU doctors are stunned by Saul's recovery. They say he's done impossible things, so they visited the surgeon to tell him what they've seen."

Yvonne still wished she could meet this man, but Roger and others seemed to respect him for his aloofness. Yvonne now admired his skill. He'd certainly earned it. After all, this man had saved Saul's life. Hopefully she'd get to meet him one day.

An amazed expression spread over Daniela's face as she listened to Roger. "The ICU doctors couldn't believe a person who'd had part of his brain removed could wake from a coma so quickly and move all his fingers and toes. The surgeon told them there'd been a miscommunication. He didn't remove part of Saul's brain."

"You're kidding!" Jim said.

Daniela shook her head. "No. This morning they explained everything to Dr. Ménard."

All five of them burst into a happy dance in the middle of the market. Yvonne motioned for Daniela to give her the phone.

Yvonne held it to her ear. "So they didn't do the invasive surgery as we were told?"

"Definitely not," Roger said. "The surgeon thinks he may have disturbed some exterior brain cells, nothing more."

Her son was whole? Yvonne wanted to scream for joy. "This means he might be able to do everything he did before?"

There was a pause. "I'm not sure about everything. Remember when you told me you wanted Saul never to ride again?"

Yvonne searched her memory banks. "I said that?"

"Yes. On the day you arrived in France."

"Well, if you say so I'm sure I must have, but I don't remember it. Not at all. It doesn't matter what I said, though. If Saul is cleared to do those sorts of things it will be his decision and I'll support it. I'm never going to tell my son which goals he can or can't pursue. I'll be as nervous as ever … more nervous actually … but I wouldn't think of standing in the way of his dreams."

"No wonder Saul is amazing person." Roger sounded thoughtful. "He gets it from his mama and papa."

Yvonne chuckled. "I don't know about that, but I do know I'd like to get him back home where he can really recover. That's our next goal."

The idea of returning to Georgia, basic as it seemed, had hardly crossed Yvonne's mind until she made the comment. Now that she thought about it she realized getting Saul back to America was something they had to do as soon as possible. She'd move heaven and earth, if necessary, to make it a reality. Saul needed to hear his mother tongue and be around his family. If it meant selling everything the family owned or even going into debt, they needed to do it. At home their chances of getting Saul well would increase significantly.

Yvonne knew the medical staff was giving Saul the best of care, and they were doing their best to communicate the information she and Jim needed. She could tell the French doctors were sometimes as bewildered by her expectations as she was confused by the doctors' words and methods. It wasn't anybody's fault. She simply longed for the ability to discuss her questions in detail.

After their walk Jim started researching what it would take to bring Saul home. Would Crédit Agricole's insurance cover his care? When would he be well enough to travel? How could he travel? What hospitals near Dalton were equipped to care for him? There were so many questions.

Before their visit with Saul they again met with the lady doctor in the private room. "Saul's doing better than expected, and that enables us to direct more attention to challenges beyond his brain."

Yvonne was surprised by the positive tone. She'd learned to accept the differences in bedside manner between the doctors in France and those she'd become accustomed to at home. The language barrier had something to do with it, but culture did, too. Europeans tended to be a lot more blunt than Americans. They saw no need for the sugar coating people in the States usually added when delivering bad news. The news was what it was, simple as that.

The doctor continued. "Today we attempted to wean him from ventilator."

"You're taking that tube out of his throat?" Yvonne asked hopefully.

The doctor nodded. "This process was conducted normally with assisted pressure after decrease of sedation. That led to removal of breathing tube today."

"Thank God," Yvonne said.

The doctor held up her hand. "Reintubation was necessary two hours later because left lung has collapsed and oxygen levels dropped too low."

Yvonne's spirits deflated. "How serious is this setback?"

"Not too bad. Maybe it was to be expected." The doctor looked back at her chart. "Also today, we took a sample from his lungs. Cultures came back positive for a polymorph culture in a small quantity."

"What does that mean?" Jim asked.

"He has slight infection, very slight," the doctor said. "Not surprising, given his situation. It will be best for Saul to fight this naturally. Give him few days and we will try extubation again. He is getting stronger."

As the Raisins headed for the ICU Yvonne said softly to Jim. "Was it my imagination, or did our lady doctor actually say something encouraging?"

Jim squeezed her hand.

When they approached Saul he beckoned them with a finger. He still looked like he was in a fog, though it had lifted a tiny increment. On a scale of one to one million he might have progressed only from a two to a three, but even such small improvements were reassuring.

Saul moved around more than before, mostly just trying to get comfortable. He wasn't using his left side too much, and the more active he became the more obvious the disuse was, but he wasn't entirely neglecting it either. From time to time Jim asked him to move the fingers of his left hand and the toes of his left foot. Usually he wouldn't, but sometimes he would. That was enough for now. Knowing his brain was intact gave the Raisins new confidence that everything would be all right.

The nurses doted on Saul. They would fluff his pillow, pinch his cheek, and check on him often. As so many people seemed to do, they sensed his spirit, his innate goodness. Even though Saul couldn't talk, they spoke to him constantly. Usually they spoke in French, but sometimes they practiced their English. One of the nurses told Yvonne it felt good to speak English with someone who listened and didn't make corrections.

Before the second visit Saul's former directeur, Lionel Marie showed up. They'd spoken with him several times since he'd accompanied them to Angers and spent that first terrible day by their side. It was nice to be with him again. He'd played such a central role in Saul's European cycling success, and was probably their son's closest friend on this continent other than Daniela. Lionel had heard the good news about Saul and wanted to see for himself.

"I told the doctors that on the cycling team Saul has earned the nickname, American Dreamer. This is why. No matter what odds he faces, he always believes things will turn out well. Sometimes that is not so good, like when he wastes valuable energy on a hopeless attack, but with this injury it is different. He must fight his hardest no matter how long the odds. I think his optimism is playing a role in his recovery."

Yvonne thought about the words. Most people's lives were guided by a realistic view of the world. It made perfect sense. Their minds defined their possibilities based on what appeared reasonable given their education, wealth, and other factors. But Saul's world had never been limited by realistic expectations. His view had always been exceedingly optimistic. He usually imagined the best possible outcome and assumed he could attain it regardless of obstacles. Sometimes such an outlook worked out in his favor, and sometimes it didn't. Was Lionel correct that Saul's unrealistic view of the world was benefiting him in these hard times? She believed so.

Yvonne walked into Saul's enclosure and said, "We have a special surprise for you today."

Lionel stepped into the doorway. With great effort, Saul's raised a thumb. His eyes lit up slightly.

The two friends shook hands gently. Saul looked fragile and exhausted, but mildly content at the same time. Yvonne knew he probably wanted to talk with Lionel, but the tube in his throat made that impossible.

Lionel didn't mind. He had so many messages to pass on and so many stories to share. He spoke mostly in French. Saul listened. Even that seemed to take extreme effort. A couple of times, as when Lionel told him about the success of a teammate, Saul gave the thumbs up sign.

"Has Saul always been such a loveable guy?" Lionel asked.

Yvonne grinned. "He's been a joy. I could give you a million examples. When Saul was in kindergarten a little girl fell on the playground—"

Jim chuckled. "You need to let Lionel know I was a fireman at the time."

"Oh yes. That's important. Jim was Fireman of the Year, in fact. He went into a burning house, and while the rest of the crew went one way he went another. He discovered a little girl about Saul's age, unconscious in a smoke-filled bedroom. He carried her out and saved her life. Saul admired his daddy so," Yvonne said. "So at Saul's kindergarten, when a little girl fell on the playground and got bark in her mouth, Saul knew exactly what to do. He hurried over and gave her mouth to mouth resuscitation."

"You sly dog," Lionel said, eyeing Saul.

Saul lifted a hand weakly for a high five. Lionel touched Saul's fingers.

"Oh, you two!" Yvonne said. "He wasn't making any sort of moves on her. They were five years old, and he was trying to help out the way he knew his daddy would have."

Lionel winked. "I know that, but I can still give a fellow 'ladies man' credit for a smooth move. Did Saul ever have any enemies?"

Jim thought for a moment. "Remember that time the school called because he'd been fighting?"

"I'll never forget it." Yvonne grabbed Lionel's hand to increase the connection while she related the story. "An older, bigger kid had been harassing Saul every day. One day the teacher called and said something had happened between the two of them and we needed to come pick Saul up. When we got there she told us she was just tickled to death with what our son had done."

"She was happy he got in a fight? What grade was he in?" Lionel asked.

"Fourth, I think. Maybe fifth," Yvonne said. "The teacher had been pretty frustrated about this bully picking on a lot of the smaller kids. She couldn't hide her smile as she told us what happened. The big kid had backed Saul into a corner and was pushing him saying, 'What you gonna do about it?' Saul asked him to stop three times, but the boy wouldn't stop so Saul just wound up and clocked him right in the nose. There was blood everywhere. The bully ran away crying and never once bothered Saul again."

"A couple of years later they became friends, so he doesn't really count as an enemy," Jim said.

Lionel looked over to Saul for confirmation, but he was dead asleep. Lionel laughed. "His brain becomes so exhausted that when his concentration drifts, even for a moment, it just shuts down on him."

Jim grinned. "That's right. He's got a lot of healing to do."

"Do you think he knows what he has come through?" Lionel asked.

Jim shook his head. "I doubt he realizes he's even been hurt."

Yvonne knew her husband was right. Saul was too confused to make any sense of the things he was going through.

Lionel left the hospital with the Raisins. "Where are you eating tonight?"

"We planned to return to Logis Ozanam and make a salad," Jim said.

"Can I join you? We must drink a toast." He opened his jacket to reveal a bottle of wine.

Looking at the bottle, Yvonne felt an odd trepidation. She was still worried sick about Saul. She knew Jim felt the same. A toast seemed celebratory, and they weren't ready for that yet. Even though their son was officially out of the coma he remained in grave danger and could die at any moment. Finally she answered. "We will share a toast with you, Lionel, because we know this is the French way and because you are such a wonderful friend to us and to Saul, but I have to say, we do this with great caution."

"Caution is good," Lionel said. "We must toast the good things in life, no matter how small. It is for good luck."

Yvonne nodded. "That's a good point. Saul needs all the luck he can get."

Day 11 – Friday, April 14, 2006

Roger had called early. He was in Angers and wanted to meet for coffee. Yvonne and Jim were surprised by the unscheduled visit, but they knew he looked forward to seeing Saul now that he'd regained consciousness. They were anxious to meet with him.

They arranged to get together for lunch at a nearby bar that had become one of their regular lunch stops. They liked the sandwiches despite the smoky atmosphere. When they arrived with Daniela they noticed Roger already seated at a corner table. Daniela signaled the bartender who nodded. He would prepare their usual order without exchanging a word, three chicken sandwiches and three Coke Lites.

Yvonne and Daniela traded hugs and *bises* with Roger.

"It's good to see you again," Yvonne said.

"Yes, always," Roger said. "Today I must have important talk with you and Jim. I prefer it be in person."

Jim sat down to the table. "Okay, talk."

"Yesterday on the phone Yvonne mentioned your goal to get Saul home."

"Yes," Jim said. "We've started working on it."

Roger nodded. "I would like to talk you into leaving him here."

Yvonne felt her jaw drop open. "Why?" Yesterday her first thoughts of taking Saul home took her by surprise; but today the idea of leaving him in Europe to complete his recovery absolutely stunned her. She was prepared to stay with her son for as long as it took, but they couldn't stay away from home forever.

Roger touched his left thumb with his right index finger, apparently preparing to tick off the reasons. "First, Saul is already getting the best care available. You've seen that."

Yvonne knew in her heart that he was receiving great care, but how she wished she could take him home, if only to remove the language barrier.

"Second," Roger said touching his left index finger, "A trip like that would be very costly."

Yvonne nodded. That point couldn't be argued, though hopefully insurance would pay.

Roger pointed to his middle finger. "Third, nobody can say for sure how much longer Saul might need care, but once he leaves France he will lose his coverage entirely. Every remaining expense will be yours to bear. I am concerned for you financially."

Jim suddenly looked like a punch-drunk boxer.

Roger answered his unspoken question. "That's how our system works,"

Roger said. "Medicine is socialized, so there's no need for Crédit Agricole to insure their riders on French soil. Once Saul leaves this country he won't receive anything else from France."

Yvonne could barely process the words. She just listened and felt hollow inside.

Finally Roger touched his ring finger, "Fourth, and I cannot express how much it pains me to bring you this news, once Saul leaves France our sponsors at Crédit Agricole can continue to pay his salary a little longer, but at some point they must choose to stop." His eyes pleaded with them to understand the bind he was in. They knew Roger had to answer for the expenses the cycling team incurred. His looked like his heart was about to break. "I am so sorry. There is nothing I can do about this."

Jim's head bobbed slightly in recognition of the dilemma. Yvonne put her face in her hands. She'd hardly thought about financial concerns to this point. Her mind had been too occupied with life or death. At this moment, if a Mack truck had run over her she might feel more optimistic about the future. She couldn't imagine staying in France indefinitely, but she couldn't consider leaving her baby behind either.

The bartender placed the sandwiches and drinks in front of them, but the Raisins' appetite was gone. Financial concerns dominated their thoughts for the rest of the day.

"It's frightening that his salary might end at any time," Daniela said. "With the financial uncertainty, maybe you need to think about leaving him here."

Yvonne shook her head. "I can't leave my child behind in a foreign country. What mother could? And I can't stay here with him in France forever. We have lives and obligations. Being stuck in a foreign land is so hard. I need to take him where I speak the same language as his doctors. We need to be surrounded by friends and family. I love France, but not under these circumstances. We have to go home."

Jim scratched his chin. "Saul should still be covered by that private policy we held on to. I'll call my sister and ask her to look into it."

Since Jim's sister was an attorney, she was the perfect person to investigate alternative coverage. Jim phoned her and then made numerous other calls with some apparent progress. He hung up after one conversation, looking discouraged.

"What is it?" Yvonne asked.

"Remember the evacuation insurance Saul had through USA Cycling?" Jim asked.

"I'd forgotten about that." Yvonne's spirits lifted. "They offered it as a service to all of their athletes. That will help us, won't it?"

Jim shook his head. "It would have. Saul let it lapse two months ago. I just spoke with USA Cycling and they feel terrible. Saul told them he was insured by Crédit Agricole for the same thing. They had given him medical transport from

Strasbourg to Nice after his Trans-Alsace crash. Remember when he told us that two nurses escorted him on a commercial flight?"

Yvonne nodded.

"Well, it turns out his Crédit Agricole transport insurance covers only taking athletes back to France. For $30 we would have been covered for the year for emergency transportation from anywhere in the world back to the USA."

"So what does this mean?" Yvonne asked.

"It means if our personal insurance won't pay for it, we'll have to come up with the money out of our own pocket," Jim said.

Yvonne sat down heavily. "Every time I think we've handled the important challenges a new one crops up."

"Yeah, Roger's news this morning hit hard, and this just adds a little extra sting," Jim said.

That evening, inspired by the good news circulating about Saul's recovery and obviously unaware of the burgeoning financial concerns, Francis Van Londersele and his wife Carole, arrived. They were wonderful people. Carole was normally happy and Francis, normally serious, but today they both teared up when hugs were exchanged. They gave the Raisins candies called, "Sweets for the heart." The name had just the right ring to it.

Francis and Carole had driven 500 kilometers to show their support. After visiting with Saul the couples went to dinner at a nice French restaurant to speak by candlelight. A cozy flame blazed in a stone fireplace at one end of the room. Landscape paintings decorated the mahogany walls.

Francis was the directeur sportif of Cofidis, another major French cycling team and a primary rival of Crédit Agricole; but in this tight-knit business, everybody knew everybody. In fact, Lionel now worked for this team. He'd introduced the Raisins to the Van Londerseles on an earlier, more enjoyable trip to France.

Francis selected a 2004 bottle of Saumur-Champigny Rouge from a vineyard just down the road.

Yvonne took a sip that brought to mind violets and raspberries as she looked at the menu and then glanced at Jim. "Maybe Carole would be willing to choose something for us?"

"Are you feeling daring?" Carole asked.

Yvonne grinned. "I've never been daring before, but maybe tonight is a good time to start."

"What have I got to lose, except my appetite?" Jim said.

Carole called the waiter over and put in the orders.

After he left the table she turned back to them. "Isn't it wonderful that Saul is improving?"

Jim nodded. "We're very happy he's out of the coma, but we never understood how long and difficult the waking up process would be. He still has so far to go."

"He'll do it. He's tough," Carole said.

Francis unfolded his napkin and set it in his lap. He didn't speak much English so he said something to Carole.

She translated. "Do you know the most amazing race he's ever seen Saul ride?"

"Was it last year's World Championships?" Jim asked. Saul had been in a four-man breakaway that built up a margin of over fifteen minutes. Even when two of the men fell off the pace, Saul and another cyclist held onto the lead until the penultimate lap. Not only had he been in position to win, but he'd put his American teammates in a tactically superior position because they didn't have to help chase the breakaway down.

"He was great that day," Carole said. "But Francis' favorite was, Milan-San Remo last month."

Saul had once explained to Yvonne that cycling's five most important one-day races were referred to as The Monuments. Milan-San Remo's history stretched clear back to 1906. At 294 kilometers it remained the longest of all one-day professional bicycle races. Saul had been very excited to participate.

"He didn't tell us he was ever in the lead that day," Yvonne said.

"He wasn't. Francis thinks Saul played the perfect support role when his team missed the break of the day."

Yvonne nodded. A typical race started with lots of attacks, where opportunists tried to separate themselves from the field in an all-or-nothing bid for victory. Once a group finally freed themselves from the almost gravitational pull of the peloton, their separation was referred to as "the break of the day." After those cyclists were out of sight up the road, things tended to calm down while the favorites strategized and saved their team's strength to help them charge for the line and overwhelm the escapists. Winning a race wasn't so much a matter of being the strongest as it was of using strength judiciously.

Carole continued. "Saul was one of a handful of riders who spent 200 kilometers at the front of the peloton, pulling everybody else back into contention. It's a beautiful thing when a guy works that hard in an effort to earn glory for somebody else. After watching Saul's performance, Francis said, '*Ce sera son année de percée*,' 'This will be his break-through year.' The crash was such a terrible disappointment."

Jim nodded. "That's putting it mildly."

The food arrived. Yvonne laughed at Jim's entrée. Beside a small mound of spinach and another pile of diced pear was something that looked like cat food dropped straight from the can. "What is that?"

Jim touched the cylindrical piece of processed meat with his fork and then looked at Carole curiously.

"That's a liver pâté made from foie gras," she said.

"Foie gras?" Jim asked.

"Geese are force-fed to enlarge their livers prior to slaughter," Carole explained.

Yvonne's nose curled. "I can't wait to see you eat it."

Jim took a bite. He swallowed it thoughtfully and said, "It's very good. How's your meal?"

Yvonne looked at her plate. The presentation was extremely artistic, with green snap peas and yellow potatoes framing mushrooms in gravy with butter beans. Yvonne tasted a bean, but the moment her tongue sensed the rubbery texture she knew this was no bean. It had to be some sort of meat. It wasn't bad, but she wasn't crazy about it, either. Besides that, it was undercooked. "What did I order?" she asked.

Carole finished chewing the bite in her mouth. Then she said matter of factly, "I chose a special dish for you, lamb kidneys. Do you like them?"

Yvonne's stomach grumbled.

Jim laughed joyfully. "You've finally expanded your culinary horizons. And this from a Southern belle who won't even touch pork rinds. Next you'll be ready to take a taste of Bambi." He looked thoroughly amused.

"Very funny, Jimmy," Yvonne said. "I hope you don't mind sleeping on a cot tonight."

Jim put his hand on Yvonne's and they both laughed, harder than ever. Logis Ozanam was a Godsend, but it was yet another reason they needed to return to America. They certainly weren't going to miss those cots. Oh, how they needed to find a solution to the insurance concerns.

"Maybe I could send my meat back to be cooked a little bit more." Yvonne raised her hand to get the waiter's attention.

Carole took her forearm and pulled it down. "*Non, non, non*. You cannot insult the chef."

"Insult the chef? It's my food. Wouldn't he prefer I was happy with it?"

Carole gazed at her as if trying to decode a language she'd never heard before, and in that moment Yvonne came to a realization. In America she'd become accustomed to the philosophy, "The customer is always right." That motto had always been a core value at Raisin Textiles, but in France things were different. This chef was the artist. A customer asking him to alter his creation would be equivalent to an art gallery visitor ordering revisions on the Mona Lisa. Did the same philosophy extend to medicine?

Yvonne nodded in understanding as Carole released her arm.

Day 12 – Saturday, April 15, 2006

Outside the Raisins' Logis Ozanam bedroom window rain came down in sheets. A long walk was out of the question. Yvonne took a dirty towel to the nun and pointed to it. The nun nodded her head, understanding that clean towels were needed. She gave them to Yvonne to take back to the room.

When she returned Jim was talking to Roger on the telephone. He waved her over. She leaned her head against his so both of them could hear and speak to Roger.

"… Saul's doctors now expect him to make a nearly full recovery," Roger said.

Yvonne looked at Jim in amazement. She knew the medical staff felt Saul was doing well, but a nearly full recovery? She'd almost forgotten that could even be a possibility. Until today, life in a rest home had been the best case scenario.

Jim pulled his wife tightly to him. "Yvonne's at my side now. You can't imagine how happy that news makes us."

"I think maybe I can. I am thrilled, too."

"What else did they tell you?" Yvonne asked.

"They are amazed at how he is regaining awareness, movement, and memory but there is still very long way to go. They expect him to continue improving gradually for a year or more. The doctor you call The Philosopher also says the bicycle will be good for Saul during rehabilitation."

Yvonne drew a sharp breath. "Riding bikes still scares the hell out of me, but it's going to be Saul's decision. I'm just thrilled to be talking about recovery. A week ago this conversation wouldn't even have been conceivable."

"I know. This is wonderful news. I doubt you can imagine what this has done for the esprit de corps of our entire team. They have followed every detail, good and bad. They will be very happy to hear today's news."

The hours rolled by slowly, and if anything the weather got worse, but the Raisins and Daniela were so happy nothing could dampen their spirits. Finally the time for the day's first visit came. As the three of them approached the bed Daniela said, "I wonder if Saul knows how good the prognosis is?"

"He will soon." Yvonne looked toward Saul as she spoke.

Something was obviously different, and it wasn't good. His hands were tied down. The moment his eyes met hers he began to struggle. A green oxygen mask covered his face, and the respirator tube was no longer in his throat. His breathing was rapid, like it would be at maximum effort on a climb in the Alps, except for much more ragged, less disciplined.

"What's wrong, Saul?" Yvonne asked.

His eyes were wild and angry. He looked like he wanted to grab hold of somebody and make them answer for a terrible insult, but his movements were slow and weak.

"Ask the doctor why he's restrained," Jim said to Daniela. The physician on duty didn't speak English.

Yvonne felt anxious about the answer as they communicated in French. Finally Daniela said, "He's tied down so he doesn't pull out any more wires or tubes. He pulled his breathing tube out about an hour ago. The doctor says that figuring out how to remove it shows his mind is working, but his lungs aren't ready. Still, the doctors have decided to let him go without it for awhile to see how he does. They are monitoring his blood oxygenation, so even though he doesn't look or sound good doing it, they're certain he's getting the air he needs. The tube is very irritating, and the sooner he can do without it the better."

Yvonne looked back at her son. His eyes were more crazed than ever. It was so hard to watch, even though she now understood there were positives to this situation. She stroked his hair and soothed him. His breathing only got worse. It was loud, like he was starving for oxygen and sucking it in through a straw. Sweat soaked his hospital gown, and he appeared frightened to death.

Daniela had been talking to the doctor some more. Then she explained to the Raisins. "There's no way he can sleep while breathing like this. That means he's probably going to be reintubated, and the only way to do that is to sedate him with drugs."

Yvonne realized her fingernails were between her teeth.

Daniela continued. "When someone comes out of a coma the last thing they want to do is put them back to sleep, but they'll keep the dose low and make sure its effect lasts only a short while."

Saul lashed out like an injured but frail badger. He was furious at everyone and everything, but too weak to do anything effective about it. He pleaded with his eyes to be freed from his restraints. After the most stressful hour in Yvonne's life the nurses ushered them out of the room.

When they reached the hallway Yvonne couldn't hold back tears. "I'd been looking forward so much to seeing him today, and then to have a visit like that … this is killing me."

Jim held her in his arms. "Yeah. I know what you're saying. Me too."

"I'm trying to be thankful that he has so much fight in him," Yvonne said. "That's good, right?"

"Of course."

They left in sadness, but they understood. Their presence was making it harder for Saul.

When it came time for the late visit they approached cautiously, watching him through the big window that served as his wall. Saul lay in bed, still restrained, but not fighting. His eyes were open and he calmly surveyed the room.

"He's better now," Jim whispered.

Yvonne nodded and stepped into Saul's view. The crazed look immediately returned to his eyes and he started flailing just like before. It seemed like he was trying to get out of bed.

She grabbed his more active right hand and held it down. It amazed her that she could control him so easily. He was very weak. "No, Saul. Don't do this. They're trying to help you. You've got to rest and recover. Please calm down."

"He thinks since we're here we can help him," Jim said.

"I know. I know. Please calm down, Saul. We can help you, but it's not time to get out of bed. We're staying in a building just up the street. We're paying attention to everything that happens. We're here for you. Please relax and allow yourself to heal." She wanted to crawl in bed with him and hold him like she had when he was a baby. He still had so many tubes and wires hooked to him, though; even touching him required great care.

"I wish I could swap places," Jim said. "I'd do it in a heartbeat."

Saul's breathing got worse, and he looked at Jim like he was trying to say, 'How can you leave me here, Dad? Take me home.'

It crushed Yvonne to watch Saul go through this, and she could see it was equally difficult for her husband.

Saul wouldn't quit fighting. Although the nurses had changed his bedding and clothing since the previous visit, he was already drenched in sweat again. He just wouldn't calm down. Yvonne, Daniela, and Jim kept trying to comfort Saul, both physically and with words, but he refused to pay attention. He struggled and fought through the entire visit, and soon the time neared 8:00 PM. Time to go.

At some level Yvonne knew Saul was better off without her there at the moment, but she just couldn't leave. It would hurt him too much. "I can't walk away tonight."

Daniela took her hand. "You must. We aren't doing him any good right now. Saul's going to be all right. They take good care of him here. He needs his sleep."

Yvonne allowed Daniela to push her toward the door. When they moved out of Saul's sight he started struggling even harder. His breath sounded like an urgent plea. No mother should be required to endure this. Yvonne stepped toward him again but the Philosopher came from nowhere and held her back.

"He will be better in morning. Time to go," the doctor said.

With that, she was escorted from the ICU. The door swung shut behind her, but she could swear she still heard Saul's desperate breaths, even from the hall. The sound didn't leave her for the entire night.

Day 13 – Sunday, April 16, 2006

The Raisins approached the ICU doors. It had been a heartbreaking twenty-four hours. Yvonne couldn't quit thinking about the stress Saul was under, or regretting she had a role in causing his panic attacks. He appeared to be fine until he caught sight of familiar people. Would he be better off, at least for the next little while, if they didn't visit him and cause his emotions to spike?

Saul was asleep when they reached his bedside. He wore a small green oxygen mask. It made him look like a fighter pilot. Yvonne took a seat and watched. She appreciated quiet time at his side more than she ever would have before yesterday's experience. In a way, she hoped her son would sleep through their entire visit. "Everything's going to be all right, Saul," she whispered.

Eventually he stirred and then his eyes opened. It took a moment for them to focus on Yvonne, but when they did he started fighting the restraints again. A vein bulged in his forehead, his respiration soared, and the alarm on the oxygen monitor started beeping. His breath had the same rasping quality as the night before. A nurse hustled into the room and made adjustments.

Yvonne spoke to Saul, practically nose-to-nose, while Jim held onto him so the nurse could do her work. "Please, Saul! You can't do this again. You've got to allow these people to help you." She smoothed his hair with a hand, pleading with him to be calm.

Then another alarm went off and another nurse came in. This one made a sweeping motion with her arm, indicating the door. "You must go," she said.

Yvonne wanted to cry. "See what happens when you won't behave? We can't visit if you won't stay calm, Saul."

"We'll return to try again in a few hours, Son," Jim said. "Please calm down."

His tone reminded Yvonne of two decades earlier when they sometimes had to reprimand their little boy. Reluctantly, they left.

"I've got to get some fresh air," Yvonne said.

Jim led her by the hand through the corridors and then guided her down a street they'd only walked a few times before. They came upon the Château d'Angers. Leaden clouds swirled above the stone ramparts, but the place had a unique peacefulness. Yvonne looked down into the gardens at the bottom of the old moat as they walked past. A family of rabbits munched on the flowers and expertly trimmed shrubs.

"I hear there's a museum inside that includes the world's largest tapestry," Jim said.

"It looks like a lovely place. I hope we can return in better times."

They sat down on the stone wall that separated the moat from the street. "I feel so helpless, Jimmy," Yvonne said. "At least before I could be there for him, even if I was confused by the care he was receiving and unable to make things any better, but now it's as if we're a negative complication. What are we going to do?"

"I don't know. I guess it's just a stage of recovery he has to go through." The cell phone rang. "Hello," Jim answered. Looking at her, he mouthed, "The Shepherd Center." Then he devoted his full attention to the telephone conversation.

Yvonne watched the rabbits while listening to Jim's half of a complicated conversation. She felt hopeful. Jim's sister had volunteered to search for a rehabilitation facility in America and had come across numerous references to the Shepherd Center. She even discovered a family friend who had connections with the facility. She became convinced Shepherd's was one of the best, if not the best, facility in America for this type of injury. The center specialized in brain and spinal cord injuries, and unlike most rehabs, it had an ICU on site. That meant Shepherd's could accept a patient very early in his recovery. Best of all, it was in Atlanta which was within easy reach of Dalton. It was an expensive place, though, and beds were in high demand. Even beyond those considerations was the challenge of getting Saul to Atlanta in the first place. How do you transport a critically ill patient across an ocean?

Jim ended the call.

"Well?" Yvonne asked.

"That was Laura Brown. She's our case worker at the Shepherd Center. They've gone the extra mile. When Mrs. Shepherd heard about Saul's accident she told the staff, 'Get that boy in here.' I told her about our insurance situation, and she said she felt confident they could accept it. I asked about transporting him, and she promised to put me in touch with the best people. She says the critical piece of the puzzle is getting Saul's doctors here in France to release him to their care. Since he's breathing on his own she thinks it could be accomplished quickly. She said we should get him into their facility as soon as feasible. They have an intensive rehab they like to start the moment a patient is able to leave ICU. The sooner his therapy starts the better. Laura will contact CHU d'Angers and figure out how to make the transfer."

∗   ∗   ∗

Saul lay staring at the wall when Daniela and Yvonne cautiously tiptoed into his room for the 6:30 visit. "Please, Saul," Yvonne said.

Her voice startled him. He searched the room for her face and then stared at her with palpable tension.

"Please stay calm this time," she pleaded. "The doctors aren't going to let us visit if you get so stressed every time we come by."

Saul's eyes softened a bit, seeming to question her, but given their cloudiness she wasn't sure how well he understood the situation, so she sat down beside the bed and tried to explain the circumstances. "You were in a terrible bicycle accident. It nearly killed you. But these kind doctors and nurses have brought you back to life. They don't want to have to tie your arms down, but if you pull out your wires or tubes they must. I know all this equipment is uncomfortable, and I understand how badly you want to get out of bed, but your body and mind aren't ready for that right now. Trust me."

His lip quivered, as if he was trying to cry. No tears would come. He relaxed another increment.

"Oh Saul. Thank you," Yvonne said.

They held hands quietly for awhile. Then Yvonne smelled a repulsive odor. "Saul, did you …" She hugged him while Daniela went to find the nurse. "That's your first bowel movement in two weeks! It's proof your internal organs are returning to normal function. I never imagined something so putrid could make me so happy!"

After he'd been cleaned up Jim stepped into the ICU, taking Daniela's place. "Hi Saul. Something came in the mail today you might like to see." He held up a Crédit Agricole team photo.

Saul pointed to it.

"You want to take a look?" Jim asked. He steadied it where Saul could easily inspect the picture. Saul's eyes lingered on each of the three dozen or so faces, one at a time, team staff, ownership, elite riders, promising prospects. Then he pointed to Thor Hushovd, the Norwegian sprinting sensation. He and Saul had formed a special bond from the day they became teammates. Saul let out a long, melancholy sigh. It sounded like a cry of despair for what he'd left behind, but in his current state, Yvonne doubted he could really focus on anything but the present.

Still, he'd loved that life so much. He'd been so happy. Yvonne desperately wanted his life to be a good one. She wondered again, as she had so many times, what sort of a life could he live now?

Day 14 – Monday, April 17, 2006

When the Raisins reached Saul's room he slept soundly, but moments later a technician arrived and adjusted Saul's bed to put him in a seated position. Saul woke. The technician pantomimed coughing, and pointed to Saul. "Must cough."

Yvonne looked at him curiously.

He repeated the act.

"We need to get Saul to cough?" Yvonne asked.

The technician smiled. "Yes."

"Can you cough for him, Saul?" Yvonne asked.

Saul's expression looked resigned to pain. He'd been poked and prodded, tested and analyzed. Now he was being asked to cough, even though his throat had been severely irritated by a breathing tube for almost two weeks.

"Cough please," the technician encouraged.

Saul coughed weakly. His face knotted into an expression of pure misery. It hurt Yvonne to watch.

The technician collected mucus with a suction tube. "More please," the technician said.

Yvonne could tell he wasn't satisfied with the quantity Saul had produced. That meant more pain. Yvonne understood the technician's concern. She cringed at the rattling sound in Saul's breathing. Whatever was in his lungs had to be cleared. The technician was trying to help Saul help himself.

Saul looked at Yvonne for confirmation. Should he try to cough again? She nodded.

Saul's eyes dropped sadly. Then he coughed as hard as he could, trying to bring up everything possible from his lungs despite the pain in his throat. His misery tore at Yvonne's heart. Finally he lay back, defeated and exhausted.

The technician checked the reservoir the suction tube emptied into. Yvonne could tell there wasn't enough.

"I must put tube into lungs," the technician said. Saul froze in fear. Yvonne could tell he'd been through this before. His eyes pleaded with her, but she could only stroke his hair and return his gaze. She did her best to help Saul keep his eyes off the technician's preparations.

The technician laid sterile materials out on a rolling tray and prepared a clean tube. He mumbled to himself in French as he worked.

"Can I help somehow? Does he need to be held steady?" Jim asked.

The technician couldn't understand the question, but Saul could. He shook his head; then he pursed his lips, a look of resolution on his face.

The technician attached his new sterile tube to the suction outlet on the wall. "We run suction tube through his nose to his lungs. This be a little painful." Then he looked at Saul. "I am sorry. I will be quick."

The technician fed the sterile tube into Saul's nose, mumbling the entire time. Saul winced in pain.

The technician kept sliding his tube in. Yvonne couldn't believe how long it kept going. Sometimes the tube would catch on something. Saul squeezed his eyes shut but moisture still ran from them in heavy streams. He looked so uncomfortable as the technician worked past the obstruction.

The suction sounded like a padded jack-hammer. It sucked and released in rapid succession. The technician continued manipulating the tube, searching the lungs for pools of liquid.

Saul quivered in pain. Yvonne soothed him with soft words as she stroked his arm, trying to simultaneously control the chaos going on inside her head.

Eventually phlegm appeared in the tube where it exited Saul's mouth. The secretions accumulated in a measuring beaker where the suction tube was attached to the wall. The technician glanced at it with satisfaction as the contents reached higher and higher levels.

Long after the secretions had stopped accumulating the technician continued probing around, looking for more. Finally he said, "Good job."

Saul relaxed and opened his eyes slightly while the technician removed the tube. Saul let out a big sigh when it was finally out.

The technician wiped his patient's face with a towel. "Saul est fort." He flexed a bicep and pointed at Saul's bicep in admiration.

Saul smiled, ever so slightly, at least with the right side of his face. The left side of his mouth looked like it was numbed by Novocain.

"Yes. Saul is strong," Yvonne said. In reality he had almost no physical strength at all, but that weakness revealed an underlying mental strength that amazed even her. "Saul est fort."

* * *

During the break between ICU visits Jim and Yvonne met with a French attorney. "Is there any way to transfer his health benefits to an American facility?" Jim asked.

The attorney shook her head. "None whatsoever. The moment he leaves France he loses all coverage."

Yvonne put her head in her hands. She wanted so badly to take her son home, but that was beginning to look like an unreachable goal. How much more of this could she take? At least they had a nice home and other assets they could sell to give Saul the care he was going to need.

Dejectedly, the Raisins returned to their son's room. The familiar rhythm of the ventilator greeted them when they entered his enclosure. His left lung still wasn't functioning well, so the doctors had reintubated him. They'd had to give him sleeping medication and Morphine to do it.

Yvonne felt her son's forehead. "He's starting to get a fever."

Dr. Fesard shook his head. "We have run a culture. It is not serious."

Saul had a tendency to get bad sinus infections which settled in his chest. This would be the worst time for those sorts of complications. "What are you giving him for it?"

"Nothing. We prefer to allow him to heal naturally," the doctor said. "We will check him for infection four times a day."

Yvonne didn't believe in curing everything with drugs, but she still wondered about withholding antibiotics from a weakened immune system. She doubted her opinion would be well received, and the doctors must have legitimate reasons for their methods, so she remained silent.

The euphoric days of Saul taking steps in the right direction seemed like a distant memory. Now setbacks had become the norm. Yesterday Laura Brown of the Shepherd Center had told Jim she believed Saul was nearly well enough to be transported. Since that time Saul had been returned to the ventilator, put on increased pain killers, and might have an infection.

On top of that he'd become frighteningly emaciated. Like all pro cyclists he'd started out extremely thin. During cycling season he carried only 145 pounds on his 6-foot, 1-inch frame, but now he couldn't weigh much more than 125. His eyes were sunken and dark, his cheeks were caved, his coloring was flushed. In fact, his skin looked similar to a bed sheet draped over a framework of bones, every rib visible. Yvonne worried they were moving in the wrong direction. Should she and Jim should be looking for an apartment in Angers where they could stay long-term rather than for a hospital bed in America? She almost couldn't bear the thought.

Day 15 – Tuesday, April 18, 2006

Yvonne and Jim stopped by the Internet café. Daniela hadn't joined them on their walk today.

When Jim logged onto Saul's site the Raisins were amazed by the number of people who'd left messages. The thousands of notes of love and encouragement strengthened them. After reading for more than an hour and realizing they couldn't possibly review all of the messages, they left a note of their own:

It has been 15 days since Saul's accident. The first 8 days were very dangerous for him. Now he is stable. Because of the coma he will be sleeping hard for awhile. We plan to move him to the states in a few weeks for rehab. He is showing improvement every day, but he still has a long road ahead of him. Your prayers and love have truly helped him and us get through these hard days.
Thank you, Jim and Yvonne

Before leaving Jim checked his e-mail. He found a detailed message from his sister saying she and the Shepherd Center had worked out preliminary arrangements with the family's insurance company in America. "If we can get him there, he'll be covered," Jim said. "Am I ever glad we kept that policy in effect!"

Yvonne couldn't contain her smile. The insurance situation had been so frightening. It relieved her beyond words to have that safety net replaced. "That's wonderful! What a relief."

"One problem," Jim said as they headed for the door. "They won't pay for his transportation from France."

"Maybe we can pay that part ourselves. Do you know what it will cost?"

Jim shook his head. "I'm not certain yet, but it looks like it will be more than thirty thousand dollars."

That was more than the condo down payment would have been, not that she cared about that place any more. She hadn't even thought about it in weeks. It seemed like a dream from a lifetime ago. She kissed it goodbye without another thought. She'd sell their current home in Dalton if that was necessary to save her son. She stepped onto the Angers sidewalk. "And we thought our flight over here was expensive."

Jim's stressed expression had an oddly happy tinge. "Easy come, easy go."

Yvonne thought how poorly those words described this trip as they walked the streets of Angers hand in hand. Their lives had been on hold for a long time now. All their normal responsibilities had been turned over to others. Neighbors were taking care of the yard, Jim's mom was handling the bills, brothers and sisters were picking up slack wherever they could. Still, appointments were going unmet and costs of being away from home were accumulating. With every passing day Yvonne became more anxious to leave France behind, and every time they discussed logistics it only increased her determination to reach that happy day.

They'd been walking for a long time when Jim asked a surprising question. "Do you know where we are?"

"No idea. I was just following you," she said.

They looked around themselves. They were in the modern outskirts of the city. It may as well have been an Atlanta suburb, except the cars were much smaller and none of the signs were in English.

"Hôpital?" Jim asked a passerby.

The woman pointed in a direction Yvonne thought couldn't be right and gave a detailed list of instructions. The only recognizable words were a smattering of "à gauche" and a couple "à droite." Go left, go right. Not so helpful if you couldn't figure out how many blocks to walk between turns.

"Parlez-vous anglais?" Yvonne asked.

The woman shook her head. No, she didn't speak English. The Raisins began walking in the direction she'd pointed them. Eventually they found themselves entering the old part of the city again. A maze of streets confronted them. European towns had been designed to confuse invaders, and the strategy worked just as well with tourists. They asked directions several more times with similar results.

"If we just keep going downhill we'll eventually reach the river," Jim said. "Then we can look for the hospital dome or the church spire."

The strategy eventually worked, but by the time they reached the hospital they'd put in a fifteen mile day. Yvonne stepped into Saul's room, physically spent. "Is the tube hurting your throat?"

He nodded.

"You know it's helping you get better, don't you?"

He nodded again.

"If I talk the nurses into letting me untie your hands will you promise not to yank any of the tubes out?"

Saul nodded again, this time with enthusiasm. He didn't like the equipment he was attached to, but he disliked being tied down even more. Yvonne went to the nurses' station and explained the deal to Dr. Fesard. A nurse followed her back to Saul's bed and asked him some questions in French. Saul nodded his head to some statements and shook it to others. Finally the nurse untied his arms. He immediately rotated his right shoulder and elbow as far as he could in every direction, clearly grateful to be free. Then he looked at his left arm. It seemed partially dead. Yvonne hid her disappointment in his inability to move it while she helped him stretch it out.

"Would you like a massage," Yvonne asked.

Saul nodded.

Yvonne moved toward the bottom of the bed to begin. She kissed his foot before starting. Saul pressed his toes against her cheek three times: "I … love … you."

Jim pulled up a chair next to Saul. "Do you want to play a little game?"

Saul gave a thumbs up.

"I'm going to make statements. You tell me if they are true of false."

Saul nodded ever so slightly.

"You're from Atlanta, Georgia," Jim said.

Saul gave a thumbs down."

Jim smiled. "You're from Dalton, Georgia."

Saul gave a thumbs up.

"Very good! Two plus three is four."

Saul thought for a moment, and then tentatively pointed his thumb down. Jim kept asking simple questions in all sorts of categories. Saul answered all of them right.

Dr. Fesard tapped Yvonne on the shoulder. "Before you two leave, I'd like to talk."

Jim and Yvonne nodded. Throughout the rest of the visit as Yvonne massaged her son she kept glancing at the doctor, wondering what he had to say. When visiting hours ended she stood reluctantly and went to find the doctor. He led them into the familiar conference room.

"The ventilator tube has been in Saul's throat too long. It's causing inflammation which can lead to infection. I think it is time for a tracheotomy." Dr. Fesard wore a serious expression.

"Like they do for heavy smokers?" Yvonne asked.

Dr. Fesard nodded. "Yes. A hole in the windpipe so that we can force air into his lungs without going through the throat."

"Would they also use it to suck fluid out of his lungs more easily?" Jim asked.

Dr. Fesard smiled. "Correct. We have a team of four doctors who make decisions on his case. I'm in favor of this now but the others haven't decided yet. I want to be sure that when we do go ahead you're aware of it."

"Thank you," Yvonne said. The doctors were the decision makers, but she appreciated this small opportunity to voice her opinion. Even though she didn't know much at all about tracheotomies, her gut told her it was the right thing to do.

"We'll do it soon. Saul's throat is hurting very bad," the doctor said.

Once they were outside the hospital Jim called Laura at the Shepherd Center and told her about the conversation while Yvonne listened in.

"Trachs are good," Laura said. "It would allow Saul to be ventilated without constant irritation to his larynx. The only long-term side effect would be a scar on his throat."

"Saul wouldn't care about a scar. So, you think we should do it?" Jim asked.

"Yes. Frankly, I'm amazed he's endured the ventilator tube as long as he has. Not only will a trach reduce the pain in his throat, but it will enable him to clear his lungs. Those little throat clearings you and I do without a thought many times daily would be an incredible luxury to Saul. He might even be able to start talking."

"That's really possible?" Jim asked.

"Yes. He could hold his hand over the opening and it would enable him to whisper."

"Oh, that would be wonderful." Jim hugged Yvonne. She loved seeing her husband happy.

"There's something else I've wanted to ask you about, Laura," Jim said. "Saul is really, really thin. Should we be concerned?"

"It's normal. I'm sure they're feeding him through tubes," she said.

"Yes. He has an IV plus they give him white liquid through another tube in his nose," Jim said.

"He's being treated correctly. You don't need to worry about it," Laura said.

"Thank you. We thought it was probably all right, but it sets our minds at ease to hear your answer."

"Don't hesitate to ask whenever you have questions," Laura said. "I'll do my best to get you an answer. There's one other thing before you go. We've been trying to offer assistance and make transport arrangements with CHU d'Angers by phone and e-mail, but we can't seem to get through the bureaucratic channels to speak with his lead physician. We gave them all the information they should need, but we aren't certain our messages are getting to the right person. Can you let them know what we're trying to accomplish and ask them to respond?"

Yvonne felt Jim tense. One of Saul's doctors had finally asked their opinion about his treatment, and now they were being asked to request a favor from him. Yvonne knew as well as Jim this might not go well and their efforts to move him to Atlanta probably wouldn't be well received. The thing they'd learned the doctors liked least was being told what to do by outsiders, but the Raisins needed to do whatever they could to help this process move forward.

Jim swallowed hard. "Okay, Laura. We'll do our best."

Day 16 – Wednesday, April 19, 2006

Yvonne carried a chocolate éclair with a single lit candle into their room where her husband still slept. "Happy birthday, Jim."

He opened one eye. "You're kidding." He looked at the date on his wristwatch. "I'd completely forgotten."

She feathered a hand through his graying hair. "Good thing I'm here to remind you you're getting to be an old man."

"Maybe this will be a good day," Jim said.

Yvonne set the éclair down on his night stand. "That statement counts as wild optimism coming from you."

Jim sat up in his cot. "Yeah? Well, it's hard to be realistic on my birthday. It's been ingrained in my mind for fifty-one years now that April 19th is a happy day."

Yvonne kissed him on the cheek. "It will be."

*   *   *

Early that afternoon Laura Brown from the Shepherd Center called with information about transporting Saul home. She'd negotiated logistics with Midway Air Ambulance. Midway had a Learjet specially equipped for this sort of service. It would fly in a big arc from France, over Greenland and then down the North American coast to Atlanta. That way they'd be near land at all times in case of medical emergency. The plane's crew included two pilots and two medical personnel. There would be room for Saul on a stretcher and one other person, either Jim or Yvonne. She had tentatively scheduled the trip for April 27, eight days from today. Midway requested a couple days notice to firm things up.

"We have a date! I can hardly wait for April 27," Jim said.

"Don't get too set on that schedule yet. There could be changes if Saul becomes ill or if the weather doesn't cooperate, or for any of a number of reasons. The important thing is that they can be ready to move as soon as Saul is cleared to come home, once you wire them the money."

"How much money?" Jim asked.

"Fifty-nine thousand dollars," Laura said.

Jim looked dizzy. The number was almost twice his earlier estimate. "Our insurance won't cover it. Is the price negotiable?"

"No."

Jim called his mother and asked her to go to their bank. Because of the family business, Raisin Textiles, they had a well established relationship with their banker. He would need to liquidate some investments from their retirement account and then follow the wiring instructions.

Saul didn't know it, but at this moment he was receiving every present due him for the rest of his lifetime, and his inheritance as well. Of course, it was money well spent.

Several hours later they sat in the familiar conference room outside the ICU. Beside them sat Serge, a Crédit Agricole Team Manager who'd come to visit Saul. Daniela sat on the other side of the Raisins. As Dr. Fesard spoke, Yvonne was acutely aware that Jim was looking for the right moment to bring up the Shepherd Center.

"The tracheotomy has been planned for tomorrow," Dr. Fesard said.

Yvonne nodded. "Good."

"We have a small problem, though," the doctor said.

"What is it?" Jim asked.

"We have detected a subluxation extra pericardial of the heart. It is enlarged and deviated to the left with a small amount of liquid at the tip."

"What are you saying?" Jim asked.

The doctor searched for simple words. "The protective sac around Saul's heart may have ripped open and allowed the heart itself to shift out of position."

"How long have you suspected this?" Jim asked.

"Since before you arrived, but there was no reason to give you additional bad news at that time. The issues with his brain were far more urgent. If Saul hadn't survived them this never would have mattered."

Yvonne bit her lip. She was confused at the reasoning for keeping such a major issue silent for so long. She counted silently to ten while she waited for Jim to respond. He would handle this with a more level head than she would.

"How do you think this happened?" Jim asked.

"We believe it is the result of his hard fall."

Jim nodded calmly. "What's the solution?"

"We may need to repair this problem surgically."

"You're talking about open heart surgery?" Jim asked.

The doctor nodded. "Possibly."

"Whoa, whoa, whoa!" Yvonne said.

Jim covered his face in his hands as if trying to hold his thoughts back until they became coherent. Yvonne admired his composure as she bit back frightened words. They couldn't do open heart surgery. He'd been through too much. But at the same time, she knew deep down that if the diagnosis was correct, there would be no choice. Shepherd Center was certain to agree.

Finally Jim spoke. "Are his vital signs irregular in any way? Yvonne had a virus of the heart a few years ago and it affected her heartbeat. Wouldn't the same sorts of things show up in this case?"

"Usually," Dr. Fesard said, "but just because we haven't discovered adverse symptoms doesn't mean everything's as it should be. Saul's heart is very large, and it is not where we expect it to be. We can't ignore that."

"We've found a hospital for Saul in America," Jim said tentatively.

Dr. Fesard tensed. He spoke in a more authoritative tone than usual. "It is not the time to talk of transferring him. He has a lot of healing to do. That is where our focus should remain."

"I understand," Jim said, backpedaling. "Of course he needs to be healthy to travel, and this heart situation has to be cleared."

Yvonne looked at Daniela and Serge, the Crédit Agricole team manager who was visiting today. Maybe one of them could better understand this situation and offer a solution.

Finally Serge spoke. "I'm sure you are aware that bicycle racers have large hearts. You probably do not know that Saul's is larger than most. Crédit Agricole has tested this. Saul's heart is more than two times larger than a normal person, including cyclists. It is part of the reason he is so good."

The doctor shook his head as he answered. "An enlarged heart can be symptomatic of other serious problems, and what you have said does nothing to explain its odd positioning."

"Open heart surgery? I can't take any more bad news." Yvonne had spent two and a half weeks reassembling her shattered world. Like shards of a priceless vase, she'd glued a few of them back together. Earlier this afternoon returning home had finally felt within reach. Now everything was crumbling again.

"I understand how you are feeling," the doctor said. "Sorry."

Jim nodded. "It's not your fault. It's just hard to hear about this so late when you've known for so long."

"If you are keeping any more secrets from us, please tell us now," Yvonne said.

Dr. Fesard smiled. "No more secrets."

"Thanks," Yvonne said.

"Rest assured that every detail will be checked and rechecked before we turn to the surgical option. We have your son's best interests at heart," Dr. Fesard said.

"We know you do," Jim answered.

The doctor closed his chart and left the room.

Jim collapsed forward onto the table, defeated. "So much for April 19 being a happy day. I never imagined we could get hit so hard. This is a birthday I'll never forget."

Day 17 – Thursday, April 20, 2006

Yvonne woke with a start. She'd suddenly remembered a conversation with Dr. Frix, Saul's Orthopaedist, from a decade earlier. She shook her husband awake. "Saul's chest cavity has an irregular shape because of his kyphosis. Remember, Jimmy? Could that be the reason his x-rays look different than normal?"

Jim rubbed his eyes. "I assumed they took that into consideration, but you know what they say about assumptions. We'd better ask if they've thought about this."

"Let's find some old x-rays for comparison? If his heart is in the same position as the new x-rays we'll know it's not a problem."

Jim sat up on his cot. "Remember those shots that were taken showing the history of his back condition. They're between five and ten years old, but they might show something. I don't know if his heart is visible in them or not. They're filed in our house somewhere. Do you remember seeing them?"

Yvonne thought hard. "I came across them years ago, but I don't recall where we put them."

"It's five in the morning. That's 11:00 PM at home. It will be nine hours or more before we can call anybody to begin working on this, but I don't know how we'll get back to sleep now."

"Saul's been hospitalized here in Europe, too. Maybe Roger can tell us where he's been treated and we can track down those doctors first. One of them must have taken an x-ray of his chest."

Jim stood up and switched on the light. "You've got my thoughts racing so fast there's no point in trying to sleep anymore. We'd better give Roger at least three hours before we call. There must be something we can accomplish in the meantime."

Yvonne got out of bed. "Jimmy, there's something else I want to tell you. Saul is their baby too. They love him because they brought him back to life. They're proud of how hard he's fought and how fast he's healing. You've seen that just like I have. They must know the Shepherd Center is fishing around for information. I think they just want to make sure everything is okay before any transfer occurs."

Jim nodded. "I'm sure you're right, and I'm as thankful as you are they care about him so much. Still, I really doubt Saul has a heart problem, especially an urgent one. You would think and hope if the heart were out of line, it would show up in his vital signs."

Yvonne also believed Saul's heart was probably healthy. He'd already been through so much, so she wasn't going to let his chest be cut open unless they could prove there was no alternative. "Let's make a list and call everybody who could possibly know anything about this."

Jim poised his pencil over a pad of paper. He looked at her. "If only they'd told us about their suspicions earlier. We've wasted so much time that could have been devoted to searching."

Yvonne thought about it from the doctor's perspective. "Maybe they did the right thing. I'm not sure we couldn't have handled this information on top of everything else at the beginning."

When Daniela woke they told her their strategy. "It's a good plan. I wish I could help you with it."

"You can help. Your translation skills will be invaluable," Yvonne said.

Daniela looked confused. "You've forgotten this is my last day here, haven't you."

Yvonne thought for a moment. "Oh yes. Of course! I've been so overwhelmed with this new challenge for Saul I can hardly think about anything else."

Daniela nodded. "That's understandable. I can't think of anything else, either. School starts on Monday, though. I wish I could stay to help you but I've already delayed my return as long as I possibly can."

"Yes," Yvonne said. "Of course. You have to get back to school."

As the day progressed the Raisins recruited an increasingly large army to scour files looking for old x-rays. Nothing turned up in Europe, but they remained confident in their strategy because they felt certain they had some at home … somewhere. At two in the afternoon Jim called his brother Phil and listed every possible location he might find the film. Phil got right to work.

Later that afternoon they visited Saul and explained Daniela's departure to him. "Do you understand, Saul?"

He nodded, but Yvonne could tell it wasn't sinking in. Saul looked so frail. He now weighed only 120 pounds.

Daniela kissed him. "I'll be thinking about you all the time, and I'll call daily. You're going to get better, Saul. Will you promise me that?"

He paused and then nodded.

"Good, because you owe me a really nice date, something even better than sitting beside your bed playing thumb war." She smiled. "I expect you to pay up."

Saul blew her a kiss.

After they left the ICU Daniela hugged each of them again. "You're making the right decision to take him home. I can see that now. I'll visit as soon as I can."

"Thank you," Yvonne said.

"I don't know how we would have survived without you," Jim said. "We can never fully express our thanks."

Daniela reached out to hug him. "Don't be silly. I feel fortunate I found a way to help. We're family now. Closer than family, actually."

Yvonne hugged the girl. They were closer than family. Daniela had not only been their parent, guiding them around like children, but she had been their very lifeline. Yvonne squeezed tighter. "You're a great girl, Daniela. I've enjoyed getting to know you, except that I wish it had been under better circumstances."

"I feel exactly the same," Daniela said.

Yvonne didn't release her grip. Her eyes filled with tears, not because she wouldn't have a translator, but because she was going to miss Daniela's company. She'd been with them virtually everywhere they went for the past two weeks. She'd helped them through the hardest time of their lives. Daniela was young and smiled a lot at a time in their life when smiles were otherwise far too rare. Finally Yvonne released the hug.

Daniela smiled one last time. Then she turned and left. Yvonne felt like a part of her was leaving, too. She'd always hated goodbyes, but this one was worse than usual. Of everyone, Daniela had been the strongest and most positive throughout the ordeal so far. Yvonne admired the girl's purposeful, athletic stride as she walked to a waiting taxi. Then she was gone.

The moment she was out of sight the cell phone rang. Yvonne answered.

It was Phil. "I found the x-rays in the first place you told me to look. I took them straight to Dr. Delay. I'm at his office now. He wants to talk to you and Jim."

"All right," Yvonne said. "We're both listening."

A moment later she heard the comforting voice of their long-time family physician. "Hi Yvonne. Hi Jim. I don't know whether my news is good or bad. I've read the x-rays available to me and I don't see any problems with the heart."

"Are you certain," Jim said. "Even the slightest indication that it's farther left than normal would be meaningful."

"I'm not seeing that on this film. The heart's position appears normal to me."

Yvonne's own heart sank. If someone ran a chest x-ray on her right now she doubted anything would be where it belonged. She'd become so certain the Dalton x-rays would clear everything up; instead they seemed to lend credence to the French doctor's theory.

"Do you want me to overnight these to you?" Dr Delay asked.

"No," Jim said.

"Very well. If you decide you need them I'll be standing by."

After they hung up the phone Yvonne asked, "Are you sure you don't want him to mail them?"

Jim shook his head. "I'd become afraid they might be too old to do us any good. Unless we have evidence of a serious problem, the last thing I want to give the doctors here in Angers is evidence to suggest they should go forward with an operation. Even if Saul needs surgery, unless the situation is critical I'm going to do everything in my power to make sure it's done on American soil. We need to find more recent films."

Day 18 – Friday, April 21, 2006

The search for x-rays that could prove Saul's heart had been shifted to the left prior to the accident had been fruitless. They'd contacted every source they could think of, but they hadn't yet uncovered a single film taken in the last five years.

Yvonne felt lethargic as she dragged herself down the hallway toward the ICU conference room for their daily meeting. "If we're unable to prove that Saul's heart position didn't change because of the crash, and if we learn that his condition isn't life-threatening, can we refuse them permission to perform surgery?"

Jim shook his head dejectedly. "I wish I knew."

They stepped into the ICU conference room, feeling defeated.

Moments later Dr. Fesard walked through the door. He flipped his chart open. "Another CT scan of the head was obtained today. It showed a progression in healing of the hemorrhagic contusion on the right frontal lobe."

"His brain is looking better?" Jim asked.

The doctor nodded. "Now to the pulmonary concerns. Attempts have been made to find prior chest x-rays, but nothing useful could be found either at the hospital of Menton, where Saul was treated for a fracture of the clavicle, or elsewhere."

Yvonne looked at Jim. The French doctors had been searching for the same thing they had, with the same results.

"The patient was examined this morning by a heart specialist. Upon his recommendation, the diagnosis of extra-pericardial subluxation of the heart has not been kept." Dr. Fesard grinned.

Yvonne wondered if this meant they had decided Saul's heart was all right.

"We are also abandoning this diagnosis because of the absence of any heart-related issues during all of this evolution; he has had normal blood pressure and no rhythm problems. However, we cannot forget the suspicion, and follow-up will continue."

Yvonne glanced at Jim. He looked as surprised and thrilled as she felt.

"But you're not going to operate?" he asked.

"It doesn't appear to be an urgent concern," the doctor said.

Yvonne and Jim squeezed hands beneath the table. They were back on schedule to bring Saul home. Her feet did a little jig without her permission. She felt so overjoyed she couldn't resist teasing the doctor. "No more bad news. Okay? Only good news from now on."

Dr. Fesard patted her hand. "You two have had a hard time, haven't you?"

Yvonne nodded.

"I want to deliver only good news," he said. "Honestly I do. Unfortunately Saul has not successfully overcome the infection in his lungs. In fact, it has flared. This is a common outcome for coma patients, so it is a setback that does not surprise us."

Yvonne's feet stopped dancing. Every time they got over one hurdle, another one seemed to rise in their path. She wished she could have confidently told the doctors that Saul needed to be on antibiotics from the moment they discovered an infection. If she told them how to do their job, though, they would have been offended. That was the last thing she wanted to do to the people in charge of saving her son's life. She simply had to simply accept that they weren't going to do everything the way she might prefer.

The good news was that the doctors were obviously watching Saul very closely. It looked like he was getting great care. Until she saw something that suggested otherwise, her best strategy would be to remain calm on the outside, even when her insides were turbulent.

"The bacterial infection has been cultured and found to be sensitive to Methicillin. We've begun treatment with Rocephin to bring it under control. The decision has also been made to delay the tracheotomy with the goal of canceling it entirely if the antibiotics can heal the lungs and allow us to again remove the ventilator within a couple of days."

When the doctor's briefing was over they went to see Saul. Yvonne was interested in his reaction to Daniela's absence. Would he remember? Forty-five minutes into the visit there was still no indication he'd noticed.

"Do you miss Daniela?" she finally asked.

He looked around anxiously, as if confused by the suggestion. Then his eyes asked where she'd gone.

"She left yesterday. She kissed you goodbye." His reaction made Yvonne sad. The moment someone wasn't in the room he didn't remember. If Yvonne had been the one missing his reaction probably would have been similar.

She wondered how much of his mental capacity he'd get back, but she couldn't think about that for long. In the otherwise silent room Saul's lungs rattled with each exhalation, disturbing her concentration. The sound, like an engine on the verge of failure, seemed to mirror the rickety feel of her nerves.

Afterward Yvonne called Laura Brown at the Shepherd Center and shared the newest information. They celebrated the good news about Saul's heart, and then Yvonne asked whether the infection might cause new delays in bringing him home.

"If necessary we could bring him home while still on the ventilator, even with the infection. The plane is equipped to handle that sort of thing."

"I'm sure it's safer to wait, though," Yvonne said.

"Yes. Probably."

"We're anxious to get home, but we don't want to take an unnecessary risk," Yvonne said. "We'll wait."

"Do you know what the infection is?" Laura asked.

"No, only that they're treating it with something called Rocephin," Yvonne answered.

"It sounds like he's come down with pneumonia," Laura said.

Yvonne searched her memory banks. "They never called it that. I was hoping it was something less serious."

Laura sounded thoughtful. "The antibiotics should kill the infection pretty quickly. Coma patients are extremely susceptible to these complications because pooling secretions create an ideal environment for bacteria to multiply. I doubt it will delay his return by more than a week."

A week. That meant April 27 was out of play and they wouldn't return to America until May, at the earliest. It seemed like an unendurable amount of time, but enduring it was the only choice.

Shortly after their evening visit with Saul, Yvonne's cell phone rang. She looked at the display. It was Phil again.

Yvonne flipped the phone open. "You don't need to keep searching for x-rays. The doctors have decided against heart surgery."

"That's wonderful," Phil said, "but I'm calling about something entirely different."

"What is it?"

"Well, you remember that the Tour de Georgia came through Dalton today?"

It had slipped her mind in the chaos of the last few days. "How did it go?"

"There wasn't a dry eye in the place. The students from Dalton High passed out green ribbons for everybody in the crowd to wear in Saul's honor. Phil Liggett and Bob Roll and all the other dignitaries had them on. Each cyclist wrapped a band of green tape around his handlebars for Saul. Then the mayor called for a moment of silence. While we stood there in downtown Dalton thinking about the three of you in Angers, you could have heard a pin drop."

A tear ran down Yvonne's cheek. "Thank you for helping to organize that, Phil."

"Don't thank me," Phil said. "Thank Jennifer and Ron Swopes. They're the ones who came up with the green ribbon idea and made everything happen."

Now Yvonne was crying like a baby. "It really does help to know that people care."

"Yeah, they care a lot. We put up a big get-well poster, and lots of people signed it. Many of them told stories to Teresa and me about their past experiences with Saul. You know that everybody who knows your kid loves him, but I'll bet you have no idea how many people know him. It was amazing."

Yvonne grinned. "Yeah, we've been discovering that for ourselves."

"One other thing. The mayor read a proclamation dedicating Saul Raisin Woods Mountain Bike Park, and the crowd went crazy."

"They named that new mountain bike park after Saul?" Someone had mentioned the possibility back when Jim and Yvonne were helping to build it, but the Raisins hadn't taken it seriously.

"It was so cool," Phil said. "We wished you could have been here."

Yvonne patted Jim's leg. "We wish we could have too. Yesterday was rough on us, but today has been better. This is the sort of news we need to keep the momentum going. Thanks for all you've done."

"Of course. I'm just glad I could help."

Day 19 – Saturday, April 22, 2006

The Raisins took their long daily walk, still isolated by the language barrier, but increasingly comfortable with their ability to communicate about simple things.

They came upon a farmer's market and walked up to an orchard vendor. Jim held up an apple. "*Combien?*"

"*Cinquante centimes,*" the vendor said.

"*Deux, s'il vous plaît.*" Jim handed over a one Euro note, and the vendor gave him a second apple.

Strolling along, they noticed a large gathering of excited people but couldn't make any sense of what had everybody agitated. They talked about how much they missed Daniela's company, and at times like these, her ability to explain what was going on.

They left the farmer's market and walked the now familiar streets, all the while praying the medicine would heal Saul's lungs quickly so they could reschedule the flight home.

Near midday John, Jim's brother and former business partner, and his wife Kathy arrived. It felt so good to have family with them again. They gossiped about home, family matters, and Saul. Yvonne enjoyed speaking English and having old friends nearby to share their long days.

Eventually they found themselves, as they did every day, beside their son's hospital bed. Today Saul showed more agitation than usual, rocking from side to side, moving his arms and flexing his fingers. At one point he got hold of his catheter tube and pulled on it as hard as he could.

Jim removed it from his grip. "You keep yanking on that thing and you're liable to pull off something you don't want to lose."

Saul looked at him curiously.

"You're connected to all of this stuff for a good reason, Son," Jim said. "Don't pull any of it off or they'll have to tie your arms down again."

Saul seemed to understand Jim's point. After that he touched the tubes and wires that led from his various body parts to the equipment spread around the room from time to time, but he behaved himself well and didn't try to remove any of them

For the first time in several days Yvonne could see positive progress. His color had improved a tinge, and his responses, while slow, seemed slightly quicker. Though his eyes were still very dull, she sensed the thoughts going on behind them were an increment sharper. Today it felt comfortable to be at his side as he healed.

She was massaging his feet when she heard something like leaves rustling in a slight breeze. She looked up. Saul's lips were moving. He fought to whisper, even though the tube in his throat made speech impossible. She could hardly even hear the noise, but at the same time, she couldn't hear anything else. She felt Jim move in close beside her. He was as attuned as she was to the tiniest changes in Saul's condition.

"Oh, Saul. What are you trying to say to us?" She leaned her ear next to his lips.

More rustling, but she couldn't make out the words.

She combed through his hair with her fingers. "That's all right, Saul. We're here for you. We're ready to do whatever you ask. We love you more than anything."

"They're going to take that tube out soon, Son," Jim said. "Once they do you can start jabbering just like usual."

Yvonne smiled inside. Saul had always been talkative, just like her. Jim had been the quiet member of the family, at least in public. Having two silent men around was strange. They all wanted it to change.

Saul's efforts at speech wore him out, and he relaxed back in the bed. Yvonne started singing songs. She and Jim had long since exhausted their repertoire of comforting nursery rhymes. They had already repeated every one they could think of dozens of times, even though none of them seemed all that relevant to a twenty-three-year-old man. Yvonne figured at the very least the tunes were stimulating his brain, maybe even bringing back early memories. They also went over numbers, birthdays, family members, friends in the USA and France as well as their addresses, and anything else they could think of to encourage him to think.

Yvonne felt a hand on her shoulder. When she turned a nurse smiled at her, then pointed to her watch and said, "*C'est l'heure d'y aller.*"

Yvonne knew it was a reminder that visiting hours had ended. As she gathered up her things she noticed Saul struggling to climb from his bed, as if the nurse's request applied to him, too.

He wrenched his body to the right with everything he had, throwing a leg toward the floor. The nurse rushed to hold him back, and Jim hurried to help.

It broke Yvonne's heart to see her son try to rise because he was nowhere near successful. It hurt even more to watch the nurse tighten his restraints. While she did, Saul looked at Yvonne with miserable, pleading eyes. Sadly, she backed out of his room.

Oh, if only she could take his place. Saul's physical pain was certainly great, but the emotional pain that sliced at her heart at times like these was almost more than she could bear.

Day 20 – Sunday, April 23, 2006

When Yvonne's phone rang she knew without looking that Roger would be on the line. He was as reliable as springtime rain, and speaking of rain, today it poured down in sheets.

"*Bonjour*, Yvonne. It is a good day, no?" It was ironic that he always seemed to start the conversation this way when the weather was at its dreariest.

Yvonne knew from experience that his greeting meant he had happy news. "Yes. A good day," she answered, "and I have a feeling it's about to get better."

"You're right. This morning the doctors have done a slight evaluation of Saul."

"What does that mean?" Yvonne asked.

"They tell him, touch your nose with your right finger. Squeeze my hand. Wiggle your toes. Many questions like that."

"How did he do?"

"Perfect. He does everything they ask."

Yvonne grinned at Jim who was now listening in on the conversation. She felt a tear roll down her cheek. "I knew he would."

"Maybe you do not understand how good this news is," Roger said. "These are tasks the doctors thought he might never again do in his life."

Jim squeezed Yvonne. His eyes shone behind a sheen of moisture.

"We understand, Roger. We're so grateful to the hospital staff for bringing him so far. It's been such a painful experience for our family, and so confusing … Sometimes we haven't expressed ourselves the way we'd like. At times we've felt so frustrated, but it's mostly because we're often unable to understand what's going on. Will you please tell the doctors and nurses how grateful we are?"

Roger chuckled. "I think maybe they already know this. You and Jim are kind, and you both love your son very much and want the best for him. Your concern is for Saul, and you are doing everything you can to help him heal. Anybody can see this, but I will put it into words in case someone does not know."

"Thank you, Roger."

"Do you realize it can be as hard for the doctors to understand you as for you to understand them? Maybe Americans and French are very much alike, but sometimes they do not understand how to communicate so well."

Yvonne realized his words encompassed far more than Saul's stay in an Angers hospital bed. "Yes, Roger. I think you're right about that."

"So, I want for you to know something else. CHU d'Angers is one of the leading brain trauma hospitals anywhere. Saul's surgeon, he is one of the best brain specialists in the world. I have talked to many about this. We are very fortunate he happened to be the one to operate on Saul. Maybe with another surgeon the outcome would not have been so good."

Yvonne shuddered. "Yes. Thank God for his skills. We've realized there's been good fortune mixed with the bad."

"There is more good news, too," Roger said. "The doctors will try to remove the breathing tube soon. They keep holding off on a tracheotomy and now they believe it might not be necessary."

"Oh, I hope they're successful. Saul wants that thing out so badly. He needs to talk." Shepherd's had continued to be surprised that they didn't just go ahead and do the trach. At this point Yvonne wanted Saul to either have the tracheotomy and get it over with, or get rid of the ventilator all together. She was more than ready to move on to the next step.

*   *   *

That afternoon Yann Courbon, a soigneur from Saul's cycling team arrived for a visit. Soigneurs were charged with tending to the welfare of their team's athletes. They gave massages, moved luggage, handed out feed bags, ran errands, and performed all of the menial tasks necessary to keep the rolling circuses otherwise known as bicycle races moving toward their assigned destinations. Jim and Yvonne had met Yann and seen firsthand what a hard worker he was at the Tour of California and the Tour de Georgia. They'd hit it off from the very first.

Yann nodded. His mind was obviously elsewhere. "Saul will overcome this."

"We hope so," Jim answered.

Yann looked surprised at the reservation in Jim's answer. "He will. They don't come any stronger or more determined than Saul. This is only a small obstacle to him."

"I wish you were right," Jim said, "but it's not small."

Yann thought a moment. "Do you know what I love most about him?"

Yvonne shook her head.

"He's always so nice to everyone. You don't often find people like that."

"Thank you, Yann." Yvonne knew Saul would be happy to see his friend. Jim would have to wait outside. But when they reached Saul's bedside Yvonne was disappointed to find him lying in a puddle.

"Oh, Saul. What's happened here?" She felt sad as she moved the wet sheets away from his skin.

He'd pulled his catheter off, something he did quite often, but this time nobody had noticed. She called the nurse.

Experiences like these reminded Yvonne how thankful she was for the little things. Before Saul's accident she'd never felt gratitude for the ability to go to the bathroom on her own. Nowadays she didn't take much of anything for granted.

She prayed the day would come that Saul could take care of himself again.

While the nurses changed the sheets, Yann stood back, looking shaken. His gaze remained on the ground. Yvonne suddenly saw her son through a visitor's eyes. As much progress as Saul had made, he still didn't look right. Not even close. In fact, it was impossible to imagine that he could ever fully recover. Saul couldn't talk, and he could barely move. Every motion was painful and slow, and communication was nearly impossible. He'd lost twenty-five pounds, and like all endurance athletes he'd been light to start with. In Saul, Yann saw a friend on the brink of death, and he didn't like it at all.

As the nurses finished their work Yann exchanged a few words in French. Yvonne felt jealous of his ability to communicate with them. She had so many questions and so few answers.

When the nurses left, Yann stepped forward. Saul kept his eyes on his soigneur.

Yann spoke to Saul in French, holding back tears.

Though Saul's eyes were cloudy as usual, Yvonne could tell he recognized his visitor. Saul reached out for Yann's hand.

Yann held onto his friend's fingers gently and spoke in a loving way. Yvonne wondered what Yann thought about how far Saul still had to go. She'd like to know what was going on in his head at this moment. Now that he'd seen Saul as he was today, did he still feel the same about the future as he had before he stepped into this room?

Sadly, as Yvonne looked out the window that framed nothing but a rectangular chunk of sky, she already knew the answer to her question. As strong and determined as Saul was, the obstacles he now faced were anything but small.

Day 21 – Monday, April 24, 2006

Yvonne and Jim sat in the Logis Ozanam sitting room with Jean-Jacques Henry, the Crédit Agricole directeur sportif who'd been overseeing Saul's team at the Circuit de la Sarthe when he crashed. He was young, handsome, and intelligent.

"Have you learned anything about why Saul had the accident?" Jim asked. "We've heard very little."

Yvonne thought about how the effects of Saul's crash had taken over every facet of her life. She dealt with it twenty-four/seven. How could one tiny moment have had such a massive impact on their lives? She wondered if she would ever know what had caused Saul to hit the pavement.

"I can tell you all I know. The racing was very fast, full speed." Jean-Jacques wrapped his hands around an imaginary set of handlebars then twisted his right wrist back as if opening a Harley's throttle. "A small breakaway had escaped, and Saul was on the front of the peloton chasing them down. He rode powerfully and closed the gap, exactly as I had asked him to. That's when he drifted back into the pack for a breather. Cyclists I spoke to said Saul made what looked like a dirty move and he—"

"What's a dirty move?" Yvonne asked. "That doesn't sound like Saul."

"Dirty move means to force one's way back into the pace line, and you're correct that it does not sound like Saul. The cyclists who witnessed the crash said the same thing. Normally he would put out a hand to tell the trailing men he needed some room. The riders who saw him at this moment called his behavior odd, as if he was in a trance. He swerved into the line, rode into another cyclist, and their handlebars locked together. When they pulled apart Saul went down hard, flopping onto his side. This is where there is more cause for concern."

Yvonne looked out at the drizzling rain still coming down in the garden. "What concern?"

"Saul took no evasive action." Jean-Jacques must have recognized confusion in the Raisins' expressions so he added more detail. "He didn't correct his steering, he didn't put out an arm to break his fall, he didn't even try to keep his head up in a normal manner. This would explain why he hit so hard. So I have asked myself, was he conscious before he fell, and my answer is, maybe not. Of course, the racers were going full speed, so maybe we cannot rely so much on what others thought they saw him do. There are many other possible explanations. Maybe he hit something in the road. Maybe he touched tires with another cyclist. We might never know the reason for his crash."

Jim nodded. "But by the time you arrived on the scene Saul was having a seizure."

"Yes, this is also true. It frightened me. It was terrible to see … so much blood and uncontrolled shuddering." Jean-Jacques' face had become ashen simply from the retelling.

Yvonne put a hand on his shoulder. "Thank you for helping us understand."

"I only wish I could do more."

After Jean-Jacques left, the Raisins went walking, but the rain soon convinced them to step into the Internet café and check Saul's web site instead. As usual, the kind posts from fans and supporters encouraged them. When they had read all they could, Jim and Yvonne composed an entry of their own:

> Saul's doctors did a quick evaluation with him yesterday. It went well. He is waking up, but still needs a lot of sleep. He is aware of what's going on around him. He does use his left and right limbs, his left side a little less, but hopefully that should change with rehab. We will know more when he is fully awake and can be completely evaluated. Because of the coma, he has an infection in his left lung. The doctors are on top of it and that should go away soon. The doctors and nurses here are great. They are taking wonderful care of Saul. Saul wants out of the bed and we are ready to bring him home. We should be headed home when the infection is clear, to a rehab center in Atlanta. Thank you for your thoughts and prayers, they are working.

Moments after they submitted their post Roger's daily call came in.

"The tube is out," he said.

"Saul is breathing on his own?" Yvonne asked. She knew that if the ventilator tube came out and stayed out they would be going home soon.

"Yes. He is doing very well. His fever is gone, and he's trying to talk."

Yvonne's spirits soared. She hung up and threw her arms around Jim. They were going home! This major milestone had eluded them for several days; then it suddenly jumped out of nowhere, so huge nothing else was visible.

She could hardly wait for morning in America to arrive so she could call the Shepherd Center. Eight in the morning in Georgia was two in the afternoon here, though, so she had a long time to wait.

Finally the time came. "Hi, Laura. Saul's off the ventilator and his fever has passed. Can you get the ball rolling to transport him?"

"Slow down, Yvonne. You sound like you want to leave this instant," Laura said.

"We wouldn't mind it," Yvonne said.

"Well, I understand. Saul has improved with surprising speed. Have his doctors signed off on his transfer yet?"

"We haven't dared ask them. Is their permission really required? Shouldn't we be the ones with the final say?"

"If he was in America, yes, but I don't know how things work in France. I'll see if I can find someone who can assist us."

"If it helps, our impression is that Saul's doctors resent outside help. It's better if they feel they make every decision. I don't think they like sharing information, and they definitely don't want outsiders telling them what to do. They want to do things their way."

Laura laughed. "That's a perfect description of several American doctors I've met. Good insight, though, and I'll pass it along to our pharmacist. He speaks French so he's stepped in to help get this transfer finalized. In the meantime, I'll get to work finishing the transportation arrangements. My guess is we should be able to get it done sometime between Friday and Monday."

"Wonderful! Thank you, Laura. We can't wait to meet you later this week. What a beautiful day that will be." The very idea brought a lump to Yvonne's throat.

The afternoon visit couldn't come soon enough. The Raisins were equally excited to tell their son about the day's developments and to see how he was doing and hear what he was trying to say.

When they finally walked into the ICU they got a major surprise. Saul wasn't in his bed. He was sitting in a wheelchair beside it. Straps held him up. Her tear ducts opened so suddenly she could hardly find her way to her son's side.

"Saul, you're sitting!" Jim said. "I had honestly doubted I'd ever see this again."

Saul smiled weakly. His good mood didn't last, though. He started twisting and turning, looking for a more comfortable position. He was very agitated. He pointed to his bed and pleaded with his eyes to be returned. What an ironic change from his demeanor when he hadn't been allowed to get out of the bed.

"He hates sitting. Can we lay him down?" Jim pantomimed his question to a nurse.

She shook her head and pointed to the chair. Then she held up a hand as if to say stop. Yvonne assumed it meant he needed to remain in the chair for now. She knew that sitting up must be good for his lungs. Maybe it was also an early step in his rehab.

Saul tried to slide out of the chair, but the straps bound around him when he got halfway down.

"That looks pretty uncomfortable," Jim said. He lifted Saul back to a sitting position. "You might as well quit wiggling around because you'll probably hurt yourself."

Saul began moving his lips again. Yvonne leaned close, but the words were so weak she couldn't understand them for sure. She thought he said, "I don't like this."

"Are you hungry, Saul?" Yvonne asked.

He nodded and pointed toward the dresser.

She noticed a serving tray with utensils and other items.

"You're eating real food now?"

He nodded.

She went over and looked at the containers. They held several varieties of what appeared to be baby food. She dipped a spoon into one and tasted it. Very bland. She sampled the other two. They tasted the same. She picked up a container and took it to the nurses' station. "Can he eat this?"

"*Oui, il peut.* Maybe he choke a bit. Feed slow."

Yvonne brought a container back to Saul, lifting a small amount to his mouth. He sucked it from the spoon like a hungry dog, wincing as he swallowed. She could almost hear the raw flesh grating in his throat, but the pain wasn't enough to slow him down. He opened his mouth, waiting for another bite. Saliva ran down his chin.

Yvonne lifted another spoonful. Whenever she slowed Saul grabbed her wrist and tried to help her scoop up more, even though he choked on every bite. She tried to slow the pace—she'd always believed it wasn't healthy to wolf down food—but her efforts were of little use. Saul was starving. Somehow, no matter how hard she tried to be careful, he was getting food everywhere. It was worse than when he was a baby, but his appetite was much bigger. Soon she had to get the second container, and then the third.

As his stomach finally filled, his eating slowed. Now, between bites, Saul looked longingly at the bed.

A nurse stepped into the room and saw all the empty dishes. "*Bien. Très bien.*" Then she took a careful look at Saul. His breathing was rapid. Yvonne worried the food might have created the problem. Had she fed him too quickly? Maybe the nurse could solve the problem by putting him back into bed. Saul would appreciate that.

Instead, the nurse returned with an oxygen mask and fitted it around his head. Saul pointed at his bed again, but the nurse turned her back and walked away.

The extra oxygen helped. As Saul's breathing returned to normal Yvonne noticed it was time to leave. Maybe once they were gone the nurses would let Saul lie down.

She stood and kissed him on the forehead. "You're doing great. Way to go, Saul."

Jim understood the cue and stood as well. "I'm very proud of you, Son." He kissed Saul on the forehead, too.

Yvonne's nerves raced. She longed for a pleasant exit from this room, and it seemed she was finally on the verge of one. It would feel especially good to leave him in a sitting position. She turned and took a cautious step toward the door. Jim slid his hand into hers and they took a second step together. They were going to make it.

A tapping sound from Saul's vicinity forced her to turn around. Her son was knocking his right hand against the side of his chair, and his eyes were pleading. He gestured for them to take him wherever they were going, apparently emboldened by having his own set of wheels. He might hate the chair, but now he saw it as a way out of the hospital room he hated even more.

He beckoned Yvonne with his right hand. She couldn't possibly stay away when he needed her so badly. She took a cautious step toward him.

Once she came within reach he moved his lips next to her ear and whispered with all his strength, "Mom, take me home. Please!"

Day 22 – Tuesday, April 25, 2006

The Raisins stepped into the Internet café. It had become one of their favorite stops on their morning walks.

"Now, let's just hope and pray that Saul can keep breathing on his own," Jim said. "I don't know if I could take it if the doctors told me they need to put a trach tube in."

"Amen to that," Yvonne said. Saul had somehow avoided having a tracheotomy for all this time. Not only would it be a shame for him to have to go through it now, but it would create an additional delay in getting him home. She wanted no part of that.

Jim sat down at the computer and before reading any of the new messages began typing one of his own:

> Today is a good day. We did not tell this before, but Saul was not taken off the respirator earlier, he pulled it out. After 24 hours they had to reinsert it. Yesterday they took it out again and so far Saul does not need it and hopefully he will not need it. Saul is sitting in a chair for short times and talking a little. He told us he does not like it here and he is hungry. Saul is still very confused and will be for awhile. The infection in his lungs is a lot better. If he keeps improving with little or no set backs, we are coming home soon. We have a medical air ambulance ready to bring him home. Again, thank you for all the love, support, and prayers.
> Jim and Yvonne

He submitted his post and rose from his chair. "That'll do, don't you think?"

He didn't want to stay and read the new posts to Saul? At first Yvonne wanted to know what people had written, but the idea of a day outdoors did seem refreshing. She looked out the window. Although omnipresent clouds hung over Angers, the weather had become considerably warmer than when they'd first arrived. She still wasn't skilled at converting centigrade temperatures, but she estimated that today it was already in the low sixties Fahrenheit. After two days of rain it would feel good to get out and stretch her legs. She smiled at Jim. "Let's go visit the castle."

He grinned broadly in return. "Okay." They didn't have to discuss what a significant change it was that they felt like sightseeing. For the first few weeks in Angers they hadn't done anything for pleasure. They'd walked the streets but had hardly seen anything. They'd eaten the food, but other than two evenings at restaurants with old friends the taste barely registered. They'd experienced the culture, but mostly only in frustrating ways. Now they were finally ready to do something unimportant.

Le Château d'Angers sat on the shore of the Maine River. It was an imposing structure that seemed to overlook the entire valley, even though it sat on ground near the lowest point. Yvonne felt her pulse rise with excitement as they strode toward the ancient ramparts. She was breathing hard when her phone rang.

She looked at the display before answering. "Hi Roger."

"Hello Yvonne. Are you exercising?" The optimism in his tone was obvious.

"Yes. How's Saul?"

"You will be happy. He had a good night. The doctors think the tube will stay out. This means he will not have to have a tracheotomy."

"Oh, how wonderful!" Yvonne's surge of emotion surprised her, but when she passed the news on to Jim he surprised her even more.

"Time for a happy dance!" He grabbed her by the wrists and swung her around as he sang a spur of the moment tune. "The Raisins are a goin' home, the Raisins are a goin' home!" He did a little jog step and then bounced spryly on his heels.

Yvonne had a hard time returning the phone to her ear in the midst of her husband's uncharacteristic display of joy. Finally she succeeded. "We'll call you back, Roger. Thanks for the news!"

The Raisins paid their entry fee and crossed the drawbridge to the castle. English-speaking guides were available, but they preferred to wander around on their own.

The stone ramparts they had passed so many times enclosed a large courtyard filled with perfectly manicured hedges, blossoming fruit trees, and inviting spaces. Around the periphery was an assortment of stone buildings. The royal apartments had a quaint hodgepodge feel, as if they'd been built, partially destroyed, and rebuilt many times. Yvonne's eye was most drawn to the charming Chapelle Ste Geneviève, a simple stone structure with clean lines. Somehow, even from afar, it felt every bit as holy as the much more spectacular Cathédrale St-Maurice they'd visited so often outside the castle grounds.

"There's a church we haven't yet prayed in yet," she said.

Jim took her hand, and they walked over to rectify the situation. The moment they stepped through the doorway, they were overwhelmed by the shrine's fine frescoes and dazzling stained glass. Yvonne loved the little building's solemn feel.

The next structure they visited was a modern museum. Skilled effort had been made to make it look ancient from the exterior. Inside Yvonne gasped at the beautiful Tapestries of the Apocalypse. They found a brochure written in English and learned that most of the art had been commissioned in 1373 by Louis I, Duke of Anjou, brother of Charles V, the King of France. Some panels illustrated battles between hydras and angels; others showed Saints fighting to spread and uphold the word of God while mountains spat fire and ships capsized in turbulent seas. The duke's goal had been to illustrate the story of the Apocalypse with the largest tapestry ever created. He succeeded, and even to this day there were none bigger. It originally included one-hundred panels stretching 140 meters long, much longer than a football field.

Seventy of the panels had survived to the present day, their condition incredibly fine even though at various times portions had been forgotten in a musty attics, used to protect orange trees from heat and cold, and even made into rags. How inspiring to see that something so valuable had ultimately been saved and restored. Like nearly everything else in the world, this success story reminded Yvonne of her son. She wished she could explain the beauty of the tapestries to Saul during their afternoon visit, but she knew it wouldn't be possible. His mind wasn't ready for that sort of conversation.

They inspected frightening dungeon cells, a windmill tower, and several hidden gardens. Before leaving for the hospital they climbed to the top of the ramparts. The sweeping view of the regal Loire valley brought with it a peaceful sensation. Below Yvonne recognized many locations that had played an unexpectedly critical role in the last month of her life. She left the château hand in hand with Jim, happily rejuvenated and extremely grateful for a somewhat carefree day.

*   *   *

Arriving at Saul's room they were happy to see him seated once again, but he wasn't at all happy about it. His whispering had become mostly decipherable.

"Down," he told Yvonne, pointing at his bed

She patted his hand. "They're keeping you in the chair because they care about you. I know it's not comfortable, but you need to work hard to recover." She didn't know the precise reasons he needed to sit up, but she believed it was good for him whether he enjoyed it or not.

Saul scowled. "Toilet."

Yvonne looked around nervously. "Oh no!" She hurried to the nurses' station. "He needs to use the bathroom!"

Two nurses hurried to the room and moved Saul onto a portable toilet. One of them waved Yvonne's and Jim out of the ICU.

After a few minutes the Raisins returned. The nurses were proud of Saul. Simply being aware of natural urges was well beyond what some of the doctors had initially predicted Saul would ever be capable of. They'd put him back into bed as his reward. Yvonne and Jim thanked the nurses and heaped congratulations on Saul.

He looked like a happy puppy, thrilled to have pleased his master, but simultaneously befuddled about what he'd done that deserved such a fuss.

Within moments he started snoring. Though she loved watching her son sleep so soundly, it amazed Yvonne that simply sitting in a chair could use up so much of his energy.

When they returned for their next visit Saul was still in bed. He motioned his parents to come close. "We leave," he whispered, pointing at the door and indicating he needed to go with them.

"We know you don't like it here, Saul, but these people are helping you recover. You need to stay," Yvonne said.

His brow furrowed and he repeated, "We leave," as if Yvonne's explanation had been irrelevant.

"We can't yet, but we're going to go to Atlanta soon. How does that sound?"

He didn't seem to care. Yvonne wondered if he knew where they were now. She looked into his eyes. "Saul, you know you were in a very bad accident, don't you?"

She heard a pop. Saul had found his catheter and pulled it off with his right hand. Urine spilled all over the bed.

"Oh, Saul! You've got to quit doing that," she said.

Jim found a nurse and showed her the problem. She nodded in understanding. "*Oui. Un moment.*"

The Raisins left the ICU. After standing around the waiting room for a long time they realized they'd been forgotten. "Let's just go back on our own. We have limited time with him. I'm not going to spend it standing out here," Jim said.

They walked back into the ICU and went to Saul's bed. There he lay, alone and still wet. Yvonne's blood boiled.

"Ridiculous," Jim said. He strode toward the station and got the attention of a different nurse. Using gestures and simple words he tried to explain that Saul had been lying in urine for a long time.

"*Oh, pardon. Pardon.*"

As the Raisins again left the ICU to allow the new nurse to change the sheets Yvonne looked at the nurses' station. The woman who had initially promised to change Saul sat gossiping with other nurses. When she made inadvertent eye contact the nurse's gaze dropped, embarrassed at her error. At least she knew the Raisins were unhappy about her lack of follow-through. She jumped to her feet and hurried to help change Saul's bed.

Yvonne hadn't felt upset about any aspect of Saul's care before this moment, but now she felt frustrated. The communication barriers added an exhausting layer to the already life-sapping nature of Saul's situation.

She stepped into the hall and dialed Laura at the Shepherd Center. "Any more news about when we can bring Saul home."

"Your timing is perfect," Laura said, "except that we still haven't heard back from anybody at CHU d'Angers, the air trip is set for Sunday, late. We'll send them a new round of messages and make sure the urgency is obvious."

Yvonne felt a wave of relief. Their trial of isolation by noncommunication was almost over.

Day 23 – Wednesday, April 26, 2006

Jim and Yvonne had been visiting the ICU for so long it seemed almost ordinary to walk through the antiseptic hallways to visit their son, connected to the hospital fixtures as he was by wires and tubes. They would dress in the sterile clothing, wash their hands, and then page the nurses' station to give them Saul's name. The nurses would say either "*oui,*" or "*un moment.*" Once inside they would nod to the nurses as they crossed the room to Saul's enclosure. The nurses always nodded back.

Yvonne gave the nurses' station her usual nod on the way to see Saul for their afternoon visit, but this time it seemed to incite a commotion.

Dr. Fesard hurried across the ICU and cut off the Raisins' progress. He held up a piece of paper. "What is this about?"

Yvonne tried to read the paper. It looked like an e-mail, but she couldn't tell for certain.

Dr. Fesard pointed them toward the door. "We should discuss this in the conference room."

Reluctantly, Yvonne walked in that direction, away from her son.

They stepped into the conference room and the doctor said, "All right, now. Please explain."

"Explain what?" Jim asked.

The doctor handed him the paper. It was a message from the Shepherd Center informing CHU d'Angers of the air ambulance arriving on Sunday. Yvonne recalled how stern the doctor had become a week earlier when Jim mentioned transferring Saul to America. She thought about all the difficulties the Shepherd Center had experienced communicating with the French hospital.

"Who are these people and what is their business with Saul?" the doctor asked.

Jim studied the document a long moment. Yvonne worried he couldn't come up with a response. Finally he said, "They want to transfer him this Sunday?"

The doctor nodded.

"The Shepherd Center is the hospital we have chosen for Saul, but we have explained to their staff that when he leaves is your decision. The whole situation confuses me."

Yvonne's nerves raced as she listened to Jim carefully skirt the truth. He hadn't lied, but he had phrased words carefully, almost assisting the doctor in misinterpreting them in a specific way. Her palms sweated for fear the doctor would block the transfer.

"They are doing this on their own?" Dr. Fesard asked.

Jim avoided the question. "You are the most knowledgeable person in this situation. It might be helpful if you speak with the people at the Shepherd Center and suggest a plan. It's the number one facility in the United States for brain injury rehab, but you are in charge of our son right now. We'll support your decision."

Yvonne squeezed Jim's hand beneath the table. She didn't have the strength to maintain a neutral expression, so she looked toward the door as she tried to collect her thoughts. She wondered where Jim had learned to bluff so well.

Dr. Fesard thought for a while. "Things are moving too quickly. It would be foolish to move this patient if he has a fever, breathing problems, or remains in serious danger. I will not allow that to happen."

"We don't want to take unnecessary risks, either," Jim said. "If you decide Saul isn't ready to move please let us know by Friday. The air ambulance costs a lot of money, and once it leaves for France the charge is nonrefundable. We've got to stop them from coming if they won't be able to return with Saul."

Dr. Fesard reread a portion of the e-mail silently, tapping his fingers while he thought. Finally he spoke. "Very well. I'll speak with them. We will see if it is possible to move Saul." He left the room.

Yvonne waited until she was certain the doctor wasn't coming back before collapsing onto the table. "Jim, you amaze me. It looked so bad, but once you convinced him he was in control and that we supported his decision his attitude changed."

Jim wiped his brow. "Yeah, and we will support his decision ..."

Yvonne felt her jaw drop.

"... as long as he makes the decision we are trying to get him to make," he added. "Now, we'd better call Laura and tell her what's up before Dr. Fesard makes his call."

Yvonne dialed Laura Brown and explained the situation.

"Thanks for letting me know. The air ambulance is all set. They'll arrive on Sunday but won't be able to take off until 3:00 AM on Monday because of mandatory rest time for the pilots. You'd arrive in Atlanta at about eleven in the morning on Monday. That's fourteen hours of flying with the time change."

"Oh Laura, how will we ever repay you if you successfully convince them to discharge him?" Yvonne asked.

"Don't get your hopes too high. Saul could still have a medical setback and the trip would be canceled."

Yvonne gritted her teeth. "I won't let that happen. I'm going to give him all my strength, and I'm going to give you a big hug when we reach Atlanta. Thank you for all the work you've done."

"You're welcome, Yvonne. I look forward to hugging you, too."

Saul was sitting in his wheelchair when they reached his room. He looked more alert, but less happy about sitting than ever. He pointed longingly at the bed.

"Can we move him?" Jim asked a passing nurse.

She nodded and helped them transfer him to the bed.

Saul settled in contentedly. During their entire visit Yvonne's thoughts were preoccupied with the conversations that might be going on at that very moment between the French doctors and the staff at the Shepherd Center. She didn't dare mention her distraction to Saul. She wondered if he could sense that she wasn't entirely there.

Saul pointed to his throat. "Sore," he whispered.

"Drink this," Yvonne opened a can of orange juice, slid a straw in, and held it where he could suck on it.

He took a long draw, draining the small container in a single sip, but choking as usual when he swallowed. "Home."

"We're going to take you home, Honey, but it takes time. We're trying to make the arrangements. It's very complicated. We're in a French hospital, you know."

Saul scrunched his brow. "Fly half day."

Yvonne stared at Saul in amazement as a nurse entered the room and began prodding him for yet more tests. He'd just guessed their travel time almost perfectly, though it was surely a coincidence. She stepped against the wall to give the nurse more space while she thought things through.

"I can't help but think that when the fog leaves, he'll be OK," Jim whispered.

Yvonne nodded. "He looks a little better today, doesn't he?"

"Yeah. Brighter, and he's gained a little weight."

Visiting hours came to a close. Reluctantly they said goodnight to Saul and left the room. As they strolled from the ICU, Dr. Fesard indicated for them to stop.

"I have just spoken with the Shepherd Center."

Yvonne's heart froze between beats. Jim stayed silent as well, waiting for the doctor's decision.

"They have put a great deal of work into this transfer already."

Yvonne tried to look surprised and concerned.

"I told them my conditions for the transfer, and they promised to meet them all, but if you are uncomfortable about this moving forward so quickly I can put a stop to it. If he continues like he is now he will be able to go." Dr. Fesard paused, obviously waiting for a response.

In her entire life Yvonne had seldom found herself at a complete loss for words, but she did now. Her legs begged to jump for joy, but her brain told them they must be on their best behavior, and her face had to act as if she was mulling a difficult decision.

"We trust your judgment," Jim finally said.

"Well, my judgment is that he might not be ready yet. We can make that decision on Friday."

Jim nodded. "If you decide Saul is ready, what conditions are you requiring of the center?"

"I have given them a list of the medical equipment the plane must carry, plus it needs to be staffed with a *medican* and a nurse."

Yvonne looked at Jim, mostly because she felt certain her expression would betray her at any moment. They might be going home Sunday night!

Jim extended a hand. "Thank you for all you've done for my son, Doctor Fesard. We owe you and the staff here his life. There's no way we can ever repay you."

The doctor shook Jim's hand. "You're welcome for everything. You owe us nothing. Just make sure Saul keeps on fighting."

Day 24 – Thursday, April 27, 2006

Jim had purchased round trip tickets on Delta when they left Dalton under emergency conditions. At that time he chose their return flight out of thin air. Now, amazingly, it turned out to be the exact flight he would take home. With everything out of their control, the chances of that happening must have been astronomical.

He couldn't suppress a grin as he hung up the phone after confirming his Sunday afternoon flight on Delta. "Ouch. We wire sixty grand from our accounts for a private jet to fly us home, and I don't even get a seat."

Yvonne patted his back. "You're sure you don't want me to take the Delta flight?"

"Of course not. Saul needs you beside him on his journey. I'm actually happy about the whole thing, even if my wallet isn't. I don't think a small plane would agree with my stomach all that well."

Yvonne nodded. She agreed that, all things considered, it made more sense for her to fly with Saul.

Jim tossed his blue and green fleece coat onto the bed. "I'm leaving this ugly thing behind. I don't know what I was thinking the day I bought it."

Yvonne chuckled, but decided not to remind her husband she'd tried to talk him into taking enough time to find a coat he liked. There was nothing to gloat about because the gray sweater she'd purchased on the same shopping trip had shrunk to a useless size when she tossed it into the dryer without thinking.

"I'm not taking these running shoes home, either," he said. "They were new a month ago. Now they're trashed."

Yvonne looked at her own shoes. There were no more miles left in them, either. She'd shed fifteen pounds from the stress and the walking over the last three weeks. Jim looked like he'd lost at least twenty.

Her husband looked at the rest of his clothing for a minute and then shook his head. "We've got all of Saul's stuff to take home. Why don't we just give our clothes to Logis Ozanam. Our pillows, too. Unfortunately, someone's bound to come along who could use them."

Unfortunately was right. As wonderful as Logis Ozanam was, Yvonne felt heartbroken for anybody who had to stay here. Donating their clothing was a great idea.

She looked into the mirror in preparation to leave their room and saw something startling. "Oh, look Jimmy. I have a gray hair."

Jim grinned sympathetically. "Join the club."

She was about to mention that she wasn't interested in joining this club, but her phone rang. She looked at the display and connected the call. "Hello, Roger."

"I have good news today, Yvonne. Saul continues to amaze," he said. "This morning they asked him if he wanted to try walking, and he said, 'Yes.' With the help of two strong nurses he went to the foot of his bed and back."

"Oh, I wish I could have seen him!"

"I'm sure it won't be long until you can. They are not exactly saying he walked. They said his left foot just flopped along. I believe they mostly carried him, but it is a good sign that his desire to get on his feet is strong."

"That's Saul," Yvonne said.

"I am coming to Angers this afternoon to visit the three of you," Roger said. "I want to wish Saul well on his journey home."

"Wonderful. We can't wait to see you."

The day rolled by quicker than most. Yvonne and Jim talked a bit more than usual, and they laughed a lot more than had become customary—at least since Saul's crash. At three o'clock they entered the ICU with Roger. At this point Saul could have been transferred to a regular ward, but since the staff knew he was leaving soon and his bed wasn't in demand, he remained in Intensive Care. It probably felt nice for the doctors and nurses in this quadrant of the hospital to actually see one of their charges get better.

Saul's face lit up when he saw his team manager. "I ride Giro," Saul whispered.

He was talking about the three-week-long Giro d'Italia he'd been targeting his fitness toward before the accident.

Roger looked confused. "I know you were looking forward to riding your first Grand Tour, Saul, but I am sad to tell you it won't be this year's Giro. Next year, maybe."

"No, this year," Saul insisted.

Roger smiled. "The race starts in a week. You're just learning to stand again. You could not possibly ride a bike at this time."

Saul did some sort of mathematical calculation on his fingers. Then he looked Roger in the eye. "Okay. Next year."

Roger patted Saul on the shoulder. There was a loving tenderness to the gesture. "Yes, next year. I can't wait to watch you ride it."

There were hugs all around as Roger said goodbye.

"We couldn't have made it through this without you," Yvonne said. Roger's fanaticism for detail had helped them in so many ways. From day one he'd followed up on every conceivable item. Even now he knew precisely when the ambulance was scheduled to land, where it was supposed to refuel along the way, and what time it was supposed to touch down in Atlanta.

"Saul's accident has changed me. I'm glad I found a way to help," Roger said. "I've told you many times before, it is the hardest thing I've ever been through with one of my cyclists. I am very grateful for the progress he has made so far. Now it is your job to keep me informed of where things go from here."

"Of course we will, and thank you again." Yvonne held Roger's hand in hers and leaned in to trade a *bise*. Jim joined them in a big family-style hug. They'd gone through such hardship together. Roger had shown himself to be the best of men. Saying goodbye was very hard. They'd always share a special bond.

After Roger left, the Raisins strolled around the campus, enjoying the fine spring day while waiting to return for their evening visit. When the time came they walked back into the hospital.

Yvonne did a double take as they exited the elevator. "Saul?"

He sat in a wheelchair while a nurse pushed him along slowly. He fought to raise his head toward the sound of his mother's voice.

"What a surprise." Jim looked at his son in amazement.

"I show Saul sun," the nurse explained, pointing toward the window.

"Yes, it's a beautiful day." Yvonne looked at Saul. "Don't you love the sun?"

Saul bent his head back, indicating he wanted to return to where he'd come from. "Bed."

Yvonne knew that, as much as Saul hated it, it was good for him to be up and moving around. "Don't you want to see the waiting area and conference room where your dad and I spend so much of our time these days?"

"No."

Jim smiled. "Well, you're going to." He pointed out random details: the locker where they stored their things, the box where they got their shoe covers, the spot where they'd been standing when they learned Saul had awakened from his coma.

Saul didn't care about any of it, but that wasn't the point. They needed to keep him up and stimulated as long as possible. He kept wanting to kiss his parents and hold their hands like a small child. He kept begging them to return him to his bed.

Soon Saul's pleas were too strong to ignore.

Jim looked at the nurse and the nurse nodded.

"All right, Saul. You're going to get your way," Jim said. "We're taking you back to your room."

Yvonne felt grateful for the brief opportunity to see Saul far from his life support systems. What better proof could there be that he was getting better?

They returned him to his room, fed him, and helped him into bed. He looked exhausted.

Yvonne moved her cell phone from one pocket to another as she prepared to sit down. Saul noticed it. He motioned with his hand and held it to his ear.

"You want to make a phone call?" Yvonne asked.

Saul nodded.

"To who? Daniela?"

Saul nodded more enthusiastically.

Yvonne got Daniela on the phone and gave it to Saul. He whispered, "I love you." He grinned as he listened to her voice and repeated his same line three more times, but his already fragile whisper weakened further with each repetition.

Yvonne took the phone back. "Did you hear him?"

Daniela laughed. "Oh yes. Only barely, but I heard. I can't believe he's talking!"

"Whatever you said made him very happy," Yvonne said.

"I told him I loved him and asked him to promise to get well. I know for sure he can do it."

Saul lay in the bed watching his mother talk to his girlfriend. He looked content. Soon he closed his eyes and drifted into a deep sleep.

Yvonne stepped into the hallway alongside her husband. "Jimmy, do you feel like I do?"

There was a tear in the corner of Jim's eye, so he didn't need to answer in words.

"Our son has been returned to us," she said. "He's coming back."

Jim nodded. "Yeah. It's a miracle. I just wonder how far he's going to recover."

Yvonne's phone rang. "This is Dan with Midway Air Ambulance. Are you going to be ready for us?"

"You couldn't possibly imagine how ready," Yvonne said.

"Sounds good. We'll be there soon to take you home. It will be Saul, you, two pilots, a nurse, and an EMT. I think you're going to like our little plane."

Yvonne hardly heard the last sentence. "An EMT? It was supposed to be a doctor."

Yvonne heard papers shuffling. "Nope. Says here the doctors in France are requiring a medic. That's the same as an EMT."

Yvonne's heart sank. "*Medican* is what they asked for. That's French for doctor. They won't like this. Is there any way we can get a doctor instead?"

"You'll have to talk to the Shepherd Center about that. They set this up."

Yvonne immediately called Laura Brown and explained the misunderstanding. "This could cause big problems. We've got to have a doctor on that plane."

"The EMT and nurse are husband and wife. They travel around the world doing this sort of thing. I assure you, they're very skilled. Maybe even more skilled than a doctor in these circumstances."

"My confidence in their skill level isn't the problem. It's the comfort levels of the French doctors I'm worried about. They'll shut this trip down if they decide we aren't following their rules." Yvonne's head hurt.

"Let me find out what it would take to get a doctor," Laura said. "I'll call you back tomorrow."

Yvonne disconnected the call and turned to Jim. "What are we going to do?"

Jim shook his head. "I don't know. We could stay quiet. Maybe they won't know the difference."

Day 25 – Friday, April 28, 2006

Laura called early in the morning, Atlanta time. "I doesn't look like a doctor is possible, Yvonne. Even if one was, the costs would be enormous. Not only that, but I really believe this EMT is the better choice."

"We're fine with him," Yvonne said. "But can you make sure the French doctors are as well?"

"I'll take care of it," Laura said.

Not long afterwards Jim sat in the Internet café typing:

> Hopefully this will be our last report from France. Saul is strong enough to move home and we have started the ball rolling. Saul is improving every day. He is sitting, walking with help, eating, and whispering. All the people here in France have been great to us and especially to Saul. Saul still has a long hard road to travel, but we all know he can do it. Thanks to everyone for your support. If you see us, we need a hug.
> Jim and Yvonne

"That ought to do it," he said.

Beside Jim sat Kilian Patour, munching on a pastry. Kilian was one of Saul's teammates who had come to visit shortly after the accident only to be turned away by the Raisins. They had decided it would be too hard on him to see Saul in a coma. He was a young cyclist who didn't need to have images like that in his mind. "I'm glad I am going to see Saul before he leaves. I think about him often."

"We appreciate that," Yvonne said.

Kilian wiped his mouth with a napkin. "You know, Saul may be most honest person I have ever known."

"Yeah. Too honest if you ask me," Yvonne said. "Even when Saul was a little bitty stink bottom he never held back. He told it like it was from day one, and he's never changed. He once called from a strip club on the French Riviera. He said, 'Mom, you'll never guess where I am.' I didn't even try but he told me anyway, and I said, 'Saul! You're not supposed to share that sort of stuff with your mom!' Sometimes I don't know about that boy."

Kilian laughed hard. "He always make me smile."

"Well, I'm sure he'll be happy to see you, too," Yvonne said.

Just as they were about to visit Saul, Laura's call came in. "Everything is set. The French doctors are satisfied with the EMT's qualifications. I've asked him to bring along all his papers just in case. The ambulance will be airborne within a couple of hours."

Yvonne was no gambler, but she felt like she was pulling the lever on the world's largest slot machine. Fifty nine thousand dollars was at stake. To hit the jackpot Saul had to stay at least as healthy as he was right now, the French doctors had to remain comfortable with the transfer, and most important, the trip had to be safe and successful. "Okay," she said. "Let's do it."

They walked into the ICU. Saul smiled lopsidedly when he saw his friend. Kilian spoke to Saul in French. Saul responded with a word here and there. Yvonne stood back, wondering what the friends were discussing. A nurse walked in and said something. Kilian and the nurse laughed. Saul smiled again. An intern looked in the door and made a friendly comment, and an orderly peeked in and shared a laugh.

In the three weeks Yvonne had been visiting this ward she'd never experienced such a lighthearted exchange involving the staff. It occurred to her that this wing of the hospital dealt only with the worst patients. A large percentage of those who came through here made their next stop at the morgue. Saul had come within a hair's breadth of that fate. Only the tiniest fraction of the patients in this part of the hospital returned to active lives. Even for the sort of person who drew great gratification from helping others, this must sometimes be a depressing place to work. Maybe in Saul they found the glimmer of hope necessary to continue functioning in such a bleak environment. For whatever reason, Yvonne could see her son had become a favorite in the ICU. She could also see that many of the employees here were emotionally invested in Saul's recovery. The staff genuinely cared about him.

Kilian turned to Yvonne. "I ask him many questions. He answers them all correctly."

"It makes me happy to hear that," Yvonne said.

Saul smiled his widest grin so far.

Kilian leaned down and kissed him on the forehead. "*Bon courage*, My Friend. Travel safely."

Day 26 – Saturday, April 29, 2006

Yvonne and Jim were in a good mood when they made their afternoon visit to Saul's room. Home was within reach.

Saul immediately pulled the nose prong style oxygen mask from his face.

Yvonne put it back in place.

Saul's eyes became fiery as he tried again.

Yvonne moved it for him. "Why do you want this off?"

"Not working," Saul said in a loud whisper.

"Are you sure? You really ought to wear it." She put her finger over one of the openings to test for air flow. Saul was right. Nothing was coming out. No wonder he didn't want it on his face. Yvonne could imagine how uncomfortable those prongs felt.

Saul smiled. "Talk better with it off."

"You've made a big improvement in your speech today, Saul," Yvonne said. "It's not just that your laryngitis is a little bit better."

"I like talking," Saul whispered. She could tell that even constructing a short sentence like this took all his concentration and energy.

Yvonne knew what it felt like to want to talk. Saul must have gotten those genes from her. In Saul's position Jim might have been content to stay silent. It would give him even more reason than ever to stand back from the crowd, watch, and analyze. She looked toward her husband.

Jim wiped his eyes and approached Saul's bed. "I'm leaving for America tonight, Son. I've got to prepare things for you in Atlanta."

Yvonne knew Jim felt nervous about leaving his family behind. He'd travel to Paris tonight by train and then fly clear through to Chattanooga in the morning. After a brief visit to their home in Dalton to handle business and gather supplies he'd drive to Atlanta. He was very stressed about what might happen if anything went wrong while he was away. What if Saul's health took a turn for the worse? It would be disastrous if the doctors refused to release him while a 60,000 dollar nonrefundable air ambulance sat on the tarmac. That thought made Yvonne nervous, too. Seeing Saul's improvement today helped settle her nerves, and she figured it would make Jim more comfortable as well.

"What do you think of Malaysia?" Saul whispered to his dad.

"I've never been to Malaysia. I don't think anything of it, except I was really happy when you won the race there." Jim gave Yvonne a concerned glance. "We're in France now. Your crash occurred here. Remember?"

"It's so hot," Saul said.

Jim shook his head. "The temperature is fine."

"Hot for racing," Saul said. "One-hundred-fifty degrees and one-hundred percent humidity."

Jim shook his head. "Whoever told you that was exaggerating. That was in Malaysia, anyway, a few months ago. It was only about 60 degrees here in Angers today."

Saul's brow creased. "I don't remember Angers. Is it in the north of France?"

His confusion panicked Yvonne. He'd been so coherent yesterday. Why couldn't he accept this simple fact about his location? How come every time he progressed he immediately seemed to regress in a different way? Could this disorientation complicate their plans to take him home? "Saul, you're in Angers right now. It's in the west of France. That doesn't matter, though. The important thing is that if you can keep the doctors happy with your progress, by Monday morning you'll be in Georgia."

"You're taking me home with you?"

Jim nodded. "Yeah. That's what we're working on."

Saul smiled contentedly. "Good. I'm sick of Malaysia."

Yvonne dabbed a tear from her eye. "Oh Saul. Just keep getting better."

Saul nodded. "What's wrong with me, Mom?"

"You hurt yourself real bad, Saul. It's going to take your body a long time to repair itself. Now, please get a lot of sleep in the next thirty-four hours or so. That's when we leave. And give your dad a hug. You won't see any more of him until then, and not too much more of me, either. Just like you, I need to rest up for the flight. It's going to be a long, hard travel day."

"Dad?" Saul asked.

Jim leaned in close.

Saul concentrated all his strength and lifted his right arm over his father's neck in the best impression of a hug he was capable of. "I love you." Then Saul puckered his lips and kissed his father on the forehead.

Day 27 – Sunday, April 30, 2006

Yvonne had slept restlessly all night. The cots had prevented her from cuddling with Jim for the last three weeks like she normally did at home, so she'd become used to simply holding hands with her husband while she fell asleep. Last night there hadn't been anybody to touch.

The silver lining to sleeping poorly was that it might help her sleep later than usual, and that would assist her in adjusting to the time change in Georgia. She remained in bed as late as she could, but by ten in the morning, which would have been 4:00 AM at home, she had to get up.

She took a short walk around the town. By now she knew Angers like the back of her hand. She'd become accustomed to walking alone like this in Europe because Jim and Saul were off riding bikes so often. Eventually she sat down beside a fountain and read her book.

Finally the time approached to visit Saul. She returned to her room, packed her bags, and carried them to her son's room. The doors to Logis Ozanam would be locked at 10:00 PM, and for all Yvonne knew the doors to the hospital might close around the same time. She couldn't take the risk of finding herself stuck on the wrong side of either door, so she needed to stay near Saul's room from here on out.

She found him lying in his bed, wide awake.

He looked at her luggage. "We go now?"

"Soon."

"Has Dad gone?"

"Yes."

"When we go?"

"Not until two in the morning." She ran her fingers through the hair growing over the incision on his scalp. "Now please, relax."

"We go soon?"

"If you can't calm down, Saul, I'll have go to the waiting room until the time comes."

"No!" His eyes were panic stricken. "No! Stay, Mom."

"I want to. Just please, be calm. I feel bad I'm getting you agitated."

He shook his head. "Stay."

A nurse entered the room with a tray of food.

"All right," Yvonne said. "Let's get something into your stomach."

Saul licked his lips and began to drool. He seemed incapable of keeping the saliva in his mouth since the accident. His appetite clearly wasn't affected by nerves. He ate as fast as she was willing to shovel the food in. Even though he had obvious trouble swallowing each bite he hardly slowed down at all. He didn't stop until his tray was empty.

Afterward he drifted off to sleep. Yvonne settled into the chair beside him and tried to find a comfortable position. She felt thirsty but didn't dare drink anything because she'd learned a couple of days earlier the plane she'd fly home on had no toilet. She tried to sleep but couldn't.

A tapping sound in the door frame caught Yvonne's attention. It was Dr. Fesard. Yvonne looked at her watch: almost 10:00 PM. She hadn't expected to see him so late on a Sunday evening.

"How are you doing?" she asked.

"More important, how is our patient?" Dr. Fesard asked.

"Go to Atlanta," Saul said sleepily.

The doctor nodded while studying his chart. "Yes. I am aware of the plans." Then he turned to Yvonne. "I'll be back at two to talk with the American medical team."

Yvonne felt sorry for putting him to the trouble. "I'm sorry you have to stay so late for us."

He smiled. "It is no problem. Getting to say the final goodbye to our new American friends is my reward for speaking English better than any of the other doctors."

Day 28 – Monday, May 1, 2006

In the early morning hours of *Fête du Premier Mai*, the French equivalent of Labor Day, nurses, doctors, ambulance drivers, and airport workers stood by to help Saul leave the country. He was costing a lot of people their vacation time. Yvonne moved aside as two nurses stepped into the room to begin readying Saul for the trip. They cleaned him, put him in fresh hospital clothes, started a new IV, and fed him one last time. The American medical team had called ahead. They would be here soon and planned on a quick departure. A very expensive plane sat on the tarmac.

Yvonne put on her coat, ready to go. Her blood raced when she finally heard the voice of an American man. He spoke with a slight Southern drawl. Yvonne loved hearing the cadence of home. She looked toward the nurses' station and saw him talking to Dr. Fesard. He was with a nurse she'd never seen before. They were both wearing medical clothing that didn't match the uniforms in this hospital. This was obviously the American team. They crossed the ICU toward Saul's room.

"You must be Yvonne," the woman said. "I'm Pat." She was probably in her fifties and wore her sandy hair cropped short.

"I'm Bill," said the man. He was about the same age with a full head of gray hair including a mustache and beard.

Everyone shook hands.

"Where are you from?" Yvonne asked.

"Atlanta," Pat said.

Yvonne smiled. She'd been right. A little piece of home had come to her.

"Do you have your passports?" Bill asked.

Yvonne handed them over. He glanced at each of the photos and checked the expiration dates to make certain everything was in order. "Please give these to the pilot when we board the plane. He'll hold them until we're through customs in Maine."

Bill and Pat checked Saul's vital signs and made notes in a chart.

Yvonne enjoyed listening to their conversation simply because of the familiar language. In the doorway a French nurse and orderly now stood beside Dr. Fesard.

"Everything is set," the French doctor said. "Saul is healthy enough to travel, and I've briefed the American medical team on the relevant details."

Yvonne hurried out of the way as a stretcher was brought alongside Saul's bed. With practiced efficiency the French and American teams moved her son onto the stretcher and then wheeled him from his room.

A nurse handed Yvonne two diapers and some packages of pudding.

"*Merci*," Yvonne said.

Nurses, residents, interns, doctors, orderlies and others stopped what they were doing to hug them and say goodbye. Someone handed Yvonne a card with the hospital's address on it. The ICU nurses asked her to promise to write. They needed to know how their patient's recovery progressed.

Yvonne felt such gratitude to these people, but at the same time utter excitement to be leaving the ICU for the last time. "Yes, we'll write. Of course. Thank you all so much for the loving care you've given my son. You saved his life. We can never repay you."

They responded with beautiful sounding words, many of which she couldn't understand.

After Dr. Fesard finished a conversation with Bill, the EMT, he stepped over to Yvonne.

"Is everything all right?" she asked. As nice as the goodbye had been so far, she couldn't shake the impression the staff at CHU d'Angers would prefer to keep Saul under their care.

"I've come to a realization," Dr. Fesard said, handing her Saul's medical chart and an oversized envelope stuffed with x-rays. "I understand why you are taking your son home now. He needs to go to the USA to get better. You are doing the right thing."

"Oh, thank you," Yvonne said. "You can't imagine what a relief it is to hear you say that."

She reached out for a handshake. The doctor took her hand and clasped his other hand over the top. It was all good.

"Au revoir, Yvonne," Dr. Fesard said.

"Au revoir," Yvonne said.

Saul didn't understand what was going on. He wanted his mother's full attention. He held her hand tightly and kept asking her to explain every detail. His nerves were making this a challenging and exhausting experience.

They entered the elevator and descended to the ground floor. Yvonne thought about how long it had taken her to memorize this simple route through the building. In all this time, she hadn't set foot anywhere in this hospital except along this direct passage to and from Saul's room.

"Are you excited to go to Atlanta?" Pat asked Saul.

"Atlanta?" Saul asked, totally confused.

As they exited the hospital next to the waiting ambulance Pat turned to Yvonne. "I bet this has been pretty hard on you, too."

"Yes. Very hard." Yvonne watched them load Saul's stretcher into the ambulance.

"Mom! Mom!"

It was only a whisper but to Yvonne it sounded like an urgent scream.

She hurried to her son's side. "What is it?"

"Don't leave me." His breath turned to vaporous clouds in the early morning cold.

She squeezed his hand. "Of course I won't leave you. I'll be in the front seat of the ambulance."

The tense sinews in Saul's neck relaxed. "Stay, Mom."

"I'll keep my eye on you, Saul. Don't worry. Just because you can't see me for a moment doesn't mean I can't see you."

Throughout the ambulance ride Yvonne kept looking over her shoulder at Saul. She listened to him talking with Pat in the back of the vehicle.

"Ambulance?" he asked.

"You got hurt real bad," Pat said. "We're working on fixing you up."

"I'm not hurt," Saul said.

"You crashed and did a lot of damage. You broke your collarbone, you—"

"I did not!" Saul's interrupted.

"Yes you did, on your left side." Pat squeezed Yvonne's shoulder over the armrest.

When Yvonne looked back at her, the nurse winked and indicated Saul with a twitch of her head.

He reached up and felt his left collarbone with his right hand. His eyes went wide with confusion when he discovered the fresh knob of calcium. "It's already healed?"

"Yep," Pat said.

"It never even hurt." He sounded incredulous.

"You slept through the pain," Pat explained. "Your injured brain might even have been incapable of registering the pain."

Saul looked like he was trying to comprehend a miracle, but soon his concentration faltered and he gave up.

Yvonne smiled and turned back toward the front window. She liked Pat's calm demeanor. Saul was in good hands.

In the pitch darkness Yvonne clutched the medical chart. Within these pages were sure to be answers to many mysteries that had troubled her over the last month. She looked forward to having them translated and learning the details of Saul's ordeal.

They reached the airport and drove directly onto the runway. The place was deserted, except for one small jet with shining lights. The pilots climbed out and helped Bill and Pat load Saul into the plane. Yvonne boarded behind them, amazed at the interior of the tiny aircraft. This wasn't the sort of plane she'd imagined. Most of the fuselage was crammed with medical supplies, in case of emergency. Each person would apparently be wedged into their own small, no-frills, position.

One of the pilots pointed to a seat. Yvonne handed him the passports and sat down. Saul's feet were toward the back of the plane. She sat beside his head, only an arms length from the pilots. Pat and Bill were behind her. She tried to get comfortable, but a cooler in front of her prevented her from stretching her legs. Then, not that she was complaining, she discovered the seat wouldn't recline. She wondered if Jim could have wedged himself into a spot this small. It was a good thing she was the one traveling with Saul.

She could hug her son just by bending at the waist. In fact, his head was only six inches from her knee. It made Yvonne happy to be close enough to talk easily with him. She felt fortunate they hadn't relegated her to the claustrophobic seat Bill occupied at the back of the plane. All her life confining spaces had bothered her, but right now it was all about getting Saul home as comfortably as possible. She'd do whatever had to be done to accomplish that goal.

Saul's eyes darted from side to side as Pat strapped him in. She handed him a couple of pills and a cup of water. "Take these for pain."

"There's no bathroom on board," Bill reminded Yvonne. "Don't drink anything."

Yvonne nodded nervously while Saul looked confused

"That doesn't apply to you, Saul. You're wearing a diaper," Pat said.

"I am? How come?"

"Just take the pills," Pat said.

Saul took the pills, choking on them even though they were tiny.

"Swallowing problems are normal for a brain-injured patient," Pat said. "Especially one who has had a tube in his throat for weeks. It's a good sign that he's willing to endure the pain."

Yvonne put her hand on Pat's. "I've been so concerned and often unable to understand whether his behavior is normal."

"Have you ever flown in a small jet?" one of the pilots asked.

"I thought I had, but I was wrong. I've taken a little commuter plane in and out of Chattanooga, but that was at least ten times as big as this," Yvonne said.

The pilot smiled. "Don't be nervous. Learjets are excellent aircraft, but I will warn you, you're going to hear some noises you aren't used to. Don't worry about them … unless I tell you to." He chuckled.

Yvonne nodded apprehensively.

"Also, we'll accelerate really fast, sort of like riding a rocket."

"Thanks for the warning."

Saul looked around. "This is nice."

"I'm glad you like it," Yvonne said. "It's sure to be the most extravagant flight we ever take."

"Wish we could enjoy it," Saul said.

Yvonne put a hand on his cheek. "We will. I'd enjoy this flight even if I had no window and nothing to eat. The only thing that matters is that I'm taking you home."

The pilot held out a map. "Here's our route." He traced a line up the coast of Europe, over Iceland and Greenland, and then down the coast of North America to Atlanta. "We'll stop twice for fuel. We'll be over land nearly the entire time and we have priority clearance to land immediately at any airport we need to in case of emergency."

Yvonne listened as the pilots continued talking with each other and with the flight tower. The lingo they spoke sounded every bit as foreign as the language the lady doctor had spoken, except without the accent.

The pilot looked back into the fuselage. "Ready for takeoff?"

Everyone nodded.

A hissing roar built behind them. The plane shot forward just as the pilot had warned. The thrust pressed Yvonne into her seat. Saul's stretcher jerked toward the back of the cabin. Yvonne fought the force of the acceleration to grab onto it. She looked back and saw that Pat had done the same. Farther back, Bill seemed to be locking something down. Yvonne's heart raced as every vibration from the pavement coursed through her body. She glanced out the front window between the two pilots. Shouldn't they abort the takeoff and try again? The stretcher wasn't secured properly.

Runway lights zipped past on either side. She wanted to tell the pilots about the emergency with the stretcher, but how could they possibly hear her? It couldn't have been louder directly beneath Niagara Falls. Saul's eyes were wide with confusion.

"Everything will be all right, Honey," she tried to say over the roar, but she wasn't sure Saul could hear her, and she wasn't positive she was telling the truth, anyway.

The nose lifted, and the vibration decreased; then the rear wheels left the tarmac, and the vibration ceased altogether, but the angle of the plane made it feel like the stretcher was trying desperately to return to Angers. Yvonne held on as tightly as she could. She'd worked hard for this moment, and she'd be damned if Saul and his stretcher weren't going to come along with her.

Saul tried to say something. Even though the plane was nowhere near as noisy as before, she couldn't possibly hear his weak voice. She leaned down and hugged him.

Gradually the plane leveled out, and the engines became much quieter. When they had apparently reached cruising altitude one of the pilots looked back and said. "That was easy, huh?"

His face slowly transformed as he took in the expressions of his frazzled passengers. "What happened back there?"

"The stretcher shifted," Bill said as he shimmied toward the front of the plane to check the front wheels. "I think we have everything under control now."

Yvonne collapsed back in her chair, exhausted. Saul's eyelids flickered and then closed.

Pat leaned forward. "One of those pills I gave him was really a sedative."

"Thank you," Yvonne said.

"He's been through a lot, hasn't he," Pat said.

Yvonne nodded. "It's almost unimaginable."

"Was that the first transfusion he's ever received?" Pat asked.

Yvonne wondered if she'd heard right. "Transfusion?"

"Dr. Fesard told us Saul received two units in the emergency room the day of the accident," Pat said.

Yvonne shook her head. "I had no idea. I wonder how much more I don't know."

"You probably know the important stuff." The nurse patted her hand. "You look exhausted. Can I get you anything?"

Yvonne shook her head. "I think I can probably fall right to sleep." She looked at her watch: three-thirty in the morning. She adjusted it to Atlanta time: nine-thirty in the evening. Time to go to bed.

Even though she had no blanket or pillow on this flight Yvonne tried to snuggle in. Sleep wouldn't come. She kept trying to find a comfortable position, but it was impossible. Every once in awhile she glanced at her watch. She finally started to doze.

A jabbing sensation in her ribs woke her. She opened one eye and saw Saul nudging her with his good arm.

"What is it, Honey?" Yvonne looked at her watch again. Only twenty minutes had passed since she'd last checked the time.

"Someone spilled water in my bed," Saul whispered.

Pat pulled down the covers. "His diaper has overflowed. Everything is soaked."

"It wasn't me," Saul protested.

Pat nodded. "It was you, Honey. You just can't feel the sensation. Don't worry about it."

Yvonne took her son's hand. "I don't understand. He hasn't drunk anything."

"It's the I.V." Bill reached up and closed the valve. "He'll be fine without it."

"Hold me," Saul said.

Yvonne leaned down and hugged him while Pat and Bill cleaned up. They replaced the sheets with disposable blankets and put Saul in a fresh diaper. Saul put his arm around Yvonne's back and held her to him. Soon he was snoring.

Although the position was uncomfortable, leaning forward in her seat hugging her son, sleep overcame Yvonne again. She woke now and then in fitful starts, but each time she saw Saul snoozing soundly so she closed her eyes again. He needed his rest to heal his brain, and she didn't want to disturb him by moving.

She felt a tap on her shoulder and looked up.

"Sunrise over Iceland," the pilot said. "We'll be landing in a moment for breakfast and fuel."

Yvonne gazed out at the stark landscape, mostly black rocks and patches of snow. The orange sun sat like a billiard ball on the horizon. Long, cold shadows stretched across the land. She noticed movement in a harbor below: hardened fishermen headed out for yet another day on the high seas. What challenging lives those men must lead.

The pilots guided the plane in for a smooth landing and taxied to the terminal. One of them reached back and unlocked the door, then pushed it open. A freezing breeze rushed in, but moments later a very large gentleman stepped into the opening and practically sealed it off. "Aye. What do we have here? Anybody in need of breakfast?" He handed Yvonne disposable containers containing muffins with eggs and a few cartons of orange juice.

She passed them back to Pat. "Thank you. Can I use the bathroom?"

"You want to take a bath?" the Icelander asked.

Yvonne chuckled. "No. The toilet?"

"Oh, yes. Be my guest," the large man said. He helped her step from the plane.

Goose pimples rose on her skin as she crossed the tarmac. After she left the restroom a weathered old man sitting behind a reservations desk offered her warm cookies and milk. The smell made her mouth water.

"My son will love them. Thank you," Yvonne said. She put two cookies into her purse and headed back to the plane. As she boarded she noticed Pat putting the last diaper on Saul.

This time the takeoff went much more smoothly. Maybe it partly helped that Yvonne had some idea what to expect. The noises didn't create the same panicked chaos in her brain they had the first time. The stretcher stayed where it was supposed to.

Once they leveled out she began feeding Saul. He was voracious as usual, snarfing down everything that came within reach, and in such cramped quarters keeping anything out of his reach was nearly impossible.

"Slow down, Saul. Your manners are embarrassing," Yvonne said.

"The brain uses huge amounts of energy," Pat explained. "Repairing it requires lots of fuel. Metabolism can more than double for brain-injured patients. It's good that his appetite is so big."

Metabolism doubles? Saul normally ate three to four thousand calories a day. Could he really start putting away eight thousand calories every twenty-four hours? She put her hand on Pat's. "I can't tell you how refreshing it is to have someone explain these simple things to me. For three weeks I've been confused and terrified by my son's behavior. It makes a huge difference to know he's doing what he should."

Pat looked her in the eye. "For coming out of a coma only a short time ago, your son is doing great. It's not like in the movies. People don't just wake up from being comatose and then go on with their life as usual."

"Is he awake enough to know what's happening now?"

The nurse regarded Saul carefully. "He seems to be aware of present events, but I doubt he can retain much. He probably has very little memory of what he's experienced since he woke, and I doubt he has any memory at all of the accident itself."

"But he seems happy, doesn't he?" Yvonne looked at Saul's grin.

"Yes," Pat said. "I think he's happy and comfortable today. He's going home. He's getting what he wants."

"It's what I want, too," Yvonne said.

Pat put a hand on Yvonne's shoulder. "You're fighting a good fight. There are still challenges ahead, but Saul looks good to me, and I think he'll be OK in the long run."

OK. Yvonne thought about the word. It was the message Saul had texted to her so many times before, the one whose absence had first alerted her that something had gone wrong. She nodded, hoping Pat was right, and she wondered as she had so many times before, just how complete Saul's recovery would be? Maybe Pat could help her understand.

"This has all been so confusing," Yvonne said. "Saul struggles with such simple things, but then in the next moment he seems to understand complex concepts perfectly."

"Give me examples," Pat said.

"He can't feed himself, even with his good hand, but when his dad asked him the code to unlock his cell phone he knew it. He isn't even aware he's been injured, yet when you told him his collar bone was broken he knew how to examine it himself."

Pat nodded. "It's the nature of a brain injury. There's no rhyme or reason. Victims entirely forget some things and retain others perfectly."

Yvonne thought about the statement. It described Saul exactly. It comforted her to know that, as confusing as Saul's behavior was, it was normal under the circumstances. The doctors in France had probably attempted to tell her this sort of thing many times, but simple concepts had been so difficult to convey. She felt so happy that from here forward she'd be dealing with medical professionals who spoke her language.

Yvonne noticed Pat checking Saul's diaper from time to time, and saw the concern on her face. Eventually, she started maneuvering disposable blankets into the region as well. She was giving him wonderful care under difficult conditions. Yvonne didn't have to do anything for Saul except feed and comfort him.

After Saul devoured his meal and most of hers Yvonne could tell he was still hungry. She reached into her purse for one of the fresh cookies. She broke off a piece and put it into his mouth. His eyes lit up. He wouldn't have reached a greater state of euphoria if he'd won the Tour de France.

Saul pointed toward where the cookie had come from. "More!"

She broke off another piece, and then another. Within moments both cookies were gone. She never even got a taste.

The pilot looked back into the cabin. He pointed out the window. "Greenland."

Yvonne looked down at the beautiful snow-covered scene. Stark white mountains fell precipitously into a deep blue sea. As she gazed at the beautiful countryside she silently repeated a prayer she'd been invoking like a mantra since the flight began. "Thank you God for helping us get this far. Please help us to continue our journey and land safely at home."

She knew in her heart if she could go home to the USA she could get her son well. Not that French doctors couldn't cure patients, but at home she could understand what needed to be done. She could help Saul the way a mother needs to. Also, she and Jim needed to have family and friends to hug and comfort them. They were scared too. They needed to talk to people who understood what they were going through and who could give them the sort of support they craved. They couldn't do this alone.

Saul looked up at Yvonne with unbridled adoration. "Atlanta?"

"Yes, Saul. We're headed to Atlanta."

"Give me a hug."

Saul had always been unusually loving, but now he'd taken it to a new level. He couldn't seem to get enough of her. Was this change permanent? She leaned down and kissed him, and he hugged her as tight as he could to his chest. They fell asleep in one another's arms again.

When Yvonne woke one of the pilots was looking right at her. He pointed out the front window. "It's the United States of America. We'll be landing in Bangor, Maine momentarily."

Yvonne sat up and looked at the low-lying mountains in the distance. She'd never loved her country so much. It felt so good to cross the borders of her homeland with Saul at her side. Nothing could stop them from getting home now. From here she could put Saul in a car and drive him to Georgia if she had to.

The plane landed smoothly again, and this time a pair of customs agents came out to greet them. A wind, every bit as cold as the one in Iceland, swept into the plane when the door opened.

One of the customs agents leaned in and glanced around. "Hello, folks. Everything looks fine here. Welcome home."

"Thank you. It's good to be back," Yvonne said.

With that he was gone. It was by far the easiest customs process Yvonne had ever been through. She hadn't even been required to fill out a declarations form. The only thing of real value she was returning with was her son.

"This is the end of the line for us," one of the pilots said, handing the passports back to Yvonne. "Mandatory rest stop."

Yvonne took his hand. "Thank you for bringing us across the ocean."

"Yeah," Saul whispered. He smiled as wide as he could, but Yvonne could tell he didn't even know why.

"Get well," one of the pilots said, giving him a pinch on the cheek. "We're proud to have helped in your recovery."

"Inside you can use the bathrooms and get some food," the other pilot said.

Yvonne walked to the terminal. Pat and Bill stayed behind to work on Saul's wet clothing. They were now fashioning disposable blankets into diapers.

Yvonne bought a blueberry muffin, a big cookie, yogurt, and milk for Saul, and another muffin for herself. She returned to the plane just as the new pilots were getting situated.

"Here are more diapers," one of them said. "You can't imagine how difficult it is to find adult sized diapers in Bangor at five in the morning. I don't think there's a single all night store in this entire town."

"How did you know we needed them?" Yvonne asked.

"The other pilots radioed ahead."

"What do I owe you?"

"Nothing." The pilot smiled. "It finally occurred to us to ask our taxi driver to swing by the hospital. When we told them our story they gave us a bag for free."

Yvonne wanted to hug the men. She felt so blessed that they would go out of their way for her and her son. She looked at Saul. "Want to call your dad?"

He nodded.

Jim answered the phone in a panic. "What's gone wrong?"

"Nothing. Did we wake you?"

"Yeah. I got to bed just over an hour ago. How's Saul?"

Yvonne chuckled. "He's going to surprise you. He's more alert than before and trying to talk a lot."

"That's wonderful! Where are you now?"

"We're in America. Bangor, Maine to be exact, two hours ahead of schedule," Yvonne said.

"Oh, good." Jim had flown back to Chattanooga, and then Phil had driven him to Dalton. He still had a two-hour drive to Atlanta ahead. He sounded very tired.

"It's nice to hear your voice, Jimmy. I've missed you so much," Yvonne said. Talking to her husband meant the world to her. They'd rarely been apart in nearly three decades of marriage, and because of the massive hardship they'd been going through this was by far the most difficult separation they'd ever had. She couldn't cry because she didn't want to upset Saul, but she surely wanted to.

"I've missed you too," Jim said. "We've taken big steps toward recovery in the last few days, though."

Yvonne smiled. It warmed her heart when Jim made optimistic statements like that. It felt comforting to imagine a time when their world might settle on its axis once again.

As the plane taxied toward the runway Saul spotted Yvonne's muffin. He beckoned it toward his mouth with a finger.

"That's mine. I bought food for you, too. I'll feed it to you once we're airborne."

Saul couldn't take his eyes off the muffin. He looked at Yvonne and pleaded with his eyes.

Eventually she couldn't bear his obsession any longer. She unwrapped the cellophane and broke a piece off for him.

Saul chewed it quickly, choking as he swallowed. Then he opened his mouth for more. The muffin was gone before they left the ground.

Her stomach rumbled and she kissed her son. "Hallelujah! You're getting better, Saul. I'll have more food for you once we're in the air."

"Thanks, Mom."

She smiled. "You've done well so far. Just three more hours to Atlanta."

Saul ate his breakfast quickly and asked for more once he finished. Not only did Yvonne not have any, but she was starved herself. She hugged Saul and said, "I'll get you all the food you need once we're home."

"Here's something for him." Bill handed her a donut.

She thanked him and started feeding it to her son.

They stared at each other as she did. Yvonne treasured the love in Saul's eyes. She'd nearly lost him earlier this month. She wouldn't take the little things for granted ever again.

After awhile his eyelids grew heavy and he fell back to sleep.

Yvonne sat, eyes open but looking at nothing, reviewing the last few weeks in her mind. Eventually she glanced at her watch. The long flight would be ending soon. Then the plane began weaving, tossing the meager contents of her stomach around. Yvonne put a hand on the airsick bag. The aircraft swayed side-to-side and then up and down, as if in a dogfight drill.

Yvonne felt irritable. "We don't need an amusement park ride."

The pilot chuckled. "Enjoy it while it lasts because you'll probably never get treatment like this again. We have priority clearance through some of the busiest air space in the world. Everybody else has to circle while we thread our way through traffic and get on the ground as quickly as possible."

"Well, it's a good thing my stomach is so empty or I'd already have thrown up."

Finally the plane settled into a steady descent. "Nothing left to dodge," the pilot said.

Yvonne looked at her watch again: nine in the morning. She gazed out at the countryside. It had the unmistakable feel of home. Her eyes filled with tears yet again. She wiped them away, not wanting Saul to see her lose control.

"It's okay to cry," Saul said. He spread his right arm wide for a hug.

"Nothing's wrong, Saul. I'm crying because I'm so happy."

"I'm happy, too."

"I'm going to kiss the tarmac when we land," Yvonne said.

Saul's expression became concerned. "Don't."

She chuckled. "It's just an expression."

They stared at each other's faces. Saul was the first to blink. "You're silly, Mom."

"Yeah. Silly and grateful." Silly was a word they probably hadn't exchanged in this way for fifteen years or more. In many ways Saul seemed to be a little boy again, yet at the same time he had clear memories of life as a twenty-three year old man. What a strange combination.

The plane landed and taxied toward the executive terminal. Yvonne climbed out and hurried across the tarmac to the restroom while an ambulance approached from the east. As she returned to the plane she did a double take. Saul was walking off the aircraft. She clambered for her camera and snapped a shot.

All right, he wasn't exactly walking. Pat and Bill were supporting him. He was mostly being carried, but they were trying to make it look as much like walking as they could. Yvonne ran to them.

Saul's face had contorted in pain. His breathing was ragged. "I am hurting."

Bill and Pat eased him onto a stretcher.

Yvonne caressed her son's cheek and spoke to Bill. "Is he going to be all right?"

"He'll be fine. That was a tiny taste of what therapy will be like," Bill said. "But I can tell Saul's a fighter. He's going to do great."

"Ohhhh," Saul moaned.

"Everything's going to be fine," Yvonne comforted.

Saul's stretcher began to roll. Panic filled his eyes. "Don't leave me, Mom. Don't leave."

"Of course I won't leave you. Now you're the silly one."

They loaded Saul into the back of the ambulance and Yvonne climbed into the front. She talked loudly as they drove so he'd know she was nearby. "I can read these road signs, Saul. It feels so good. I even know where these streets go. If I took this exit I'd end up at Lenox Mall. If I headed north on the freeway we're approaching I'd end up in Dalton. I can take any road we can see from here and I'll end up in a place I expect to be. That makes me happy in a way I can't really describe. We made it home!"

I vividly remember this moment. I was two-years-old and this was my first time on a bike. I never even used training wheels.

Dad fought fires when I was little. He's always been my hero.

A trip to San Francisco. My parents showed me the world.

I'm ready for the Barnsley Gardens Mountain Bike Race.

What a day! It was one of my first races. I came in last place, but I never gave up.

I skipped most of the school dances, preferring to race my bike, but I went to the Senior Prom with Hara Rana. We stole the dance floor.

I won the blue Best Young Rider jersey at the Tour de Georgia in front of my home state crowd. My career really took off from here.

At the 2003 Trans-Alcase I slid face first into a concrete pole. Lionel Marie cleared my airway and saved my life. Three weeks later I was back in Europe racing and I signed with Lionel's Credit Agricole Developmental Team.

I have a perfectly shaped back. Because of it my chest capacity is extra large. There's room under the hood for an oversized heart and lungs. (Copyright © Pete Geyer www.cyclingfans.com)

I felt like I was flying while climbing at the Tour de Suisse. (Copyright © CyclingHeroes.de)

I won the Best Climbers
Jersey at the Tour l'Avenir.
Chris De Vos, a U-23 National
Team soigneur and very good
friend, was one of the first to
congratulate me.

I rode for Team USA in the
2005 World Champion-
ships. I led the race on the
live world-wide TV broad-
cast for over five hours, but
unfortunately our break-
away got caught by the
peloton with two laps to
go. It was still a pretty
successful day of racing for
me. (Copyright © Phil O'Connor)

Stage Three of the Tour
of Langkawi was my
first professional win.
I loved the feeling and
plan on many more to
come.
(Copyright © Bruno Bade)

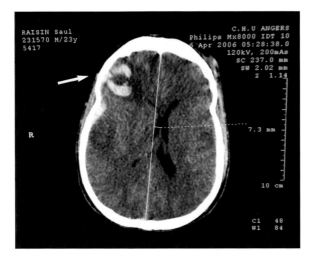

This image was taken thirty minutes before surgery. The arrow indicates the hematoma. Neurologists tell me this is a brain on the verge of death. Because of the pressure, the ventricles are swollen shut, and the entire brain has rotated in the skull.

Brain scan images are reversed. The "R" on the left side of each image indicates the right side of the brain.

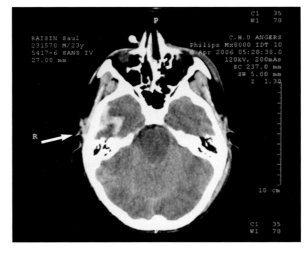

This image was taken at the same time as the one above. The arrow points to the hematoma. The brain is under intense pressure.

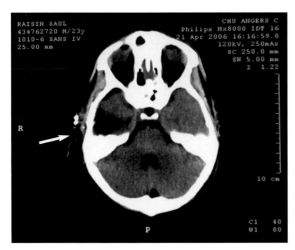

This is an image of the same portion of my brain two weeks after the surgery. The hematoma is gone. Black space filled with spinal fluid has replaced it. The entire brain is obviously under far less pressure. In fact, I no longer get headaches, even after extreme physical stress.

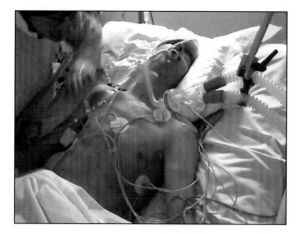

This shot hurts to look at. My dad took it with a cell phone the day they arrived in Angers. I'm deep in a coma. That's my mom tending to me.

I have almost no memory of my time in the Angers hospital. I needed strong and supportive people by my side in order to make it through. There are none stronger or more supportive than my dad. I love him so much.

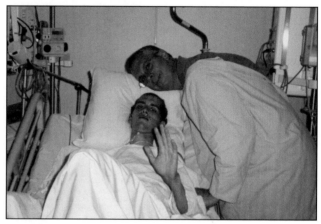

Pat and Bill cared for me on our Learjet trip to Atlanta. They helped me from the plane to the stretcher. It was only a couple of feet but it felt like miles. They congratulated me for walking but the truth is they carried me. I ached all over by the time they laid me down.

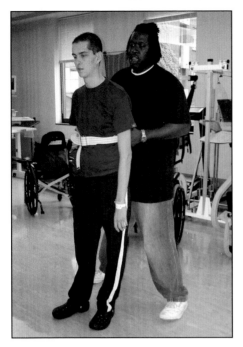

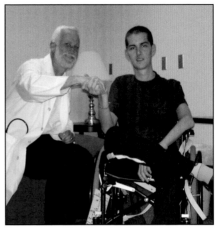

This shot was taken in my bedroom at the Shepherd Center. What a great hospital! Dr. Bilsky is one of my many heroes. He helped me return to living a normal life.

It hurts every time I see that vacant look in my eyes, but there are things I love about this photo, too. Sean the football player lent me his strength and balance when I had none of my own. Notice the gait belt he's using to support me. The staff at this place is the best of the best.

Therapy was so hard. Just lifting my arm over my head took months of work. My scapula healed while I was lying flat on my back and the muscles seized. Full use hasn't even returned yet. Looking at myself in these shots makes me sad, but at the same time proud that I've come so far.

My Mothers Day present was to walk to my mom. It took everything I had. After four excruciating steps I collapsed into her arms.

When I finally visited Dalton for the weekend the entire neighborhood had been decorated. We cried. We are truly blessed.

Dad set up my stationary bike in the room above our garage. For many weeks I had to be supervised while riding it. During the Tour de France I started putting in huge hours on the trainer, often more than five a day.

Graduation from Shepherd Pathways was one of the greatest accomplishments of my life. Here I'm goofing around with my speech therapist, Mary Ellen.

Bret Naylon was admitted to the Shepherd Center shortly after me. He broke his back in a bicycle race and is currently quadrapalegic, but nothing could ever break this guy's spirit. He inspires me.

My coach and good friend Jim Lehman came to visit me. I showed him around Saul Raisin Woods Mountain Bike Park. What an honor that they've named such a beautiful and meaningful place after me.

When I proved I could ride the rollers I knew I was going to be riding on the road soon. Some people never get the hang of balancing on these things. Can you see in my eyes that the old Saul is coming back?

This is the big day! Dad and I are getting ready to ride on the road for the first time since my accident. Mom will follow us in the car. There's nobody I'd rather share this moment with than my parents. They are my two best friends in the world.

I'm riding my bike. WooHoo!!! I blow a kiss to all the people who've supported me through this extremely difficult ordeal.

On stage at US Nationals announcer Jeff
Roake asked me to predict tomorrow's
winner. I said, "I don't know about tomorrow,
but in 2007 it will be me."

My family members have always been my
biggest supporters. Aunt Teresa, Uncle Phil,
Gram Cracker, Noah and Megan are all
in this picture.

This is my first time riding at
Saul Raisin Woods Mountain
Bike Park. I haven't been on a
mountain bike in three years. I
think I have my balance back.

Everybody would like to say they have the world's best mom, but I'm not sharing her.

I'm kissing the world's best dad at the top of one of the world's greatest climbs. What could be better than that? A few short months before this shot was taken it was inconceivable that I'd ever ride my bike again.

Thor Hushovd inspired me with several victories while I was recovering, including a win on the Champs-Eleesys. I told him that I dreamed of the day we'd ride side by side again. He told me he did, too. Our dreams came true faster than we had ever imagined.

Zach Phillips and I have a lot in common. He was hit by a speeding car and suffered injuries very similar to mine not long before my bike crash. We became friends at Shepherds, then went through outpatient at Pathways together as well. We used to marvel at the beautiful nurses for hours at a time. I'm certain we'll remain friends for life.

Credit Agricole team manager, Roger Legeay came to Dalton for a weekend visit. I showed him around my home state including the Georgia Aquarium. Roger is a special man who truly knows the meaning of loyalty. His support means the world to me.

Lionel Marie is my best friend from Europe. He's done everything for me. He offered me my first pro contract, saved my life after an accident, and helped watch over my parents while I was in my coma. I'm blessed to have a friend like him.

This is the road my parents took between Logis Ozanam and my bed in the ICU every day. Walking it with them was almost a spiritual experience. I felt like I'd been here before.

Here I am with some of the wonderful people who took care of me during that first tough month at CHU d'Angers. I don't remember them from my stay here, but when I returned they looked at me like I was their child. They are my heroes.

Professor Mercier touched my brain. Can you believe that? Imagine my incredible luck at having one of the best neuro-surgeons in the world available in just the right place at just the right moment.

Life is good again! I'm leading the first annual Raisin Hope Ride up
Fort Mountain on the one year anniversary of my crash. Not long ago the
experts said I'd be in a wheelchair for life. Well… it *does* have wheels.

Blue skies ahead!

Part II – Believe It Or Not It Is Me, Saul

Below is Saul's first blog entry since Sunday, April 2, 2006. He composed it from his hospital bed with Yvonne's help. She wrote it on a piece of paper, took it to the Shepherd Center computer room, and typed it in.

> *Believe it or not it is me, Saul*
> Contributed by Saul
> Tuesday, 02 May 2006
> Dictated by Saul, typed by Mom: Well here I am no racing for me … Only racing to get well … Got the new Pro Cycling Giro Edition Mag … Too bad I'm not doing the Giro … I want to thank everyone for their support and get-well thoughts … I hope to be leaving the hospital in a couple of weeks … I am in a super nice hospital and the staff here is TRES BON … Check my web site for more updates and pictures … I love you all … Saul

Chapter One

I am so tired. The fatigue I'm feeling goes beyond exhaustion, but at this hospital I'm stuck in they refuse to let me rest. I've been here for who knows how long. Every day of that stay they've been pushing me to do one thing or another. Honestly, I can't figure this place out. Aren't hospitals places you're supposed to come for rest?

The phone beside my bed rings. I reach for it with my right hand and bring it to my ear.

"Is this Saul Raisin?" a voice asks.

"Mmm hmm," I say.

"I'm glad I tracked you down. I'm on deadline for a story on your crash and just wanted to ask you how things are going."

A gorgeous woman crosses my field of vision. Her name is Ruth Ann. We've met before but I haven't gotten to first base. I follow her with my eyes. It's not easy. For me, even moving my eyeballs is hard work. Every tiny small motion I make taxes my concentration to its limit.

"Are you there, Saul?" the voice on the phone asks.

"Yeah. Sorry," I say.

"What's the next step in your recovery?" he asks.

It exhausts me to process even simple questions like this. I think hard about what he has asked and try to put together the best answer I can. "Riding again in a few days."

"Who are you talking to?" Ruth Ann asks.

"A reporter." He's about the fifth one who's called this morning.

Ruth Ann takes the phone from me and hangs it up. "They should be ashamed of themselves for chasing down a guy in your condition. I'll talk to the switchboard and make sure they put a stop to it."

What's she talking about? I've always liked talking to reporters, and they like me because I try my hardest to give them a good interview. I turn my head to watch Ruth Ann work. "I like your curves. What's your number?"

"My number?"

"Yeah. So I can call you. We'll get it on."

She scowls. "I'm going to forgive that comment along with all the other insinuations you've made to me and every other female who comes near, because I know you can't help it at the moment."

"I can help it." I wink. "Give me a chance to show you."

She shakes her head. "Your brain injury has removed your inhibitions, but just so you're aware, ladies don't appreciate being talked to that way."

I frown. I didn't mean to make her angry. "I'm just telling you what I think."

"That's exactly what you're not supposed to do."

What sort of a place is this? "I'm stuck in a hospital to learn how to lie?"

She starts to laugh but then she puts her hands on her hips and tries to appear tough instead. Now she looks even sexier than before. I'm about to tell her that when she speaks up again. "Saul, your brain and your body have been badly hurt. It's my job to help you get better. One of the biggest challenges we'll be dealing with is your confusion."

I won't deny I'm confused. Very little in this world makes sense to me, but her comment proves she isn't exactly clear-headed. What injury is she talking about? I healed a long time ago, and these people just refuse to let me go home.

I did have a few broken bones from a bike crash in Malaysia … or maybe it was California … or France. It doesn't really matter where it happened because my injuries are a distant memory. I don't even remember the pain. Several days ago, I can't say how many for sure, I asked a nurse named Pat why I was hospitalized. She told me I'd fractured my collarbone. I checked and she was right, but it wasn't broken anymore. There was a great big calcium deposit where it had fused back together. It's as if my body has super powers or something. I heal automatically. Weird. The doctors can't understand what's going on any more than I can, and that must be why they won't check me out of this place.

Speaking of doctors, here comes one now. He sits down beside my bed and starts asking questions. "Can you tell me your name?"

"I'm too tired to talk to you," I say.

He writes something in his chart. "I know it's hard, but you need to answer my questions."

He's talking nonsense. If he had any idea how hard it is he'd leave me alone and let me rest.

"Can you tell me your name?" he asks again.

"Saul Raisin. Why can't you remember that, Doctor Dan?"

"My name isn't Doctor Dan," he says.

I point to his nametag. It says Dr. Dan something or other.

He squeezes his lips together. "Where are you from?"

The answer is in my head, but it takes a lot of effort to get it out. Finally I say, "Dalton."

"What do you do for a living?"

What's with this guy? He's asked me these same questions many times before. "I race bicycles. I've told you all this stuff."

He acts like he doesn't even hear me.

"Where are you now?" he asks.

I can barely gather the energy to answer. "In the hospital."

"How come?"

"I crashed, I guess."

"You guess?" he asks.

I let out a sigh. "That's what they tell me."

"What are your injuries?"

He's asked me this question before, too, but I didn't know the answer then and I still don't now. I just stare at him silently for a long time. If I could get out of this place I'd start feeling better. When we flew across the ocean Mom said she was bringing me home. How come we came here instead? I told them I'd be willing to stay for three days, but I'm sure that's up by now. "I want to go home and ride my bike. Two weeks, tops, and I'll be ready to race again."

Dr. Dan shakes his head. "Saul, you can't even walk. Your brain has been badly hurt, and it isn't correctly processing the signals your body is sending to it. I understand this is all confusing but you've got to cooperate."

He thinks he understands my confusion? That's impossible, because 'confusion' doesn't begin to encompass what I'm going through. My wonderful life has somehow become scrambled beyond repair. I can't imagine how I'll ever get it back. Somebody has to be blamed for this mess, so I choose to blame Dr. Dan.

He flips to a new page in his chart. "Do you have any long-term memory loss?"

"*Je parle encore français.*"

"What?" he asks.

"I just told you I still speak French."

He stares at me for a moment, as if he's mad I passed his little test; then he gathers up his stuff and walks away.

More people come into my room while I just lie in bed like a rag doll. One pushes me onto my side while somebody else puts something cold against my back. I try to pull away.

Bend this way, bend that way, open your mouth, wiggle your toes. I do my best to follow all the instructions, though I don't know why I'm trying. There doesn't seem to be any point to it all.

"Okay, Saul. You're doing a good job," someone says. "Just one more test."

"After that will you promise to quit experimenting on me?" I ask.

"Yes, we'll be done soon. Now I need you to take in a deep breath and hold it."

I inhale. I'll bet they have no idea how deep I can breathe.

"Excellent. Hold it …"

What are these people trying to do to me? Why am I in this bed? Why can't I feel my left side? I'm so sick of being poked and prodded, tested and sampled, scanned and biopsied. It takes all my self control not to push all the doctors and nurses away. I don't know how long they've had me here, or why. All I know is I want out.

"Hold it. Just a little longer …"

Are they doubting my ability? I can hold my breath a lot longer and I'll prove it. When somebody challenges me, that's when I shine.

"Hold it …"

In my mind's eye I can see a few scattered images of the recent past. They're not exactly memories, but more like flashes of light in a sea of darkness. It's as if someone has been squeezing their hand over my eyes most of the time, but every once in a while they adjust their grip and in that instant I catch a glimpse of the outside world. I remember feeling the comfort of my mom's cheek against my forehead, and the soft rhythm of "Twinkle, twinkle, little star" in my ear … then nothing. I recall talking with Roger about returning to racing … then nothing. I remember playing thumb war with Daniela … then nothing. I remember trying to cry and discovering I couldn't do it no matter how sad I felt inside … then nothing. And I can't forget having a painful tube forced up my nose, down my throat, and into my lungs … then nothing. There are other bits and pieces, but I can't put them together in any way that makes sense. One thing I do know is that all this stuff has happened while I've been stuck in a lousy hospital bed.

I'm the kind of guy who normally rises before dawn every day. Lying around is killing me. There are only four highlights to my day anymore: sleeping, eating, visiting hours, and talking to Daniela on the phone. I can't help saying lustful things to other women, though. Whenever I see a woman, her beauty is all I can think about, but it's Daniela I'm dreaming of. I need her near me. God, I love hearing her voice. She tells me everything is going to be all right and we'll get through this. Even though I don't understand what we're trying to get through, I believe her. Our love is one of the main things I have left to hang onto. If not for that I'd be just about ready to give up.

"Nice work, Saul. You can let it out now."

I decide to keep holding my breath, just to prove to them I can. It feels good to do something on my schedule for once. Before I found myself glued to this mattress I always pushed the limits, simply because I felt the urge. I had clear goals and I chased them hard. My life was about riding bicycles fast, and let me tell you, I was flying this year!

"Saul, did you hear me? Exhale."

Damn, I want to get back on my bike. That would make everything all right again. Last season after doing so well in the Tour of Germany my career reached a new level. I finished in ninth place, the youngest rider at the top of the leader board. I'd just proven myself at the elite pro level of cycling.

After that race my motivation went off the charts. I trained like I never had before, and suddenly it was as if I found a new gear … hit a different level. I felt so powerful, especially when the roads tilted up. It was like I was riding a motorcycle. Nobody could stick with me if I didn't want them to. I started getting great results in races from little French Cup events to the World Championships. I won in Malaysia right out of the gates this year.

"Enough Saul." It's Ruth Ann speaking this time. I didn't realize she was still here.

"You're turning blue. Breathe!" she says.

I like her, so I breathe. I can't keep myself from smiling at the panicked expression on everybody's faces. Ruth Ann's too. It feels good to know there's at least one thing in this messed-up world I can control, even if it's nearly insignificant.

Ruth Ann smiles back. "You're something else, Saul."

I knew I had a chance with her. I watch her lovely curves as she leaves the room behind the others. I'm glad she turns back when she reaches the door. "Somebody will be here to put you in your wheelchair soon, and then we'll go eat."

"Tell them to hurry," I say.

Now I'm alone again. I hate this part most of all. I despise staring at these walls. My room is windowless, and I honestly can't tell the difference between day and night. Awhile ago, back around the time I talked to nurse Pat, we flew across the ocean. I've never recovered from the jet lag. I couldn't possibly tell you what day it is now, or even if it is daytime.

When I'm alone like this, though, there's one thing I can do. I can think. If I concentrate really hard my thoughts sometimes seem to make sense. I can be an intense thinker. It's something I've always liked to do while riding my bike. When I'm all alone on long training rides revelations sometimes come to me like I'm some sort of genius savant. I've solved the world's problems many times over. Don't get me started on them.

Thinking in bed is much tougher. It's just not the same when the juices of life aren't flowing. It usually takes all the mental strength I can gather just to grasp the meaning of a simple sentence. Even then, I can't hold onto a thought long enough to give it meaning.

Here's an example. If I concentrate on my left hand, I can make myself aware I can't feel it at all. If I touch it with my right hand it's nothing more than an object that happens to be in my way. It might as well be a piece of wood lying in the bed beside me. But if I look away, it's as if what I just learned about my hand no longer exists, and the next time I try to use the hand I have to rediscover all over again that it's nothing but a useless piece of flesh. It's kind of like when I raced in the Tour of Austria through a snowstorm. We went up and down mountains in freezing weather. Both my hands were completely numb back then. This time it's as if the left one won't warm back up.

That might sound bad, but here's something much worse. I'm often content. In fact, until recently I was almost always content. Some people might like that feeling, but I hate it.

You can't imagine how frustrating it is to lie here in this broken husk of a body, not knowing or even caring what's gone wrong with my previously fine-tuned machine … and feeling okay with the situation. And when I say I haven't cared what's gone wrong, I should explain that it's a different sort of not caring than you probably know about. That's because at the surface level it's as if I can't care, but at the deepest level, where thoughts are formed and goals are made, I care more than anything else.

Here's the weird thing. That thought, no matter how real or passionate, doesn't matter at all because it gets locked beneath layers and layers of useless brain tissue and it can't get out. The synapses have all come unplugged, and there's no longer a route to the surface. It's not even a thought at all in the normal sense, yet I always know its there. Sometimes it feels like it's the only thing there.

The good news is, I think it's getting better. I'm starting to figure out how to express my true feelings more and more. Still, there are many times I simply can't figure out how to experience what I'm going through. When my sheets are dry and my stomach is full, I'm often powerless to wipe the goofy grin off my face. It pisses me off when this lousy situation doesn't piss me off at all. It's like I've got the happy but dopey brain of a lost mutt. My world may be in total disarray, but the instant somebody acknowledges my existence the only thought I'm capable of thinking is, "What a wonderful life." Meanwhile, deep in my heart, I'm sadder than I ever imagined being, and I'm getting sadder by the hour. I'm devastated and depressed and confused and disoriented, and I can't tell a soul about the problem. Not even myself. Does that suck, or what?

So here I lie in this hospital bed, powerless. There's glazed crud on my teeth. It tastes horrible, but I can't get it off. They brush my teeth for me but the glaze returns in no time. My chapped lips make it even worse. From time to time, I find myself eating the flaking skin. I don't want to, but laying here with nothing else to do, sometimes I just can't help it.

Someone painted butterflies on several of the institutional ceiling tiles. The care they took is starting to make me happy, so I roll my head away. The walls aren't any better to stare at because mixed among the usual charts and machines are little bits and pieces of art. I can tell that whoever placed them there did so with love. I drop my gaze to the floor, hoping it will look as miserable as I want to feel. Unfortunately, even though it's the hard, smooth, easy-to-clean sort of surface you'd expect in a hospital, it's a nonreflective earthtone instead of the ugly, shiny, fluorescent-light-reverberating, sort of surface that could really help make me depressed. To top it all off, this place smells good, at least for a hospital. It has a cozy feeling that makes me feel content. Can you see my problem with that? Damn, I hate feeling content. I hate it with a passion.

Last night I slept soundly for I don't know how long. I must have crashed for fourteen hours or more before Ruth Ann finally woke me. Then Doctor Dan showed up. From that moment forward I felt like a rag doll some little kid was dragging around. Ruth Ann helped the others do all sorts of unpleasant things to me instead of climbing into bed like I wanted her to. It goes on and on. Did I already tell you about that? I think maybe I did. Oh well, my short term memory is shot, too.

I hear a noise at the door. A big bear of a man wearing his hair in the coolest dreadlocks walks in pushing a wheelchair. "Ready to eat, my friend?"

"I was born ready."

He picks me up and hoists me into the wheelchair. I like that he's more of a teddy bear than a grizzly.

"What's your name?" I ask.

"Sean. I'm a football player turned nurse's tech, but I'm not here to do all the work," he says. "I hear you'd like food."

I nod vigorously.

"Okay," he says. "Let's see you get yourself to the dining room."

I look up at him, confused. "You're supposed to push me."

"No I'm not. You've got feet. Use them to pull yourself forward."

Incredible. What is it costing to stay in this place where they expect the patients to take care of themselves? They don't even tell you how to use your wheelchair right. I've been in one of these things before so I know the best way to move is to push the wheels with my hands.

I start to try that … but my left hand doesn't work. Oh yeah, it's a damn piece of wood. I push my right wheel only and the chair makes a sharp left hand turn. "Help me, Sean."

"Help yourself, Saul."

I'm so mad I start doing what he suggested at first. This piece of junk chair doesn't even have footrests. At least they won't be in my way while I'm trying to pull this contraption around with my feet. Using my right foot only I drag the chair, bit by bit, toward the door. Then I try the left foot. What's wrong with it? It's just like my left hand. Dead. I use the right foot again. Tripping over the left one is half the battle. I'm exhausted by the time I've moved a meter.

"Pretty good," Sean says. "Now, if you'll promise me you'll go farther on your own the next time I'll push you the rest of the way."

What choice do I have? "I promise. Just get me some food."

We reach a table where I vaguely notice other patients already seated. Sean parks me in an open space. He puts a tray of food in front of me, uncovers a dish, rearranges the utensils, pulls up a chair, and stares at me.

I want to tell him to hurry up, but I'm worried that would produce the wrong result, so I just wait. Saliva pools in my mouth. I can feel it starting to dribble down my chin. I love eating, except that no one's ever willing to give me the food as fast as I want it. I always wish I could grab the spoon and feed myself. I can't. I can't do anything for myself.

"Why are you just sitting there?" Sean asks.

"Why are you?" I ask. Has someone told him to pace my eating or something? I keep staring at the spoon, waiting for him to pick it up.

Instead he says, "Make sure you hold the utensils in your left hand. Only the left."

I glare at him incredulously.

"Can I have some coffee?" I ask.

He opens a packet of powdered cream.

"No. Black please," I say.

He shakes his head, uncovers a cup, and dumps the powder in. "This isn't cream; this is thickener, and this isn't coffee; this is prune juice."

I'd like to take a swing at him. Why would I want to drink prune juice with thickener?

"You know how much you choke on solid food?" he asks.

I nod, even though I can't say that I do.

"You'd be far worse with thin liquids." He sets a straw in the cup.

I can tell he's not about to lift the cup to my lips, and I'm not about to try and pick it up. I lower my head to the table and take a sip. I choke as I swallow, even though it's thick.

"Nice work," Sean says.

The juice is a lot better than I expected. In fact, it reminds me that everything tastes great to me these days. I wonder why that is.

I pick up my spoon and dip it into a bowl of oatmeal.

"Left hand only," Sean says.

I glare at him for a moment but he just repeats, "Left hand."

I pick up my left arm with my right hand and put it onto the table. I watch myself put the spoon into the fingers at the end of my dead appendage. I can hardly feel the metal, but my eyes tell me I'm holding on. I pivot my wrist to scoop up some food then duck my mouth down to catch it before it falls off. Soon I'm scooping and slurping as fast as I can. Man, it tastes good!

"Well done, my friend. Well done," Sean says. "Only about half of it is actually ending up in your mouth, so you might have to take a shower afterwards, but that's all right."

I feel myself smiling inside, though it probably doesn't show on my lips. There's no time for that. I'm still shoving food into my mouth. I'm feeding myself for the first time in a long time, and even though I'm choking on every bite, it does feel pretty damn good.

I used to think of myself as a grateful person, but back then I never even imagined giving thanks for the simple sorts of things that have been taken away from me now. Oh, what a pleasure it would be to easily scoop spoonfuls of oatmeal into my mouth. What sheer joy I'd feel if I could walk across the room to wash my own face. Can you imagine thinking true ecstasy would be wiping your own rear end? Well, it would be for me.

I keep pushing the food from the bowl to my mouth. Sean puts a new bowl in front of me when I finish the first one. It doesn't take me too long to finish that one off, too. After I swallow the last bite Sean starts covering the dishes, but before he even lifts the tray, a new thought overrides everything. I want to go back to sleep. Words can't express the level of fatigue I feel, and it's constant. I crave sleep more than anything else in the world, except maybe food.

I close my eyes but a voice interrupts me. "How are we doing today, Saul?"

"Go away. I want to sleep."

"It's not bedtime," a man says.

"Don't you understand English? I need sleep. Please take me back to my bed." I let out a long, mournful moan. It comes from the pit of my gut. I don't know if I've ever moaned from such a deep place before.

"We're doing you a favor by keeping you up," the man says calmly.

"Damnit! Let me sleep! You don't understand how badly I need sleep." I feel hateful inside. "Please put me to bed. Please, please, please."

"Calm down, Saul," the man says. "That's not how we do things around here. It's ten in the morning and you're required to be awake. Your brain needs to get used to routines and activity. It's time for you to get on the Shepherd Center schedule. What are your goals for today?"

I struggle to find an answer his question, but I can't even make complete sense of what he asked. Every thought is an epic exertion. I can't come up with anything. I open my eyes, realizing that it's Doctor Dan again. Is he running some sort of boot camp? "I'm tired."

"That's understandable. Doesn't change anything, though. Do you want your parents to see you acting like this?"

No. I don't want that. I want them to see me as strong. I want them to know I'm okay. I look at him and realize I'm showing my happy puppy expression. I can't help it. His attention makes me feel good, and the sensation of mattering pushes everything else out of my mind.

"When can I get out of this place?" I ask.

He shakes his head. "Don't think that way. You'll only frustrate yourself. Besides, this isn't such a bad place."

"It is for someone who should be racing a bike. How soon until I can ride?"

Doctor Dan sits down and looks me in the eye. "Saul, I admire your determination but you're going to have to start accepting some realities. We're going to do everything we can to help you get better, but you need to be patient and realize some things might never be possible again."

I shake my head, trying to get this thought to settle … or maybe I'm trying to make sure it can't settle. "What kinds of things?"

"Well, for one, you might never walk again. If you don't, you'll need to learn to be okay with that. It's not the end of the world."

I turn my head toward the wall. I'm not okay with it. I'll never be okay with a thought like that. This guy ought to keep his reality to himself, because I'm not interested.

"Saul, are you going to pout, or are you going to accept your situation? You might never be able to use your left side again."

I look back at him. "But I can wiggle my left ear."

He looks incredulous. "I don't believe you. Show me."

So I wiggle my left ear with no problem.

The doctor's eyes go wide.

"I told you so," I say. "You can't believe your eyes, can you?"

"No. I can't."

"Well then," I tell him, "Get ready to be amazed a lot."

Chapter Two

I wish I could let you know if days or hours or weeks passed between the last story I told you and the present time. I do not know. My mind is in a fog. For me, all days are unplanned mysteries.

I lie here in the mornings, wishing I could get out of bed and start my day, but instead I'm helpless and feel like somebody beat me to a pulp. Is my soreness from work I did yesterday, or from injuries deep in my bones, or from something else. Honestly, I don't know. I can't figure out what's wrong with me, but unlike a few days ago, I do know something isn't right.

This morning it's Amy who comes to get me for therapy. She's my speech therapist. She has a happy, round face that barely seems able to contain all her joy. I love being around her. She makes me drag my wheelchair using my feet for awhile like all the others, but then I say, "You can't hide how good you are from me."

"What's that supposed to mean?" she asks.

"It means I know you're going to start pushing this wheelchair for me soon."

She laughs, and then she starts pushing the chair just like I'd hoped. "Ah, Saul. You're an international lover." When we get to the therapy I expect she's going to have physical exercises for me to do. I'm anxious for them because I like to work hard. What I'd really love is to sweat. As tough as therapy has been, I haven't broken a sweat the whole time I've been here, or at the hospital before this, either. I can hardly wait to be able to push my body that hard.

But then she says, "We're going to start out with some mental problems. Recovering your mental strength is going to be even more work than recovering your physical strength, and it's going to make you even more tired."

I don't believe her. How could solving a problem be more exhausting than climbing a mountain? I'm going to prove her wrong. "Let me hear these mental problems."

"Okay, Saul." She opens a book on the table. It looks like a kids coloring book, but there are math problems beside the pictures of zoo animals. "What is five plus two?"

I think and think. I need to show her I can do the sorts of problems they print next to zebras. I want to tell her the answer, but I don't want to be wrong. "Lets see … five, six, mmm … I think it is seven."

"How sure are you?" she asks.

I doubt I'm fooling her, and I decide there's no sense in trying. "I'm not very sure. Just twenty-five percent sure." You can't imagine how frustrating it is to be asked children's math problems and not know how to do them. I'm looking at a simple equation and I have almost no idea how to figure it out. Just thinking about the problem is exhausting. She was right about that part after all. I lay my head down on the table.

She lifts my head back up. "Twenty-five percent must be good enough because you got it right. Now, tell me what this one is."

She points to a problem but doesn't say the equation out loud. I concentrate to try and make sense of it. There's the number three and the number five, and lines going this way and that. Beside it there's a tiger with a smile on his face. I wonder if he's happy because I can't solve his problem. I don't even know where to start. "Can we do some exercising and come back to this later?"

"No, Saul. This is your exercise."

I know the problems are easy but I just can't do them. My eyes keep wandering to the little animals and pictures and that keeps reminding me that these problems are for a kid. But I still can't do them. "I don't like this book. Can we try a different one?"

Amy won't listen to me. Every time I make a guess about one problem she asks me to do another. I want to give her a hug and a kiss and talk her into getting rid of this book, but I can tell she'll have none of it. By the time Amy finally closes the book I'm so exhausted that if my eyes blink shut I feel like they're going to stay that way. I fight to keep them open because I know lunch has to come soon and I don't want to miss it.

"Are you hungry?" she asks.

"Starved."

She smiles. "Good. Your food is here. Get yourself over to the table."

I do as she says, and quick. Distances like that are a lot easier to cover when there's a reward at the end. Ruth Ann is unloading the trays from a tall cart. "Here's yours, Saul."

"Thank you," I say, hoping she'll just put the tray down in front of me and quit talking about it. I'll be happy to listen all she wants while I eat. Finally she does and I prepare to dig in.

"Uh uh," Ruth Ann says. "You can't lay your head on the table and shovel the food in. You need to lift it to your mouth using your arm."

Who makes up these rules? I hadn't even realized I'd been putting my head on the table until she mentioned it, but what does it matter? If the goal is to get food into my mouth, my method is better. Has she forgotten my left arm doesn't even work? "How am I supposed to do that?"

She pantomimes a method with her arms. "Put the spoon in your left hand. Use your right hand to lift your left arm up to your mouth."

Good grief. I'm too hungry to argue, though, so I do as she says. I pour the first spoonful down the front of my shirt. The second one ends up in about the same place. I'm starving and drowning in food at the same time. This is ridiculous.

I'm changing back to my old method. I lower my head toward the table, hoping Ruth Ann won't notice.

She waggles a finger. "Uh uh, Saul."

I try to straighten back up and eat by her rules again. I feel myself wavering, and then I smell gravy. I'm climbing a mountain of mashed potatoes. Someone grabs my shoulder from behind. I panic. They're trying to pull me off the mountain.

"Wake up, Saul."

They pull me backward and I open my eyes. I'm surprised to find myself sitting up.

Ruth Ann starts washing my face with a cloth. She chuckles as she speaks. "I turned away for a moment and you fell asleep in your food, Saul. Are you too tired to eat?"

My stomach rumbles. I try to make sense of things. I lick around my lips and taste strawberry topping from shortcake. I look at the tray in front of me and see the indentation in the food where I've been resting. I really did fall asleep while eating.

"Saul, are you okay?"

I nod. "Please take me back to bed. I'm too tired to eat by these rules. Please."

She dabs a napkin in water and washes a bit more off my face. "You can put your head on the table and scoop your food in, but this is the last meal you'll eat that way so prepare yourself."

Finally I get to eat. I push the food in as fast as I can. When I'm done Sean takes me to bed. I quickly fall into a deep sleep.

Just as I'm getting comfortable someone shakes my shoulder. I open one eye. It's Sean. "Time to get up, Saul. You've slept an hour. That's all you get."

This place sucks. As I lie there collecting my thoughts I make a resolution. I've got to regain the use of my left hand and arm. They'd sooner let me starve to death than feed myself with my right hand, so it's pretty urgent that I figure out how to use the other one. I concentrate on lifting the arm. It will barely move. It feels like there's a hundred pounds strapped to my wrist. I try again, then again, and again. It isn't long before I'm grunting from the strain, but I keep doing it. I need my arm back.

The effort drains me, not just physically, but mentally. It's as if my brain has to retrain each individual muscle fiber exactly how to do its job every single time I put the arm in motion. The motor memory that used to make most actions seem simple is now gone.

The harder I have to work the more I take the unwillingness of my arm to respond as an insult to my independence. Maybe there's something about the way my brain is wired that forces me to seek out pain and attempt to master it. I've done that for years by climbing enormous mountains as fast as I can on my bike.

Now I experience an even greater level of exhaustion, an overwhelming mental weariness, just by moving my arm.

In the evening my grandmother, or Gram Cracker as I like to call her, shows up. I can't stop smiling whenever she talks to me, but she's so sad. I don't know what the problem is, but I wish I could make her feel better. I ask her to bring some chocolate cookies next time she returns. I tell her we could eat them together. She says she will. I can already taste them. I do love chocolate. I crave it. I don't know why. It's not the sweetness I'm after; it's something else. If someone would bring me unsweetened cocoa I'd devour that, too.

The next morning Lauren enters my room. She's a babe. She's also my physical therapist. I've wanted to make all sorts of comments to her, but I keep biting my tongue. I've been a bad boy around women lately, but I'm trying really hard to fix that. Whenever a woman comes near I use all my concentration to not say the wrong thing. I wink at Lauren, and she winks back. Sean is with her. My mom and dad step in behind them.

"You ate everything in your basket last night?" Lauren asks.

"What basket?" I say.

She holds up a basket of empty wrappers she found beside my bed. I suddenly recall it was full of apples, cookies, Ensure drinks, chips, yogurt and pudding when I went to bed last night. Now I vaguely recall waking up and eating all that stuff. "Even if I did, I'm still hungry," I say.

She laughs. "Don't you remember you just finished a big breakfast?"

I shrug.

"Good gravy, Saul," Dad says. "I saw how overloaded that basket was last night and I told Mom there was no way you'd even make a dent in it. You're eating like an elephant!"

"He needs it. Saul is consuming 10,000 to 12,000 calories a day. His metabolism is racing as his brain heals. Not only that, but he needs to gain weight. He weighed only 125 when he arrived here. He's already putting on some pounds, but he could use a lot more," Lauren says.

"Does that mean we can go to lunch now?" I ask.

"No. You can eat more later. Now it's time to work," Lauren says.

"Will work get me out of this place?"

"Eventually," she says.

I smile. "Then I want to work harder than anybody you ever did therapy with before."

Lauren hands me a pair of socks. "Put these on. We're going to walk today."

I feel my jaw drop, but I don't let it go too far because I don't want them to change their minds.

I concentrate very hard on pulling the socks apart. They're folded into one of those little bundles. I usually need two hands to undo them, but I've learned my left side isn't going to be very cooperative. I feel an odd satisfaction in being able to retain that knowledge instead of having to be surprised by the weakness of my left hand yet again. I think of a trick. I use my teeth to hold onto the socks and pull the bundle apart with my right hand. The expressions of the people watching make me smile inside. I don't think they expected me to solve this so quickly.

"Put them on," Lauren says. "Sandals will be next."

Have you ever tried to put on a sock using only one hand? Maybe it's not that hard, but it is for me. I finally get the sock over three toes and decide that if I pull hard enough the rest of them might slip in. Instead the three toes bend, the sock pops off, and I'm back at square one again.

I get four toes in this time but then I can't resist the urge to pull and the same thing happens with the sock as before. After many tries I look up. Mom is crying. When I look at Dad, he's crying, too. Disappointing them makes me feel so bad. I understand why it hurts them to have a son who can't put on his own socks. "I'm sorry. Can I just rest for a moment?"

Lauren nods. "Take your time."

I do. Each time I fail I vow to be a little more patient on my next attempt. Finally I slip a sock over my left foot. I feel like dancing but I know that's not going to happen. Eventually I get the other sock on as well as both shoes.

Dad looks at his watch. "Thirty-five minutes. A week ago it would have been impossible. Nice job, Saul."

"I need to go to the bathroom," I say, proud that I've recently started being able to sense the need. I wait for somebody to give me a handheld urinal.

"Great idea. Let's walk," Lauren says. "You're wearing shoes."

They want me to use a real toilet? I like that idea, especially because I always spill at least a little bit with the other method. I also like that she's challenging me. "Okay. I will."

Lauren takes my right arm. Sean takes my left. Even with their help it's an enormous struggle to get to my feet. I've been in that bed for so long. Eventually I reach a standing position. I lick my lips while waiting for a wave of extreme wooziness to go away. Slowly it ebbs. "Okay. Let me go. I can walk."

They let go and I instantly fall back to my seat.

They lift me back up and Sean says, "We're going to help you balance."

I nod and stand there for a minute.

Lauren says, "Okay, Saul. Take a step forward."

So I think, *move your right leg. Move your right leg.* I look down at my right foot, willing it to step forward. It feels like it's stuck in wet cement. I try harder. Finally I move my right leg. The effort makes me lose my breath and get light headed again. I feel like I've just done an interval on the bike. It took every bit of strength and concentration even though I only moved it a little.

Lauren says, "Good job. Okay, now move your left foot."

I look at my other foot and I can tell it's of no use. That thing isn't going anywhere. It doesn't even really feel like a part of me, but I'm not going to give up, and I'm not going to look into anybody's face and start feeling sad.

I finally discover I can move it by twisting my body clockwise. That drags the left side far enough forward that I can take another step with the right. In this way I inch toward the bathroom door. It takes a long time, especially because I have to pause often for rest. I'm thankful for the increasing help that Lauren and Sean are giving me. Even with their assistance, I'm totally exhausted by the time I reach the entrance to the bathroom, but the exhaustion doesn't matter because I feel so proud I've reached my goal.

I look up, ready to celebrate, but a horrifying sight almost knocks me back to the bed. A man is already in the bathroom, and he's staring at me. He looks as scared as I feel, but his eyes are frighteningly vacant with dark circles beneath them. He has the complexion of a ghost, and his body is contorted. As I take in his glazed expression my blood begins to chill. I'm uncomfortable being near this man, but I can't look away from him, either. What is he doing in my bathroom?

Then slowly it dawns on me. There isn't a man in there. I'm looking into a mirror.

Chapter Three

I'm shattered by what I've seen. The reflection of my own face haunts me more than any demon ever could. My tears won't stop. I haven't been able to cry until this moment, but now I can't quit. I moan with sadness. I don't like what I've become and I can't figure out how it has happened. For the first time I really understand all the concern surrounding me. I think back to those swatches of recollection from the hospital in France and suddenly see them in a different way. New memories come to mind: My aunt bragging about my little cousin Noah riding without training wheels for the first time, my friend and teammate Killian kissing me goodbye on the forehead, my parents and Daniela standing at my bedside again and again and again.

At the time I was obliviously happy whenever a friend visited, but also confused by the concern written on their faces. Thinking back, everybody who's looked into my eyes since this ordeal began has seemed worried. Now that I know what they've been seeing I can't believe their expressions were so composed. After all, they were looking at a ghost. While I lay there, content but confused, my friends were being put through hell. Each time visitors came by we had been experiencing nearly opposite emotions, but I didn't have the slightest clue until now. Oh, what have I done?

I can't focus my thoughts on this for long. Somehow, I find myself back in bed with the covers pulled around me. I'm alone in the room again. In addition to the frightening sight in the mirror I hurt so badly from walking I can't get comfortable. It feels like the world heavyweight champion has pummeled me. My body throbs with pain. "Please, can somebody help me get some sleep?"

A nurse steps into the room. She gives me two sleeping pills. I love these pills. They allow me to forget everything and fall straight into a deep sleep. As exhausted as I am, I'm not sure I could relax enough to sleep without them.

*   *   *

Someone is shaking my shoulder. I open my eyes to find Dr. Bilsky. He's a kind gentleman with a face framed in white hair. His beard and mustache are neatly trimmed. I love the mixture of passion and compassion I always see in his eyes. Of all my doctors I like him the most.

"I heard you tried to walk yesterday evening," he says.

My legs are still sore. I look toward the bathroom. "You can't really call it walking. They kind of carried me."

"It's a step in the right direction." He has a stethoscope draped over his shoulder. He takes it into his hand as he talks. "Baby steps. We emphasize that around here. It takes accomplishing lots of little goals to reach your big goals, just like it took lots of little steps to build your career as a pro cyclist."

"I don't take baby steps. I jump."

Dr. Bilsky smiles. "But you didn't reach the pro level overnight. Correct?"

"Correct."

"These things take time. How did your balance feel?"

"I had no balance. First the world felt like it was leaning to the left; then it swirled around to the right."

He nods. "That's to be expected at this point. You can't get your balance reoriented if you don't try. It's going to take a lot of hard work. Keep it up."

I chew on my lower lip for a moment before asking a question that's been on my mind for a long time. "Would it be possible for me to use a computer? I'd like to check my e-mails."

"I think we can arrange that. There's a computer room down the hall. I'll ask Amy to take you there today."

"Thanks, Dr. Bilsky."

The doctor checks me in all the various ways I've become used to. Now that I've seen myself in the mirror, his interest in my condition makes a lot more sense to me than it did before. I do my best to cooperate.

After he finishes I call Daniela.

"How are you today, Saul?" she asks.

"I love you," I say.

"I love you too. What are you doing?"

"I love you," I answer.

She chuckles. "I know that. You already told me. Thanks for the poems you texted. They're sweet, even though in all honesty, they don't make that much sense."

"*Ich liebe Dich*," I say in her native German.

My parents walk into the room and say hello. Daniela must be able to hear them because she says, "It sounds like you have company. I ought to let you go."

We end our conversation and I turn my attention to my parents. I'm always happy to see them. They both give me a hug and a kiss. Grandma is with them and so is my Aunt Linda. Grandma pulls some chocolate cookies out of her purse and shows them to me. She acts funny, like they're some sort of illegal drugs she's smuggled past security.

"Good job sneaking those in, Gram Cracker" I say, playing along. "Let's eat 'em."

She gives me one. She doesn't know that I'm not supposed to be using my right hand to eat, and I'm sure as hell not telling her. I can shove the cookie in as fast as I want and I'm done in no time. It tasted so good.

Then she gives me the second one, too. "Go ahead. You eat it," she says.

I don't want to take her cookie but I can't resist. She nods her head at me. I bite into the cookie. I love my grandma.

"Your web site is getting thousands of hits, Saul. So many people are leaving messages for you we can't even read all of them," Mom says.

"Your traffic even shut down the servers one day. All your provider's customers were out of business for awhile because of you," Dad says.

"Yeah, I'm a superstar," I say.

Mom frowns. "Saul, you never had a big head before. Don't you go getting one now!"

Dad is looking kind of disappointed in me too, and for some reason that's always made me want to prove my point even more. "I don't have a big head. I'm just telling the truth. People respect that about me."

"Saul," Dad says, "if you can't quit bragging about yourself long enough to listen I won't read you the new message we posted this morning."

He's got me in a corner. I shut my mouth.

He reads:

Saul Update
Contributed by Saul's Parents
Thursday, 04 May 2006
Saul Update. Saul is in Rehab now … He walks with assistance and his left side is still weak … He eats up a storm … Calls Daniela every night … We know that his recovery will take some time … Saul is aware of everything … With brain injury the healing process takes 9 months to 1 year to know the outcome. Saul says he will do it in 6 months … we will tell you Saul is working very hard and we have no doubt that if anyone can do it Saul can … Saul's parents.

Their post doesn't make complete sense to me, but I thank them anyway. It also makes me happy to hear that people are leaving messages. I'm glad that people care about me and I can't wait to read what they have to say.

Lunchtime comes. Ruth Ann sets a transparent cylinder on the table in front of me. I pick it up. There's some sort of colored liquid sloshing around inside. It's a simple and spectacular work of art. I stare at it, mesmerized by the way it bends light.

"What is this beautiful thing?" I ask.

"Put it to your lips," she says.

I do, but nothing happens.

She reaches over and tips it so that the liquid runs into my mouth. Oh yes, I remember what this object is. It's called a drinking glass.

As I set down my drink an attendant rolls in a tall cart full of food. It's like a mobile dresser with a meal on each shelf inside. He pulls out tray after tray and keeps setting them down in front of people other than me. As the other patients take the lids off their dishes I see that some have a hamburger, some have a hot dog, and some have one of each. My mouth is watering so badly I can't hold the saliva inside. Finally the cart is empty, but I still don't have any food. I'm the only one who hasn't been served.

"Where's mine?" I ask.

The attendant takes a tray I hadn't noticed before off the top of the cart. It's so loaded with food it wouldn't fit inside on the shelves with everybody else's meals. I uncover my plates: two hamburgers and two hot dogs, plus fries.

I dig in, very happy to have food that doesn't require utensils. My throat kills me every time I swallow but the burgers taste so good I don't care. I reach for one of the French fries.

Ruth Ann grabs my hand. "No, Saul. You have to eat those with a fork. Left hand."

The rules they dream up around this place!

I glare at her for a moment but she won't even look back, so finally I decide I'd rather eat than make my point … whatever that point was … I can't even remember.

I use my right hand to get my left hand into position. I hold the fork and look at the fry. I concentrate all my energy. I feel like an archer aiming his arrow at a far-off target. Moving the fork forward, I miss the fry. I reposition and try again. It takes me a long time to stab each fry, put it into my mouth, and line up another target. By the time I've eaten them all, lunch has totally exhausted me, both physically and mentally.

Later that afternoon Amy walks up to me. "I hear you'd like to use the computer."

I feel an indescribable excitement as she points down the hall. I drag myself the whole way with my feet.

Amy opens the door to a room I've never entered before. It's a sort of studio apartment with its own kitchenette, dining table, and a bed. She points to a computer on the counter.

"Go ahead," she says.

I hurry over. There's an Internet window already open, and the address bar has been cleared. The cursor blinks at me patiently. This feels like one of the first familiar activities I've done in a long time. I try to begin typing, but I soon realize it's going to be harder than usual. While I can lift my left arm a little bit nowadays, I can hardly feel my fingers at all and I can't feel the tips one bit. There's no way I can use that hand to type.

Using my right hand I hunt and peck through the keyboard. It takes a long time to navigate to my inbox at wanadoo.fr.

"You can read all this?" Amy asks.

"Yeah. It's in French," I say. Finally I type in my password and hit Enter.

"How do you remember your password?" she asks.

I shrug. "Why wouldn't I?" I've always had a great memory. On my home page there's a photo of me riding a bike at age two. I vividly recall the day that shot was taken. I can recite the specifics of test results that were run years ago, and I know thousands of people who I've met only in passing by name and face. Remembering my password is pretty simple compared to that.

She watches over my shoulder as my e-mailbox opens. When it does the display tells me that there are more than 1200 unread messages. What happened? Have I been spammed? My service provider is usually pretty good at stopping this kind of stuff.

I look at the unopened files. They seem legitimate, and many are from addresses I recognize. I open one titled, "praying for you." It says:

Dear Saul,
I have been praying for you every day … I ask for God to heal you in every way. You are a dear friend, and I ask why this happened to you. I know with God's grace you will get over this and come back to life.

My mind races. I have to read another. The second email is similar to the first. It reads:

Dear Saul,
Fight fight fight, do not give up. You are in my prayers and thoughts. May god bless you and your family.

I glance over many more e-mails. They're all the same. After reading about twenty, my confusion has only increased. What exactly happened to me?

I go to Google to search for my name. I've done this many times in the past. It's an interesting way to measure the progress of my career. Last time I logged on, I remember finding about 18,000 search results. It was the largest number I'd seen yet. Winning races and showing well in others had caused my name to be spread all over the Internet.

I type in: "Saul Raisin" and hit Enter. In an instant the search is performed. The title bar reads, "Results 1 – 10 of about 550,000 for Saul Raisin. (0.06 seconds)." I do a double take. Over half a million instances of my name? Did I win the Tour de France? No, of course that's not possible. The Giro?

I know that can't be right either. What the hell has happened to me?

I scroll down the page. There's a link to an article on CNN. It says:

Raisin stable after brain surgery (04.07.2006) American cyclist Saul Raisin is in a stable condition after undergoing surgery to reduce pressure caused by fluid on his brain.

They're talking about me and brain surgery in the same article on CNN? I click on the link. The article explains how I crashed at the Circuit de la Sarthe and fell into a coma. That's why I can't move my left arm and why my hand is numb! It's why I can't eat by myself or do anything! That's why the man staring back at me in the mirror looks more like a ghost than a human! The reason I need all this help is that I've just come out of a coma!

I drop forward onto the computer, and my tears become uncontrollable. For the first time the full impact of what I've put my parents through hits me. My heart feels like it's going to burst in two. "Oh God, why me? Why was I chosen for this?"

I recall seeing mentally disabled people throughout my life. They were often put in corners where they would be out of the way and wouldn't trouble other people. I always tried to be kind, but sometimes I walked past without acknowledging them. I never really stopped to imagine their world. Now I'm one of them. I suddenly know what many of them must have been feeling all this time. Acknowledgment feels so good. They're incomplete and acutely aware of it, yet they don't have any way of understanding what's missing. I felt a whole lot better off moments ago when I didn't know for certain that there was something specific wrong with me. I guess I can't positively say that this is how anybody else feels, but it's how it is for me.

That evening when my parents walk into my room I'm still crying. "Mom, Dad, why didn't you tell me I've been in a coma?"

Mom starts crying. "We did. We've been telling you every day for over a month. You just haven't heard it until now."

I shake my head. "It never made any sense before, but if it's on CNN …"

"Saul," Dad says, "it's been a tough road. I'm proud of how hard you've fought. Now, just keep on getting better."

"I will Dad. I will. Blue skies ahead, okay?"

Chapter Four

Last night after truly dealing with what my accident meant for the first time I finally posted a message to my blog without assistance. It's a simple thing I used to do regularly, but I hadn't entered anything in over a month. Here's what I wrote:

So Hard
Contributed by Saul
Monday, 08 May 2006
Oh so I am still in the hospital … I am getting better … But I am still far away from being well … This head injury is harder than any broken bones … It is almost surreal when you need as much help to get well … I want to thank everyone for the good wishes and for following me … Soon I will be able to have visitors … I will let you know …
Saul

Mom and Dad say I'm in a fog. That's a pretty good description. I feel hung over all day long, every day. I struggle physically and mentally with every single thing I do. The lights are on, but I still can't see my world clearly or take the risk of moving quickly. I talk slowly, walk slowly, and I can't respond as fast as I wish. It feels sort of like I'm swimming, maybe in something thicker than water. Everything is in slow motion.

The suffering I'm experiencing is far worse than any bicycle race I've ever ridden. Not only is it an entirely different sort of ache, but the misery is completely out of my control. I feel like a mutt with no place to go. The sort of pain I overcome while competing is, to my mind, pleasurable. Nothing about this injury feels positive. The hurt is kind of like the hollow yearning of a loved one lost. Breaking my hip was far more physically painful than anything I've gone through here, but I'd take that any day over this hideous feeling of being dead to myself. There's never a respite from my insatiable loneliness. It's not possible to reach a summit and then roll down the other side of the mountain while the muscles recover. It's a constant and all-consuming grieving where taking a break is not an option.

Sometimes I can feel the fog lift slightly and that sad absent person I've seen in the mirror is pushed a little bit farther away. I'm not saying that I ever feel all right, or even anything anywhere close, but when you're in the condition I've been in, small improvements can mean a lot.

I'm sitting in the corner of the therapy room tossing beanbags into a bucket. They've velcroed an oversized marshmallow-type mitten onto my right hand so that I can't use it at all. I hate this damn thing and I want it off. The people here claim it will help me. I can't imagine how. I toss beanbags with my left hand. Every time I run out of them, Ruth Ann dumps the bucket in my lap again.

There's a man in the room I've never seen before. He's been working with one of the other patients. He might be a family member. I keep finding myself looking at him. When he finally comes near I say, "I can see the mesh holding your toupee together."

His face turns red and he takes a step backward. "How rude of you."

I feel terrible, but I can't understand how noticing something could be considered wrong. I know I've made some sort of mistake, but I'm not sure what it is. I would have thought he'd like to know. If my hair was combed badly it wouldn't bother me if somebody mentioned it.

I'm learning that I've forgotten so many simple things. I can't do kids' math problems. I can't walk. I couldn't control my bodily functions until recently, and I still can't clean myself. Apparently I've broken some sort of rule with this man, too.

I think of a way to apologize to him. "I hope you'll soon be able to afford a better one."

He scowls, and I can tell he's madder than before.

"What have I done?" I really want to know.

"You just think about it, okay? You just think about it," he says. Then he leaves the room.

I stop tossing beanbags and think, but I can't make any sense of what has happened.

"Are you getting bored with that exercise," Ruth Ann asks.

I don't answer.

"Let's work on flexibility in your left arm." She takes my left hand and elbow and begins rotating the shoulder.

As she lifts my arm nearly horizontal, the pain in my shoulder increases until it hits an unbearable level. "Stop!"

"Because of your broken collarbone and shoulder plus the paralysis, your arm has hardly moved in over a month. The bones healed while you were lying flat on your back, and the muscle beneath the scapula is locked up with adhesions." Ruth Ann massages my shoulder as she talks. "You're so tight. Does that feel good?"

I smile. I'll take massages from Ruth Ann any day. Her fingers knead my flesh painfully, but I like the sensation and can tell it's going to help my arm. Soon my problem with the toupee man leaves my mind, and I focus again on my physical situation. Over the last few days I've begun to have a little more feeling in my left hand. Although the fingertips are still pretty numb, I believe the whole arm will soon wake up.

That afternoon Mom says, "We have a special treat in store for you, Saul."

"What is it?"

"Dad and I got permission to take you for a little walk through the halls."

My nerves tighten. "Off the ward?"

Mom nods. "Won't that be fun?"

I'm not so sure.

Dad pushes my wheelchair while Mom walks beside me. There are no rests for my feet, so I have to walk along the ground as the chair moves. We reach the glass doors that separate the Acquired Brain Injury Ward from the outside world. I've become very comfortable here. Through the doors I can see a waiting room couch, an elevator with a door to a stairway beside it, and a hallway that leads to who knows where.

I've sat for hours at a time watching people being buzzed in and out through those doors, dreaming of the places they're going to and coming from. But now I realize that, like a dog who prefers the safety of his kennel, I no longer want to leave this place.

The door buzzes and Dad pushes my chair through, but I brace my feet and force him to stop. "No."

"What's wrong, Saul?" Mom asks.

I can't put it into words. I've always been adventurous and loved exploring, but I don't want to explore now. I want to stay on this ward with people who understand my limitations. I'm terrified by the idea of leaving, though I don't know why. I twist my head around to look back at my home.

"Please. I don't want to go," I say.

"Saul, you'll be with us," Dad says. "We're going to take a short walk and then return."

I really don't want to go. "Please take me back to my room. I don't like it out here."

"We could head down to the cafeteria for some soft ice cream," Mom suggests.

"Soft ice cream?" I have a condo in Beausoleil, France, right on the border of Monaco. There's an Italian ice cream shop nearby. After long rides I often stop there for an energy boost. The owner jokes with me that he fears going out of business each time I leave town, or whenever I get serious about keeping the weight off. I'll admit right now, I have a weakness for sweets.

Dad has taken advantage of my momentary distraction to push me toward the unknown hallway. My legs are again absently scuffling along the floor, forced into motion by the rolling chair.

At the end of a window-filled hallway is a painting like none I've ever seen. There's a lovely little house sitting on a knoll overlooking beautiful patchwork farmland that reminds me of France. It looks like a world where only happy things could happen, not a cartoon world where bricks fall onto rabbit's heads and don't hurt, but a place where I imagine everybody treats one another the way they should.

I point to the beautiful scene where clouds pass like peaceful ships through an azure sea. "Look, blue skies."

Mom leans in toward the frame and reads the plaque. "*After the Rain* by Sergey Cherep."

"Nice," Dad says.

We stay there, looking at the painting for a long time. Finally Dad starts pushing me down the hall again.

"Do we have to go very far?" I ask.

He rolls me into an elevator. "Not far at all."

We exit across the hall from a cafeteria. As we enter the smells set off joyous sensations inside my head. I look around at the other diners. There's a mixture of wheelchairs, walkers, hospital staff, and healthy visitors.

"I'll get the ice cream," Mom says.

Dad parks me at a table and soon Mom hands me a bowl and spoon. I finish my ice cream quickly and beg for more. Dad refills my cup.

I'm suddenly feeling so much calmer than before. "I'm getting better fast, aren't I, Dad? I can leave this hospital soon."

"I don't know about that, Saul. It's still going to take some time." He puts a spoonful of ice cream in his mouth.

I finish cleaning out my second bowl and hand it to my mom expectantly. She rises to refill it, and I feel happy inside. "Two more weeks and I'll be ready to come home. Okay?"

"We'll let the doctors make that decision. I think they might want to keep you around here a bit longer than that," Dad says.

I'm not surprised that Dad isn't too excited to take the next step. That's just his way. Once I prove to him I'm ready he'll become the biggest supporter in the world. He always is. "Two weeks," I repeat. "I'm going to miss this ice cream, though. Can we get one of those machines at home?"

Dad shakes his head. "Nope. This is the best place to stay if you want a supply of soft ice cream."

I smile as Mom hands me another bowl. I have the best parents in the world.

Afterwards Dad pushes me back to the room using a different route. Along the way we pass all sorts of pictures and my parents seem to have a story about each one. I'm not interested. I wish Dad would have just taken us back in the same elevator that leads to the ward. We enter a recreation room, and then he pushes me up a ramp toward a door. Mom hurries ahead and opens it. That's when I notice it leads outside.

"I don't want to go out there," I say.

But Dad pushes me out into the dappled sunshine before I can stop him. Pollen goes up my nose and I sneeze several times. Birds and insects are making a racket, but that's not the worst part. Twenty-five meters away loud rush-hour traffic is pouring out toxic fumes.

"Let's go back to my room," I say. To me this garden seems overcrowded with other patients and their families.

Mom is pointing out anything and everything she can think of to distract me. Bird houses, art projects, and plants. She reads poetry from plaques as we pass them. None of it interests me.

"This is called the Garden of HOPE, Saul. That's a nice name, isn't it?" Mom asks.

"Who cares," I say. "I don't like it here. Let's go to my room."

Finally I convince them to take me back. Dad has just helped me into bed when Ruth Ann walks in. I wink at her, but she pays no attention and pulls Mom and Dad aside to talk instead. They whisper for awhile. Soon my parents stride toward me with stern faces. I feel like I'm at school in the principle's office. Is there some sort of problem with paying for the ice cream? I thought they said it was free for patients.

"Saul, did you grab Sarah on the butt?" Mom asks.

Sarah is another of the occupational therapists here. She's tall and gorgeous. I think for a minute then say, "I don't think so. No, I did not."

"Are you sure?" she asks.

"Well she did bend over, and her butt was in my face. It was terribly pretty."

"He did it," Dad says.

I laugh. I can't help myself. I'd been controlling my mouth all day, but now I'd been caught with my hand on the … um … cookie jar.

"Herman Saul Raisin! I'm ashamed of you." Mom only uses my full name when she's really mad, but I can sense that she's holding back a chuckle at the same time. "You can't behave like that. Just because you feel an urge doesn't mean you have the right to act on it."

"I'm sorry, Mom. I'll apologize to Sarah. I won't do it again."

"You'd better be sorry, Saul," she says. "And your apology had better be sincere. Don't even think about doing it again."

Panic strikes me. I want to be a good boy and I'm willing to work hard to behave as I should, but these rules seem unreasonably strict. "I'm not allowed to think about touching her either? The women around here are all so beautiful. How can I prevent myself from having thoughts?"

Dad grins. "Just don't act on them, okay? You need to get some inhibitions back Son, and quick."

I nod, not entirely certain which other thoughts of mine fall into the same category. I wonder how commenting about a toupee compares? It seems quite a bit different, but I'm not sure the toupee man would agree. Man, do I ever have a lot of things to relearn.

Chapter Five

I love hearing Daniela's voice on the phone every evening. I often tell her our love will get us through this and we'll emerge stronger than ever. I know she feels the same way. My parents really relied on Daniela while I was out cold. She's such a wonderful person, and I'm so thankful she was there for me and especially for my parents.

It's still so weird to think about that time. I mean, here I was sleeping peacefully, recovering from all sorts of broken bones and injuries I never even knew I had. By the time I woke up that phase of my pain was pretty much gone, and I was surrounded by the people I love most. It's strange to realize this calm time for me was mass chaos for those I care about most, but it was. I've put them through so much.

I'm going to make it up to everyone. Over the last few days I can feel myself improving by leaps and bounds. I'll be better soon, I just know it. The doctors and therapists keep telling me I should be satisfied with baby steps, but I'm not. I want to make giant strides, and that's what I'm doing.

They're giving me a lot more freedom as a result. I've talked with friends all around the world by phone and instant messages. I spoke with my former teammate Geoffroy LeQuatre who now rides for Cofidis. He sent me a link to an article he wrote which was published in a French cycling magazine. It explained how he cried like a child in the arms of another friend when he heard the news of my injury, and it asked why bad things like this are allowed to happen to the best sort of people. He said he didn't have the right to judge other men, but that doesn't mean he can't hold the opinion that I'm among the best. What a kind thing for him to say. Then he marveled that I'm driven by dreams a hundred times larger than he's capable of imagining. He said his background wouldn't allow him such optimism, and he wondered if it's an American peculiarity. Then he ended by saying he loved me.

It's not half as beautiful in English as French, but the sentiment is still there. Reading it brought me to tears. I'm honored to have friends like Geoff who care so much.

Nearly every member of my extended family has visited, and most of them can't believe how well I'm doing. They say that all the time, and it makes me proud to exceed their expectations. Aunt Louise, that's my grandma's sister, reminded me Mother's Day is coming up. I don't know where my wallet has gone, so I don't have any money for a present. My mom deserves something incredibly special. I'm sure there isn't a better mom on this planet. She's gone to hell and back for me. I've tried to borrow money from everybody I could think of, including the nurses and doctors, but nobody will give me any.

Somebody must have told Mom what I was up to. "You don't need to buy me a present," she says.

My tears started flowing just like that. "Yes I do. You deserve the world. I wish I could wrap it up for you."

Mom's crying now, too. "You've already done that, Saul, just by being here."

"But I've got to give you something, something special."

Mom dries her eyes with a tissue then says, "Okay. I'll tell you what I want most, but I've got to warn you, it won't be easy for you to give."

"Perfect. What is it?"

"I want you to walk across the room and give me a big hug by Mother's Day."

I think I've mentioned I want to win the Tour de France one day. I've put every ounce of my energy toward that goal for many years now, but let me say this: I never wanted it half as badly as I want to give my mom this gift. I've got six days to accomplish my goal. I'm going to do it. Nothing on earth can stop me.

As evening comes, after all the conversation and excitement my brain won't work any more. I feel the fog rolling in as thick as ever. It's kind of like being pushed out to sea in a small lifeboat with no oar. I become more and more isolated and there's nothing I can do about it. It scares me when this happens. Soon they put me into my bed and leave the room so sleep can restore my mind.

By morning I'm feeling much better. As Ruth Ann helps me shower I feel strong. It's not easy to avoid asking her to take her clothes off and join me, but I'm determined to resist. I try to think about something other than the fact that I'm naked in the presence of a gorgeous woman. I decide to try to stand. It will be a big step toward walking to my mom.

"Saul, what are you doing?" Ruth Ann catches me as I fall sideways into the tile wall.

"I want to walk to my mother," I say.

"I've heard that. You can work on it later with Lauren, but you can't be so impulsive. Your body isn't ready to stand on its own. Give it time." Her clothes are all wet from reaching into the shower to grab me. She's still a little bit mad as she dries me off and dresses me for the day, but Ruth Ann is a very kind woman. She gets over it quickly and tells me it's a good thing I'm so determined to improve.

She helps me shave. It's strange that I've never had to shave daily in my life, but now I could shave twice a day and still be stubbly. My fingernails are growing like crazy, and for the first time ever there is hair on my chest. I can't help wondering if these changes are related to my injury. My body is just plain different now.

Nowadays I'm pretty mobile in my chair. I like to go room to room looking for sweets. It's amazing how many goodies get left around this place. I know several spots where there are permanent stashes. I could clean them out entirely, but if I returned fifteen minutes later there would be candy again.

I'm now required to drag my chair to the scheduling board every day before breakfast. I guess it's been here all along, but I could never understand it before. It's a big metal wall with all sorts of magnets stuck to it. There's a nameplate for each patient. To the right the day is broken into time blocks and in each block the therapists have placed a magnet that corresponds to one of the day's tasks. Among the codes are "M" for meal, "PT" for physical therapy, "OT" for occupational therapy, and "ST" for speech therapy. That's the therapy I like least. It's not just for speech but for all the mental stuff. I'm much more concerned with the physical stuff. Not only is that where I get my walking practice, but it's the therapy that's eventually going to give me back my life.

There's another coded magnet I look forward to more than anything else: "BTB" for back to bed. No matter how much I want to improve, my craving for sleep remains insatiable. Unfortunately, the BTB magnet is showing up on my schedule less and less frequently these days. Today, I'm disappointed to discover that as soon as breakfast is over my day will start with speech therapy, and the only "BTB" on my entire schedule comes at eight in the evening. A midday nap would be such a huge help. I consider trying to move some magnets around, but they're out of my reach.

I write down my schedule as I'm required to; then it's my responsibility to be where I'm supposed to for the rest of the day. When I report to my first station I try to explain to Amy how important it is that I work on walking rather than talking, but she's not interested. She doesn't care about my physical problems at all. She thinks her stuff is much more important. She tells me I need to start recognizing nonverbal cues, like facial expressions. She also says my speech is too flat and she wants me to work on intonation. She says things and varies her voice in different ways. Then she asks me to imitate her and explain the differences in meaning.

"How is this going to help me walk?" I ask.

"I know you like the physical stuff, but the best athletes have to be on top of their game mentally even more than physically," she says. "Have you ever thought about that?"

I'll think about it later. "I want to walk."

"Saul," she says, "there's more to life than physical activities, even for a pro cyclist. Now we're going to work on mental skills."

I have no choice but to obey her rules, so I do, but I'm watching other patients walk out of the corner of my eye, and it's making me very jealous. I want to be doing anything other than this mental work.

"You're beautiful, Amy," I say.

She smiles knowingly. "And?"

"And you're sweet," I say.

She nods her head. "And?"

I might as well see if I can get what I want. "And can I have a cookie?"

Amy shakes her head. "The international lover strikes again."

She slides a dot to dot book in front of me and then turns her attention to another patient while I start doing puzzles. What a pain. I keep telling people how important it is that I learn to walk in the next few days, but nobody seems to care.

In my next therapy session I have to kick a soccer ball around and then do a test to see how fast I can put colored pegs into matching holes with each hand.

Finally, after lunch, the time comes to meet with Lauren. Sean, the big former football player with dreadlocks, is with her, and that's a good sign. It means he's going to be helping me stand up like he did the other day.

"I've got to work on walking," I say.

She laughs. "There's not a person in this ward who isn't aware of that, Saul. You're something else when you get a goal in mind. I've never seen anything quite like it. Wouldn't you agree, Sean?"

Sean chuckles. "For sure."

I smile. "That's a good thing, right?"

"To be honest, good and bad," Lauren says. "It's great that you're so motivated to walk, but not so good if you overlook other important tasks along the way. Your speech therapy is important. Healing your mind is as critical as healing your body. If you're not mentally sharp, you'll never be able to ride a bike."

Her explanation bores me. "I just want to walk. Can I try now?"

"Yeah. Let's get to work." She straps a thick cotton gait belt around my waist so if I stumble she can break my fall. Then she tapes up my left knee.

I look at her curiously.

"You've been hyper-extending it. This will help."

Sean stands up and holds onto the belt behind me. "Let's see how hard you're really willing to work," he says.

My balance has deserted me, but I'm able to lean back on Sean for support. I'm feeling lots more sensation in my left leg than before. All the work dragging around the wheelchair seems to have helped. The leg's still not back, but it's on its way. I also notice the tape on the knee helps. Lauren knows her stuff.

The work is very hard and painful, but satisfying. It taxes my concentration and willpower to the limit. Sean patiently supports me as I walk across the room. "Do you need a rest?" he asks.

"I'm not going to take one," I say. If he asks me to take two steps, I won't stop until I take four, or maybe eight. If they suggest a ten-minute break, I'll try to talk them into five. My professional occupation has taught me how to push my limits, and now I'm going to push them as far as I possibly can.

Lauren has been watching me closely. "I've got another idea that might help out," she says. She gets out her tape and wraps it beneath the toes of my left foot then behind my calf several times. The resulting harness holds my foot rigid.

"You're dragging your toes. This will help keep them out of your way."

We walk some more, and I can soon see Lauren was right. It's easier now, and instead of simply dragging the left foot up even with the right, I'm able to move it at least a little bit in front of me. It feels a lot more like a normal walking motion. I cross the room again.

"I can't believe I'm saying this," Lauren says as I reach the wall, "but I think he's ready for the stairs. They'll help you build strength, Saul."

I'm already very tired, but I don't want them to sense my weakness. I learned how to hide physical stress in cycling. It's one of the keys to winning. "Let's do it," I say.

They take me to the stairway that leads out of the waiting room. This time I don't feel nervous to be leaving the Acquired Brain Injury Ward. Lauren stands on the stair in front of me in case I fall forward, Sean is behind, holding me by the gait belt.

"Okay. Go when you're ready," Sean says.

"Right foot," Lauren says.

"Right foot," I repeat, telling the foot to obey. I grit my teeth as I lift it toward the top of the first step. My toe bumps into the riser and I lose my balance. Sean saves me from falling on my face.

"Lift your foot as high as you possibly can before moving it forward," Lauren says. "You'll need to lift it much higher than you think you have to."

I try again, this time as if I'm stepping onto the winner's podium at a bike race. I move my foot forward until it lands on top of the stair. Success momentarily satisfies me.

"Left foot," Lauren says.

"Left foot," I repeat so the foot will hear. I suck in air; then I lean forward to pull my left foot up behind me. I'm not worrying about staying balanced because I trust Sean for that. I just want to strengthen my legs. I get the foot onto the top of the stair. I'm now standing on level ground again. I'm already breathing hard, and I'm feeling dizzy, too.

"Good. Take a rest," Lauren says.

But I don't want to. I know momentum can be a powerful ally when attacking a slope, and I also believe my strength will be improved by pushing my limits.

"Right foot," I say. Even though my head is swirling I lift my right leg up to the next step. "Left foot." Then I pull it up behind me.

"Good, Saul," Lauren says.

Next step. My breathing is getting faster now and my legs are throbbing. It's not the burning sensation I love so much from a tough workout, but more of an ache. I'm sure it's doing me good. "Right foot," I say as I lift the right foot again. "Left foot." I drag the other one behind.

Lauren looks surprised as she moves backward in front of me. Her expression motivates me to keep her off balance. "Right foot … Left foot."

She backs up again. "Right foot … Left foot." If not for Sean I would be in trouble. I can feel him partially carrying me from behind. I'm happy for the help and willing to take full advantage.

"Don't go too fast, Saul. There's no hurry," Lauren says.

There is for me. "Right foot … Left foot." Now my legs are really nearing their limit and my breathing is ragged, but I love seeing Lauren's surprised expression as she takes a step backward so I contract my muscles again. "Right foot … Left foot."

Sean grunts. He's not completely lifting me, but he is doing his fair share of the work just to keep me balanced.

There are two more stairs between me and the landing. Cycling has taught me that the last portion of the slope usually separates the winners from the losers. The guys who really know how to push through pain are always the champions. "Right foot … Left foot."

I imagine a "King of the Mountains" banner at the top of the next step. I'll be able to take a long rest once I get there. "Right foot …" I feel my toe kick the top of the riser, but fortunately it deflects above the step. "Left foot." It takes all my remaining strength to pull it up behind me. I collapse toward Lauren's arms.

She grabs me.

"My head is spinning." It feels like I've just done a VO2 Max test, an all-out effort. My eyes roll back, and for a moment I think I might faint. I twist around in Lauren's arms and now I'm looking down the stairs. The height is frightening. It's a sensation I've never experienced before. Quickly, Lauren and Sean lower me to a seated position, and things begin to clear.

"Well done, Saul," Lauren says. "You don't have to push yourself so hard, though. We still have plenty of time before Mother's Day. I think you're going to make it."

Thinking I'll make it isn't good enough. I won't be able to relax until I actually make it. If Lauren really believes I don't need to push myself, it's clear she doesn't yet know me too well. Pushing my limits as hard as I can is the only way I know to live.

I'm almost drained of energy by the time bedtime arrives, but I have a little bit left so I lie here lifting my hundred pound hand over my head again and again until I finally fall asleep.

The next morning my legs are still aching, but they feel stronger than before. I'm returning, relentlessly, to the person I used to be. The progress only makes me want to push harder.

Amy helps me with my shower this time, and I tell her, "I'm ready to walk to my mom today."

She always wears the happiest expression, even when she says, "No, Saul. I think you need to give it a couple more days."

I look forward to proving her, and anybody else who doubts me, wrong. I'm walking to Mom today.

By the time my parents arrive I'm hearing the same sorts of things I heard the day before. "Saul, you're too impulsive." "Saul, once you get a goal in mind you can be exhausting." "Saul, you've got to take baby steps." I appreciate all the help and advice the people here have given me, but I'm not letting any of them talk me into taking things easy. I'm going to walk to my mom today no matter what they say.

I drag my chair over to Lauren and whisper, "It's time."

"I don't think you're ready, Saul, but I'm going to let you try." She straps a gait belt on me and calls Sean over.

"Don't tell my mom what we're doing. Just let me surprise her," I say.

I watch Lauren put my mom into position.

"Let me help you to your feet," Sean says.

I shake my head. "No. I'll stand up myself." I push down on the armrests of my wheelchair as hard as I can. My eyes squeeze shut with the effort, and it increases the head rush I always get when I rise, but then I'm standing. I keep hold of the wheelchair armrests behind me for support. I know I'm not going to be able to stay in this position for long though, so I'd better walk quick.

I straighten the rest of the way, and then I'm ready to walk. Right foot.

Mom's mouth drops open in amazement.

Left foot.

"Saul?" I hear Dad say.

Right foot.

Mom lifts her arms as if to catch me. A patient yells, "Attaboy, Saul!"

Left foot.

I feel my weight moving too far forward.

Right foot.

She's within reach and just in time. What little balance I had has deserted me. I throw my arms over her shoulders and lean on her for support. How many steps did I take? I think maybe twenty or so.

I'm completely spent, but that doesn't matter. I did it!

Dad is crying when he embraces us. "Those were the toughest four steps I've ever seen in my life. Way to go, Saul!"

Only four steps? I look up at Lauren and see the tears in her eyes. She kisses her fingertips and touches them to my cheek. As Sean lifts me away from my mom I hear him sniffle as well.

Of course, I'm crying. My emotions have come back over the last few days, and to say they're out of control is an understatement. I don't mind. Life is good, and there is a lot to be emotional about. I don't see the point in trying to hold anything in, especially when it comes to letting the people I care about most know how much they mean to me.

As Sean sits me back in the wheelchair I get my first glimpse of my mom's face. She's bawling harder than I've ever seen her, but it's happy crying. "Oh Saul, what a gift! You're returning to life. You're doing things the doctors once told us would be impossible. I almost can't believe this is happening."

"Nothing is impossible, Mom. I can do anything I set my mind to."

She grins. "Just set your mind to getting well."

I shake my head. "That's not enough for me. I'm going to reclaim my old life. I was given this brain injury to test my will, and I've got to prove I can conquer it."

Chapter Six

Before the day is through I call many friends to tell them about the gift I gave to my mother. I explain how everybody in the room cried, and I can tell some of them cry as we talk. I feel prouder of this than of any other accomplishment in my life so far. It took everything I had, all my strength, all my concentration, all my will power.

Roger is so happy to hear the news. Dean of Rocket 7 Cycling Shoes tells me I'm more than just an athlete they sponsor; I'm one of their family. Axel Merckx, a cyclist I admire for his ethics even more than his almost poetic ability to race a bike, says I have inspired him. His father, Eddie Merckx is widely regarded as the greatest cyclist in history. What a great day this is!

Doctor Bilsky tells my parents and me how proud he is of my recovery. He says the injury I sustained came as close to killing me as it possibly could, yet now I'm thriving. He says it's impossible to compare any two brain-injured patients because we understand so little about the mind and what the underlying damage from any particular injury might be, but he also says my rapid recovery so far indicates a total return to health should be possible. He tells my parents I've reached this point much more quickly than he'd thought possible. I'm among the top echelon of patients recovering from this level of injury. Of course, only time will tell if I'll be able to overcome all my problems.

Mom says, "Saul dreams of getting his old life back. Is returning to bike racing a reasonable dream?"

Dr. Bilsky thinks for a moment. "It's exceedingly rare to send a patient with an injury like Saul's back into a high-risk profession. I wouldn't consider putting a man who fell from scaffolding back on a precarious perch again, but maybe Saul's situation will be different. If returning to racing is the dream that motivates him to work as hard as he is, I'm certainly not going to take it away until I see something that proves it would be impossible."

"Is he at greater risk than others riding bikes, though?" Dad asks.

"He obviously doesn't yet have the balance or coordination to handle a bicycle, but it looks like those skills are starting to return. Hopefully they will return completely."

"No," Dad says. "I mean, assuming his skills return, would he be at greater risk for another head injury?"

Dr. Bilsky shook his head. "We need to take every precaution to make sure he doesn't suffer a blow to his head in the twelve to eighteen months following his accident. Until the bruising on his brain completely heals he'll be more susceptible to brain injury than a healthy person. A car crash that might be no major deal for someone with no previous impact could be more problematic. Once his brain has healed, though, I'm not convinced his risk of complications in a future injury will be so great that restricting him will be necessary."

After the doctor leaves Mom says, "Dad and I are attending family-therapy sessions. In France we often wondered why you didn't even seem to be aware of your injuries. Do you know what the problem was?"

I shake my head, not really understanding the question.

"The brain is in charge of interpreting the signals the body sends to it, but a damaged brain can't always do that correctly. Your brain was unable to tell you you'd been hurt."

I can't make sense of her words, but she apparently can and it seems to make her feel better, so that makes me happy.

Later that day another patient and I are talking in the hallway. His name is Zach Phillips, and in many ways he looks like me. Were both pretty skinny with buzzed brown hair and brown eyes, and we're also about the same age. His parents and my parents have become friends. They've told me Zach was a paralegal from Washington, D.C. They explained that he was hit by a car while crossing the street and suffered a serious brain injury very similar to mine.

Zach is proud of me for walking and I'm encouraging him to do it too. Our conversation starts to ramble, and soon we're talking about life at Shepherds, especially all the beautiful nurses. We decide it's impossible to say which one is the hottest.

I watch Lauren go into a room. Moments later she comes back out. "Have you ever wondered what's in there?" I ask, pointing to the door she just used.

Zach shakes his head. "Nope. I know what's in there."

"What?" I ask.

"Food."

I almost can't believe my ears. I pull my chair over to the door and twist the knob. It opens. I reach up and flip on the light switch. The place is filled with food. I look back at Zach. "Get in here!"

We roll inside and shut the door. I discover a six pack of chocolate pudding. There are no spoons available, and I can't express how happy I am about that. I'm sick and tired of manners. I rip the foil lid off one of the pudding packages and stick my tongue inside. Oh, it tastes so good! I lick what I can out of the corners, but there's no point in wasting time getting every bit because there are lots more packages. I toss the empty aside and grab another and then another. Zach is now eating them, too. Neither of us is talking, but we do grin at one another now and then.

Suddenly the door opens. It's Sean. "Over here everybody. I found them."

Uh oh. We're in trouble. I throw down my pudding package and try to act natural. Zach does too.

Moments later half the staff and both my parents arrive.

"What in the heck do you think you're doing, Saul?" Mom says.

"Just talking," I say.

Dad shakes his head. "Well, did you happen to notice that a case of chocolate pudding busted open and practically buried you?"

Is that really what he thinks happened? We just might get away with this. "No, I hadn't," I say.

"Saul, remember how I've mentioned that you need to start learning how to read nonverbal cues?" Amy asks.

"Yeah."

"Well," she says. "This would be a really good time to start, because you're missing out on facefuls of really good ones at the moment."

After several more hours of therapy I'm lying in my bed, aching from another long, hard day. The work here is so tough. The fatigue I'm feeling goes beyond anything I've ever experienced before, and the difficult exercise continues day after day after day. I understand it's important for me to do this work, but sometimes I can't keep myself from begging my therapists to take me back to bed.

They never do until the prescheduled time.

Instead, they push me harder. I grit my teeth and continue, often growling with frustration. Whether the therapists know it or not, it isn't their demands that are making me react this way, it's my progress. I'd expected to be back racing in Europe by now, but other than a few random steps I can't even walk yet.

Maybe I've been wrong about the blue skies. Maybe the doctor who told me to accept the reality of life in a wheelchair knows more about my capabilities than I do. Who am I trying to fool? Where am I going? Is it even remotely possible to make it? Is it time to accept that my old life will be forever dead to me, or am I going to live again?

At the same time, there are moments when I feel the energy flowing back into my body. Sometimes I believe the old Saul is returning. I think about getting my old life back constantly, and the desire only increases each time somebody sits down with me and asks to hear some of my stories.

Right now it's Amy asking me questions. "Do you think your near-death experience has changed who you are?"

I grin. "Absolutely. I'm more passionate and emotional now. I value people and friendships more than I did before. I've changed in lots of ways. This isn't my first near death experience, though. I've had several of them. Maybe God has been trying to send me this message for a long time, but it took going through the worst thing possible for me to finally understand it."

She nods. "I've heard about some of your other crashes."

"You haven't heard about this. One day while on a training ride on the coast of France between Monaco and Nice I heard a sound like a thousand thunder claps all at once. Suddenly a rock the size of a minivan rammed into the road just behind me. I turned around in shock. It hit so hard the pavement bent into the hole it made. For a moment, while I collected my thoughts, I leaned up against the rock for support. It was so large that even though it embedded itself into the earth it still stood about as high as my head."

Amy's eyes are wide. "You weren't hit by shrapnel?"

"Nope."

"You must have a guardian angel sitting on your shoulder full time," she says.

I nod, and hold back a tear. I'm pretty sure she's right, and I think I know who my angel is, but I don't tell her about that part.

"What did you do?" she asks.

"I stayed there for only a moment, looking at the cliff above and trying to figure out what had happened. Then I realized if I'd been in a slightly different spot they wouldn't have found a trace of me for weeks."

"Did you talk to the police?" Amy asks.

I shake my head. "It wasn't a safe place to hang around, so I just started riding again, but later that day I returned home on the same road. By the time I neared the rock, traffic was a mess. Cars were backed up in both directions for miles, taking their turns going around it. They closed the road for at least a week while they smashed the boulder into pieces then resurfaced the road."

Amy shakes her head. "Are you teasing me?"

I cross my heart. "No. Why would I? And even if I did, your spirit is so pure you'd see right through me."

She nods. "It might not be due to my pure spirit, but I can tell your story is true. I'm glad that rock missed you. I'm happy we've become friends."

"Me too," I say.

That evening after my hardest day of therapy yet I'm sitting in my bed when the phone rings. It's my Aunt Vera, my mother's sister. "How's your recovery coming, Saul?"

"Good. I was thinking about you today," I say.

"How come?"

"I was telling racing stories and someone said I must have a guardian angel. Of course I do, and you know who it is."

"Dustin?" she asks.

She knows she's right. Her son was special to me. Two years ago, when he was fifteen he went to a dance with his baseball team. It was supposed to be a nondrinking affair, but someone brought alcohol. That night Dustin rode home in a car with five others. It was raining hard and the driver was tipsy. He was over the speed limit when he lost control on a corner and the car slammed into a bridge pylon. Dustin didn't make it to the hospital. I feel so angry about that night. Since then I've felt Dustin's presence at my side many times.

I'm in tears again, just thinking about it. We were such good friends. I have quite a few cousins, but Dustin was the only boy who was close to me in age. Throughout childhood I recall how excited I always was to see him. I still can't believe he's gone.

His mom can't either. She's suffered bouts of depression ever since. I can hear her crying on the other end of the line. We're both in pure misery when my parents walk into the room.

I hand my mom the phone, and Aunt Vera tells her she's decided to visit us the next day. Every time I hear that somebody new is coming it increases my motivation to work hard in therapy. The more work I do, the more skills I'll have once these people see me, and the more I'll amaze them. I'm glad so many people are counting on me to recover. I love the pressure it creates.

Over the next few days I have lots of visitors. It's great to see Aunt Vera in person as well as my cousins from Dad's side of the family. I hug them all, many times. I don't think I can ever get enough of hugging the people I love.

I especially enjoy hearing firsthand from my five-year-old cousin Noah about his bike riding, and from his twin sister Megan about her ballet. I've always liked kids, but I'm crazy about them now. As strange as it might sound, I wish somebody would bring a baby to visit me. I'd love to hold an infant. To me they are so pure. I think, in a way, I'd have a unique understanding of his or her world because of the rebirth I've been through.

*   *   *

It's Mother's Day today, the day I'd initially planned to walk. I'm proud I beat that goal by a wide margin, but I expected to be walking around normally by now, so I'm disappointed at the same time. I've been working on a poem for my mom during speech therapy, and I'm very proud to give it to her now.

She takes the paper from my hand. "Saul, your handwriting is so tiny and hard to read."

I laugh. "What do you expect? I almost died. Give me a while to learn how again."

She chuckles with me as she holds the paper up and squints at my shaky lettering:

Dear Mom, I love you with all my heart.
Dear Mom, You have been with me from the start.
Dear Mom, you will always be a part.
You have a place in my heart.

Dear Mom, I'm going to be OK,
I know you will be with me every day.

"What do these next two lines say?" she asks.

I look at them and shrug. Even to me they're nothing but chicken scratching. "Go on to the end."

She starts reading again:

Dear Mom, I love you with all my heart.
You are the best mom in the world.

"What a wonderful poem, Saul. Thank you."

I hug her, and Dad hugs me too. At times like these there is an incredibly powerful feeling that flows among the three of us. I can't explain what causes it, but I know it makes me a stronger person. I couldn't imagine how I would have survived this whole ordeal without my parents at my side.

Every day I'm becoming more able to push my body. I give therapy everything I have, not just the physical stuff but the mental stuff too. Bit by bit, the thinking started to click and now I'm solving problems that confused me only a short time ago. The mental work has been ten-fold harder than the physical therapy. Amy was right about that. My body often aches from mental effort. It doesn't matter whether that makes sense. If you're brain says you're in pain, you're in pain, and that's the way it is. At least that's what I think my brain has been doing to me.

I'm still not able to do math too well, but I'll get there. I have an easier time talking, too. It's not just that my throat doesn't hurt so much, but that the words come to me more easily. In fact, Dad often tells me I have too much to say.

My walking is also stronger than it was the day I walked to Mom, but if anything my balance is worse. I haven't taken that many steps on my own again yet. Lauren says the balance will come, and it's a good sign I'm able to stand up holding onto support for long periods of time.

One afternoon John Kelley, my old coach from USA Cycling days, and Jim Birrell, the top race director in the United States, come by for a visit.

Jim hands me a Tour de Georgia winner's jersey. "This is for you, Saul. Whether you come back to pro cycling or not, you're already a champion in my book."

I hand the jersey back. "No thanks. I'm going to win one on my own. What I'm going through is making me stronger mentally than I ever could have been before. I'm going to eventually win all your races, plus the Tour de France, Worlds, and a whole bunch more."

Jim looks at me like he's not certain what to make of my confidence.

"He's doing a lot of big talking these days," Dad says. "Saul still doesn't realize the time or effort it's going to take him to heal."

"Oh, I realize it," I say. "That doesn't mean I can't accomplish those goals."

Jim gives the jersey to Dad. "If he ever waivers in his motivation, maybe you could wave this around in front of his nose a bit."

Dad nods. "I doubt I'll do that. I think most people here would like to see his motivation die off a tad at this point. Saul is doing his best to drive his therapists crazy."

I wave him off. "That's not true. My therapists love me."

"Yeah," Dad says. "Right."

After my guests leave, Lauren steps into my room. "How would you like to take a spin on the stationary bike, Saul?"

I can't imagine a suggestion that could possibly make me happier. I cruise down the hall, my wheelchair practically skidding out on the corners.

Lauren helps me onto the bike. It doesn't matter that it bears little resemblance to the bicycles I ride for a living. It has two pedals and a seat, and that's all I need.

"Let's see if you can go for ten minutes," she says.

"Good luck stopping me that soon," I say. Once I start riding I know I'll never want to stop. I begin pedaling. My right leg is so much stronger than my left, my pedal stroke is a study in clumsiness. Stroke efficiency is as important as strength in riding a bike at the highest levels, and I had perfected my pedal stroke as well as anybody. That's not true anymore, though. My legs don't move in smooth circles, but in herky-jerky stops and starts. "Can you increase the resistance?" I'm hoping some tension will help me even out my stroke.

Lauren turns a knob. "I don't want to make it very hard."

My pedaling improves slightly under the load. I feel my heart rate start to rise. Soon I'm turning the cranks at around sixty revolutions per minute and I settle into a comfort zone. This is the feeling I love more than any other. I might be on a rusty old stationary bike in the corner of a brain injury therapy unit, but the sensations emanating from my legs transport my mind to the storied roads of France. In my imagination I'm tapping out a smooth cadence as I attack my favorite European training ride, the Col de la Madone. I wonder if anybody has ever felt such an overwhelming sensation of freedom while pedaling a trainer before. It feels like I'm going to ride it off into the sky. I have wings.

My cadence has picked up even more, and then I feel a familiar trickle run down my face. For once, it isn't the trickle of tears. I've broken a sweat for the first time in well over a month. I've worked hard, but I haven't done aerobic effort until now. I wipe my right hand across my forehead and lick the fingers. The salty sensation is, to me, the taste of life; but circumstance makes this different than any sweat I've ever tasted before. It's the sweetest nectar to touch my tongue in all my twenty-three years, and it reassures me I can return, all the way.

Chapter Seven

I rode for over twenty minutes, but afterwards my legs were spent. I'm disappointed I wasn't able to ride longer, but I just don't have the strength. I wish I could have gone for an hour … or two. We arrive back at my room at the same time my parents return.

"Saul just rode the stationary bike," Lauren says. "He did great."

I feel very happy inside. "Mom, if I ever ride bicycles again I have to help people who are like me."

"That's a nice thought, Saul," Mom says.

"I want to show people they can do anything they set their mind to if they refuse to give up," I say.

Mom and Dad have big smiles on their faces as they each give me hugs. I'm exhausted, and quickly fall into a heavy sleep.

Sometime in the night I hear movement. I open my eyes and see my mom reaching into my nightstand drawer.

"What a great sleep I had," I say.

Mom looks at her watch. "Saul, you've only been asleep for five minutes. I just forgot my book and had to come back."

There are times I wonder whether my confusion has any boundaries. How could I shut my eyes for five minutes and think I'd slept through an entire night? Mom kisses me on the forehead and leaves, but thoughts are running around in my head now and I can't get back to sleep.

For at least two weeks they've been trying to teach me to walk. They hook me up in a harness supported by two parallel bars. It looks sort of like a gymnastics apparatus. My goal is to walk the length of the bars without using either my hands or the harness for support. I'm not even close yet. So far, other than my Mother's Day gift of four steps, the most I've accomplished is a single stride.

I go to bed after failing again each day, exhaustion and soreness my only rewards for the effort. The accident has stolen a lot from me, and it is very hard—harder than words can express—to get it back.

I do feel some strength returning to my left leg, though, so that's good. I don't completely drag it now, and I think the cycling is going to help even more. The bigger problem is that I still have no balance. I'm as dizzy when I stand up as I was the first time they walked me to the bathroom and I looked into the mirror. I used to think lack of strength was the main thing stopping me from walking, but now I think balance is a bigger problem.

Lying there thinking, I feel the urge to use the portable urinal. I'm very bad at holding it still, and always spill some, so I push the call button for help. Within about a minute Keith walks in. He's a giant man, at least six and a half feet tall, who often helps me in the evenings or at night.

"Need to go to the bathroom?" he asks.

I nod.

He makes a sort of shooing motion with his arm. "Get up, then. You're walking to the toilet tonight."

Hasn't he been paying attention to my progress? "What are you talking about? I can't walk by myself yet."

Keith seems a little annoyed by my comment. "Come on. How do you know unless you try?"

He reaches into my bed and stands me up. I totter on my feet for a moment and then stabilize. Suddenly I realize I'm not going to fall back down this time. I swear, it's like someone turned on a light bulb in my brain. I literally felt my balance come rushing back. I stare at Keith. "Oh my God. I have balance!"

Keith flashes me a big, sparkly grin. "You do? Show me."

So I walk unassisted to the toilet. In the span of a few hours I'd gone from walking only with constant support to walking alone. I feel triumphant. I use the toilet standing up for the first time in nearly two months. I feel like a man again!

In this moment I catch the vision of becoming a complete and healthy person more vividly than I have since my ordeal began. Before now a return to my own life was only the product of a healthy imagination. Now it's real! I can't stop smiling.

"Good job, Saul," Keith says. "I'm proud of you."

"Yeah. This is a good day. Thank you, Keith."

For a long time I've been saying I'm going to accomplish this, but it's another thing entirely to actually do it. Standing before this toilet is a luxury I haven't had for a long time, and it changes everything about my future.

All night long I dream of how I'm going to show different people my newfound skill. I can't wait for my mom and dad to experience the return of my balance, or for my therapists to see this major change. There are many, many people I can't wait to walk to, but there's one person I look forward to walking past. By morning I come up with a plan, and I soon talk Sean into helping.

He hangs around the nurses' station waiting for Dr. Dan to stop by and review patient's charts. When Sean walks into my room I can tell from his expression the timing is right. I'm so excited I can hardly control my breathing. He helps me to a standing position. I start walking out my door. Sean stays close behind, ready to break my fall with the gait belt if I stumble, but he doesn't support my weight. I know I've got a bit of a weeble-wobble gait, but that doesn't matter right now. All that matters is that I'm doing what this doctor thought I could never do again.

Dr. Dan notices me and looks up. His eyes go wide and his mouth drops open. I wave as nonchalantly as I can. I've never gotten such pleasure from a simple gesture before, and I probably never will again. I don't stop walking until I'm past the nurses' station. I'm so damned happy I could do a wheelie.

Is it wrong of me to get such pleasure from doing something partly because somebody said I would never do it again? They said I would never walk, so I say I will run. They said I could never ride a bike, so I say I'll compete in another race. I will not give up. Even if something appears impossible, today has reminded me that there's no way anybody can prevent me from trying to accomplish whatever I set my mind to.

Later in the day I show off my walking to all the other people I've dreamed of showing off to. When Lauren sees she asks, "What got into you today, Saul?" When my parents see me Dad says, "It's sudden, just like when you learned to talk again." But throughout the whole day, no step I take is half as satisfying as the ones in front of slack-jawed Dr. Dan.

That evening after therapy Dad comes to my room with tears in his eyes. "I've just received a wonderful gift, Saul." He holds out at least fifty printed pages. "Here are words of encouragement from your friends and competitors in cycling. They were written while you were at your worst. These people, more than most others, understand what you've gone through and why you want to return to endure more. They meant their messages to get to us while we were in France, but I only found time to look at them today."

I take the papers from his hand and read:

DEAR FRIENDS,

I think that you already hear what happened with our friend Saul last Tuesday in the race. Saul was in a crash, Saul fell with about 2km to go in the 193km stage from Mouilleron Le Captif to Saint Mars La Jaille, breaking his clavicle and one rib as well as suffering serious cuts and abrasions to his face.

Saul is in serious condition at a hospital in Angers, France due to injuries he sustained during the opening stage of the Circuit de la Sarthe.

Saul , 23, suffered a brain hemorrhage early Thursday morning, forcing doctors to induce a coma* to stabilize his condition and reduce pressure on the brain

I am writing you all to ask for your prayers for a close friend of us and USA Cycling. I know that miracles can happen which is what he needs now.

Saul is a strong guy and I know he is fighting hard in his bad position in the hospital in France.

Kindest Regards

Chris De Vos   Noël Dejonckheere
soigneur U-23 NATIONAL TEAM   TEAM MANAGER

*(author's note: it was initially incorrectly reported that Saul's coma was drug induced)

I flip through the pages. There are hundreds of messages, many from close friends, some of whom I haven't seen in a long time. Among the messages from former teammates, mechanics, directeurs, and others are kind wishes from some of the biggest personalities in USA Cycling. I notice names like George Hincapie, Frankie Andreu, Jim Ochowicz, Dave Chauner, Craig Lewis, Sean Petty, Marty Nothstein, Jeff Louder, Dr. Max Testa, and Tyler Wren. A message from my personal coach, Jim Lehman, says:

> Saul,
> This is a tough time, but you are an exceptional individual and I know you will fight with everything you have to get through. Know that you and your family are in my heart and my thoughts. Stay strong, my friend.

A note from Steven Cozza includes the comment:

> … you are one of the toughest, strongest humans I have ever met. You have inspired me so much and continue to do so and I know without a doubt that you will recover fully from this because you are Saul Raisin, one of the most courageous cyclists in the pro peloton.

Someone else wrote:

> A friend once told me that to move forward we need to see problems and setbacks as opportunities. That one piece of advice has been unbelievably powerful in my own life. Embrace the support network that you have in your friends and family. Take care and get well soon.

I notice a message from the fastest time-trialist in the history of the Tour de France, Dave Zabriskie. It says:

> I have never really been one to say prayers but today I tried to say one for my friend Saul. I hope that things continue to improve for Saul and that he makes a full recovery. My thoughts are with you guys. Take care and stay strong!

There are a few lines from my European roommate, Tyler Farrar:

> Of course all my thoughts and prayers are with Saul and his family. I am sure that he will be able to pull through this and make a recovery. He is one of the kindest people I have ever met and I hope with all my heart that he makes a quick and full recovery.

And then a note from Timmy Duggan catches my eye:

> God says, and I truly believe that, everything happens for a reason, as hard as it is to accept at times like this. Find that reason for yourself and your path to recovery will be far less difficult. Believe in yourself and don't stop fighting.

I look up at Dad. My eyes are filled with tears. I feel gratitude for all this friendship, and at the same time I feel renewed confusion over why this happened to me. If Timmy's right, if there is a reason, what is it? Is there a lesson I'm supposed to learn? Is there something I'm meant to accomplish? Is there a change in my life I'm supposed to make? I know there must be something. I desperately want to become a better person for having gone through this. Many people have suffered alongside me as I've recovered, and I owe it to them to make the most of this opportunity. What is it I need to do next?

Chapter Eight

I've been in my room alone thinking for a long time when my parents return. "There's something we need to talk about, Saul. Your eating habits are terrible."

"I'm trying as hard as I can," I say. "My left arm is still weak and uncoordinated. I have a hard time hitting my mouth with the spoon."

Dad shakes his head. "That's not what I'm talking about. You're over the edge on eating chocolates and sweets. Barbara and David brought by a plate full of cookies this morning. Where are they now?"

"Someone ate them."

"Yeah. I know who," Dad says. "And the nurses keep a bowl of candy at their station for visitors, but it was empty when we came in. Do you know why?"

I smile. "I didn't eat it."

He lifts my shirt. "Look at that pooch of a stomach you're developing. Where do you think it's coming from? Your mom and I are frightened to death by your desire to return to pro cycling so I don't know exactly what to say about this, because we aren't going to have anything to worry about if you keep packing the pounds on like this."

"Once they really start letting me exercise I'll burn off all my fat, no problem."

"Not a good plan. You need to eat healthy whether you're getting exercise or not. If nothing else, your brain needs good food to help it heal." Dad's happy mood when he arrived today seems to have evaporated. His voice remains serious. "I spoke with your nutritionist on the way in. He agreed with me and made a memo for the staff. No more sweets for Saul."

I don't like hearing this news, but what can I do? I'm sure I'll still be able to talk people into sneaking me a bit of candy now and then. I can see Dad has my interests in mind. "Thanks Dad. I'll do better."

"That makes us happy to hear, Saul. We've have a surprise for you," Mom says. She reaches into her purse and pulls out a cell phone.

"I just have to mention," Dad says, "I think giving this phone to you is one of the worst ideas your mom has ever had. You're not ready for it."

"I am ready. I'll prove it to you." Even as I say these words I wonder exactly how someone goes about proving they're ready for a cell phone. The only way I can think to do it is by making calls. That should be easy. I plan on making tons of them.

"We'll see about that," Dad says.

I nod and soon they leave the room. I'll bet they aren't even outside the locked door that separates the ABI Ward from the outside world when I come up with an idea. I grab my cell phone and dial their number.

Dad answers on the second ring. "Just as I feared. If you've got a phone within reach you're going to spend the majority of your time talking on it. What did you need to say, Saul?"

"I'm just calling to say goodnight, and that I love you both."

"Goodnight, Saul. We love you, too. Now please quit tempting me to come back there and take that phone away."

* * *

The next day I'm in my speech therapy session with Amy. Mom and Dad are sitting beside me. Dr. Bilsky is with us, too.

"How is Saul doing?" Mom asks.

Amy answers in her usual upbeat tone. "He's doing very well. He's already gotten back a lot of nuances, things like intonation in speech and expression that many patients don't. He's become very motivated about that within the last week. To be clear, every brain injury is unique because no two people are wired the same. Damage that appears similar on the surface will usually be vastly different beneath the skull. Not only that, but every person is an individual before their injury. That's why we have to rely on people like you to tell us if we're bringing back the same person who left."

Mom grins. "Saul's the same person, only more so. He's always loved people, but now he can't get enough of them. He's always been a talker, but now he won't shut his mouth. He's always been passionate about his goals, but now he's completely single-minded. He's always been optimistic, but now he can hardly conceive of anything negative."

Amy scribbles some notes while she listens. "We'll work on those things. It's not necessarily bad if there are some permanent personality changes. Some things might be for the better, but we would still like to see some patient awareness about what has changed. I will say, awareness is one area where Saul is well ahead of the curve."

Dad scratches his temple. "What do you mean by that?"

Amy turns to him. "Many brain injured patients want to pretend they haven't been injured. Some genuinely cannot comprehend the fact. It's common for them to become isolated and lonely. Many battle depression. None of this seems to be an issue for Saul. He's surprisingly aware of his situation and unusually driven to understand his deficits and fight proactively to erase them."

"Do you think his background as a pro cyclist has something to do with that?" Mom asks.

"I do," Dr. Bilsky says. "It's been my experience that people who love their jobs, especially those who are physically active, are at an advantage when it comes to recovering from a brain injury. Saul is the epitome of both those things. You'd have a hard time finding anybody who either loves his work as much, or who is more physically active than Saul. On top of that, Saul's youth is another check in the positive column for him. So is his great family support. He's not a smoker or a heavy drinker either. In short, despite the severity of his injury, Saul's got as many or more things going for him as any patient we've ever seen."

Amy nods in agreement. "One thing you've both caught on to very well is holding Saul accountable for his actions. It's easy to want to baby someone in his condition, allowing him to get away with unacceptable behavior. It's harder but far better to confront his errors. He can only correct his deficits if someone has the guts to tell him about them. The way the two of you consistently do that impresses me."

"He's sometimes good at listening, but at other times he isn't," Dad says. "We tell him he interrupts too much but—"

"I do not," I say.

Dr. Bilsky chuckles. "Just keep telling him. Eventually it will sink in. A light bulb will go on, so to speak."

"What deficits do you see?" Mom asks.

Dr. Bilsky thinks for a moment. "I have a few things to bring to his attention. Saul has an inordinate need for structure. Lack of external planning is tough for him. That's something you can help him work on."

Mom nods. "That's not a new deficit. I think it comes from his years as a cyclist. Saul's job has been to prepare himself for races and to ride hard. He's used to having others handle the details allowing him to focus all his energy on just that one task."

Dr. Bilsky scratches his temple. "Okay. I can see how that makes sense given his circumstances. How about this? Saul doesn't have a normal gait pattern. He walks kind of lop-sided. I assume he didn't do that before."

"You're correct," Dad says.

"Well, you can't assume Saul is aware of it now. Anytime you see his walking motion deteriorate you should call it to his attention. You'll be doing him a big favor."

After lunch comes physical therapy. Lauren takes me on a walk with my parents. Dad holds onto my belt in case of a fall. After a while I realize we're headed for the Garden of HOPE. It's the only outdoor place I've been to since checking in to this hospital, and I don't like it at all. I don't like the sunshine or the chaos or anything else about it. I almost fall over sneezing the moment we walk out the door. I know a long walk will be good for me, though, so I'm not complaining as we thread our way through the crowd. I wobble and stumble on the uneven sidewalk, but my balance is now good enough to compensate for the irregularities. We reach a street and wait at the light.

"You're going to have to stay focused and cross here as fast as you can, Saul," Lauren says.

I nod my head. She didn't need to tell me this. No way would I want to end up stuck in the middle of an intersection facing traffic. We walk through the nearby neighborhood.

"I'm very proud of you, Saul," Lauren says. "You've progressed as rapidly as anyone I've ever seen."

"What do you mean?" I ask.

"You've made hour-to-hour progress. I always see carryover from each session. That tells me how seriously you've been taking your therapy," she says. "You ought to be proud of yourself."

"Thank you, Lauren," I say.

Lauren holds my left forearm with her right hand. There's a gentleness and a warmth to her touch that makes me feel great.

"There's something else I want you to know, Saul. I've been impressed from the beginning that you've wanted to make your experience a lesson for other people. I really believe you are going to inspire others, and that in a strange way, good will come of your injury. You are the sort of guy who can motivate families to encourage their loved ones to fight harder than they might otherwise have been able to."

I smile. I like the way she put that. I want to live up to her expectations.

We cross back over the street. At about the halfway point I notice a coin on the ground. I stop to bend down and pick it up.

"Saul, what did I say about staying focused when you cross the street?"

I don't know. What did she say? I try to grab the coin.

"Saul," Dad says, "Do you want to get hit by a car?"

That statement jolts me. There's almost nothing in this world I want less. I return my attention to reaching the curb safely.

As we enter the hospital again Mom says, "How long have we been gone?"

Lauren looks at her watch. "About an hour."

Only an hour? I'm exhausted.

"The day will soon come that Saul can complete that walk in ten minutes," Lauren says.

If she says it can be done in ten minutes then that's my goal, but it seems like we went so far. Regardless, I'm doing everything I can to make that day arrive as soon as possible.

"Just covering that distance, no matter what the time, is a miracle. A month ago I couldn't even have dreamt of this moment. We should celebrate," Mom says. "Can we take him for ice cream off site?"

"I don't see why not," Lauren says. "You've proven to me you can handle him. I think it's time for Saul to start becoming a citizen of the world again."

Chapter Nine

The prospect of leaving the hospital grounds has set butterflies loose in my stomach. The next thing I know, we're in public. This is much different than walking the streets near the hospital. It's surprising to discover that the outside world hasn't changed at all in my absence. The hustle-bustle I'd all but forgotten about is alive and well. There are so many people and they're all headed somewhere in a hurry. None of them seem to even consider my presence in a place like this is at all unusual.

We have dinner at a place called the OK Café. It's the busiest restaurant in Atlanta and also one of the most fun. It has a retro 1950's feel. The food is greasy and not too healthy, but it sure tastes great. I have a Rocket Burger with jalapeno peppers and Monterey Jack cheese and a basket of French fried potatoes. I follow it up with a chocolate milk shake. Yum. I'd been thinking the food at Shepherd's was delicious, but this explosion of taste reminds me that hospital food isn't exactly the tastiest.

As I finish the last few bites, I lean back in my chair and watch in amazement as the world whirls by. Just seeing all this commotion exhausts me.

The next morning I discover a strange magnet in one of the time slots on my scheduling board. It says "FT." What could that possibly mean? I notice several other patients also have the "FT" magnet, and in the same time slot as I do.

At breakfast I ask Ruth Ann.

"You're going on a field trip to the Hunter Art Museum, Saul," she says. "Won't that be fun?"

It turns out to be both fun and exhausting. I'm definitely not making baby steps now. My life has suddenly been filled with mass stimulation and sensory overload. The museum is filled with thought-provoking and mind-bending sculptures. I stare for a particularly long time at a painting whose elements seem to reassemble in different ways each time I look at it. The man who put this together is a master beyond my comprehension. When we return from the field trip I beg for rest, and this time they relent. I'm allowed to climb into my bed for a two-hour nap. I've always been an early-to-bed, early-to-rise sort of person. My injury hasn't changed anything on that front, except I'd love to sprinkle naps throughout the day.

When I wake, Mom and Dad are in my room.

"Ready to go see the condo we're staying at?" Mom asks. "Friends lent it to us. It's only a mile from here. It seems like when we need something these days angels provide it."

We're off again. All this activity is like a whirlwind inside the mind for a guy like me who's been isolated for so long. I love it and fear it at the same time. It's like rediscovering the world. Everything feels strange and new. By the time darkness comes, I'm more than ready for bed. I'm anxious to return to the Shepherd Center.

The next morning before breakfast I send a text message to Mom and Dad. When they don't respond, I call and leave a voice mail, send two more text messages, and then I call again.

This time Dad finally answers. "It isn't even 10:00 AM yet and you've already overloaded our message box on your own, Saul. What do you want?"

"I just wanted to say hi and to tell you I love you."

Dad sounds aggravated. "I love you too, Saul, but you're proving exactly why I tried to talk your mom out of giving you that phone. Who else have you called today?"

"I called Daniela and Thor Hushovd—"

"Great. Both of those calls are to Europe," Dad says, as if I didn't know.

"And then I called Jim Lehman, and I called Lance Armstrong, but I only got his message machine, and before that I made a call to someone else, but I can't remember who."

Dad sighs. "Saul, those people all lead busy lives. You can't call them over and over. They'll get tired of you. Besides, you're supposed to be in your therapy sessions, not wasting your time talking. Do you remember promising me you would use your phone responsibly?"

"Yeah."

"Well," he says, "you're doing the opposite. If you're going to have a phone then you're going to need to resist making calls."

"Okay, Dad. Sorry. I love you. Goodbye." I disconnect the call. Sometimes, I swear, the rules of this world make no sense at all. I'm usually more confused once I know them than I was when I didn't.

My parents pick me up for lunch. These days I'm spending more of my time out of the hospital than in it. I'm also having lots of visitors, both inside and outside of the hospital. It makes me feel good that so many people would take the time to come say hello to me. I love giving all of them hugs, and I hope they'll pass those hugs on to others. The world would be a better place if that sort of idea really caught on.

While we eat, we talk about my accident. Bit by bit I'm getting a sense of what happened. Dad seems surprised the information doesn't get me down or make me fearful of cycling in the future. I really don't see why it should.

"Saul, is there a reason you need to eat that hamburger so fast," Dad says.

"Yeah. I'm hungry."

"Remember how Dr. Bilsky said we needed to call problems to your attention?" Mom asks.

Of course I do. I'm not saying I don't appreciate it, but there has to be a limit. I sometimes feel exhausted by all the corrections. "I don't see why someone who is hungry should have to eat slowly. I'm happy to obey rules that make sense, but you've got to admit, a lot of them are just plain stupid."

"Let's not get into that discussion right now. It's enough to say we'd rather you obeyed all the rules, Saul, and just trust us that eventually they'll make sense," Dad says.

I shove the rest of the hamburger into my mouth before I say, "Okay."

"I'm not kidding about this, Saul," Dad says. "Your manners are embarrassing."

The next few days are more of the same with lots of stimulation, tons of corrections, trips in and out of the ward, and hard work in therapy. But then the really big news comes: I'm ready to leave the Shepherd Center. My last night will be tonight, the twenty-second of May, 2006. I realize my ability to leave this hospital is due as much to what my parents have accomplished and learned as to what I have. They had to prove they could handle my needs. They needed to be able to get me up from and put me back down in my chair correctly and safely. They had to demonstrate they could walk with me safely. Before I could be discharged they had to show they could help me dress, go to the bathroom, shower, and do scores of other simple things I used to take for granted before I hit my head.

We go out to dinner to celebrate. On the way back in to the Shepherd Center my foot catches on a floor mat in the entry and I crumple to my knees. Fortunately, Dad's good grip in my gait belt keeps my fall from being serious. Still, that wasn't the sort of triumphant entrance I'd envisioned making.

Before Dad can help me to my feet a couple of employees beat him to it. They wear the same sorts of friendly smiles that have always greeted me at the Shepherd Center. I like that. There's something else I've noticed about this place I should mention. Many of the employees here are disabled. Once I'm on my feet again, we walk up to the reception desk and I ask the woman seated behind it, who happens to be in a wheelchair, why this is.

"Harold and Alana Shepherd became committed to the cause of rehabilitating brain and spinal-cord injured patients because their own son, James, was paralyzed in a Brazilian body surfing accident back in 1973. It frustrated them that they couldn't find the sort of care their son needed near their home in the southeast. So what did they do?"

I shake my head. "I don't know."

"They did what your parents have done. They moved the earth to improve his world. That's what provided the inspirational spark to create a facility like no other. By 1975 it was up and running, and it has been improving ever since. James Shepherd, who now walks with the aid of arm braces, is one of many disabled employees who currently work for the Shepherd Center. In fact, I've heard Shepherd's employs a larger percentage of disabled people than any other organization of its size in the country. That's important for many reasons, not just to employ the disabled. These people prove by example that suffering a serious injury doesn't have to bring an end to living a productive life. That's why I chose to work here after overcoming my own injury. I want to make a difference."

I nod. Thinking back, I realize the disabled people working here helped inspire me to fight. I hadn't even realized that as it was happening. Hearing such a comment from a wheelchair-bound woman makes me realize my reactions to Dr. Dan's advice about accepting a life in a wheelchair were immature. He wasn't trying to talk me into being a lesser sort of person; he was trying to explain to me that my life could still be full, even if it had to be lived in a new way.

I spend my last night in what have become comfortable and familiar surroundings. Then I wake prepared to say my goodbyes. They won't be permanent. I've already vowed I'll return here again and again.

The therapists and doctors talk to my parents and me about the progress I've made, and about the things I still need to do. I've heard it all before, but each time I do I better understand how to overcome my problems. I'm impulsive, my short-term memory is poor, I have problems with concentration, I eat too fast and sloppily, I have left-side neglect, I don't have proper awareness of personal space, and I repeat myself often … or have I already said that?

Every nurse in the ward is special to me. Some of them changed my sheets. Some of them brought me food. Some of them made sure I had the medication I needed. They probably did a lot more jobs for me I've never been aware of. I owe every one of them a debt of gratitude. I hug each one as I move down the line. My eyes are filled with tears, and so are many of theirs.

Amy, Ruth Ann, and Lauren are my heroes. When I arrived here I was in such a fog that I didn't understand what they were doing to me. Now I watch them working with new patients, and I really see what amazing things their love and dedication can accomplish. I give them each a hug and tell them they'll always remain part of my life. Soon we're all in tears. I feel sorry now for the lustful comments I made to every female who came near me at first. I know I was a bad boy, but they understood I couldn't help it even as they taught me to take responsibility for my actions. Now, though, my feelings for these ladies go far beyond lust. I'm absolutely in love with each one of these wonderful women.

Dr. Bilsky is a saint in my eyes. I look up to him as the mentor who rebuilt me. He's filled with intense passion, keen insight, and deep love. My respect for him knows no bounds. He and the other doctors have come to mean so much to me.

Sean and Keith stand near the edge of the room. These men and others like them are the workhorses of the ABI Ward. Without them I wouldn't be where I am today. When I could hardly move on my own, they were the ones who moved my body for me. When I had no balance, it was their muscle that kept me vertical. I give them each a hug.

After the others leave Dr. Bilsky comes up to me. "You get to give a special gift to one member of the staff, Saul. The employee you feel made the biggest difference in your recovery will get a paid day of vacation. I'd like you to put his or her name on this card, and then deposit it into the house mailbox in the hallway." He hands me the card along with a pencil, lays a comforting hand on my shoulder, and then walks away.

As I watch him leave I think back on my time here. I want to give this gift to every person involved in my recovery, but I've learned that life is about choices, so I make mine. I write down Keith's name. He made me feel like a man. No single moment will have a bigger impact on my life than when Keith told me to walk on my own, and I discovered I could.

He once told me, "I'm impressed by your accomplishments, Saul. You've broken all the rules. Way to go!"

I thought about the sorts of "rules" he was referring to and realized that they're really just expectations, not rules at all. Technically, I should be dead, but in reality I'm more alive than I've ever been before. Sometimes limits become defined by preconceptions of what's possible and what isn't. Those sorts of rules don't apply to me. I make my own rules. I believe I can do anything I set my mind to. They said I would be in a coma for three months, maybe forever, or that I'd die. I was unconscious for less than a week. They said I would stay at the Shepherd Center for over three months. I will walk out in a little over three weeks. They said the things I'm doing now would never be possible, but I'm doing them. Who are "they," anyway? It really doesn't matter. I am me.

Chapter Ten

Graduating from the Shepherd Center is equivalent to earning a Doctorate. That's how I see it. It's the biggest accomplishment of my life so far. To an outsider I'm more like a preschool graduate. I can hardly do simple math, I can't read well, I can barely write. Whenever I do write, my mom has to remind me not to make my letters so itsy-bitsy. I still drift to the left when I walk, partly because of what Dr. Bilsky calls my abnormal gait pattern. It's sort of like a limp, though I don't realize I'm doing it until someone calls it to my attention. The same thing is true of the way I often unconsciously hold my left arm close to my body while clinching my left fist. I don't know why I do that, and it's so hard to stop.

I enjoy talking, but I sometimes slur my words and I often repeat myself. I even have to concentrate on simple things, like keeping my lips stiff so I don't drool when I'm hungry. There's still a long way to go. I've learned some basic skills, but I now realize I'm nowhere near ready to return to an independent life. Fortunately there are places where I can go to get the necessary help. In my case this means outpatient therapy at Shepherd Pathways. It's located in a residential suburb of Atlanta, seven miles from the Shepherd Center. Where the Shepherd Center looks and feels like a traditional hospital, Shepherd Pathways is a transitional center that's integrated into a normal neighborhood. As we approach it, my first impression is that it resembles an older community recreation center. Dad holds my gait belt as we walk into the front lobby.

A friendly receptionist greets us. "Are you Saul?"

"Where am I supposed to go," I say.

"Not so fast." Mom puts her hand on my chest. "This nice lady asked you a question. Why don't you answer it and ask her name?"

Mom and Dad are constantly noticing things I don't do right. I appreciate that they are willing to correct me because I know I have shortcomings. The only way I can overcome them is by being aware. I extend my hand to the receptionist. "Yes, I'm Saul. What's your name?"

The receptionist takes my hand. She has a beautiful smile. "I'm Evonne, with an 'E.' It's a pleasure to meet you. And right here is the place you need to go first. Please have a seat."

I drop into the nearest chair, grateful to be off my feet.

Evonne hands me a notebook with my name on it. "This is where you'll write down your daily schedule and keep other important notes." She rips a piece of red tape from a dispenser and sticks it to the front of the notebook.

"What's that for?" I ask.

"The color code tells the therapists how much freedom you're allowed. Until your balance is reliable you'll be red. That means you'll have no freedom to move throughout the building. You must wait for your therapist to come get you after every session, and you must wear your gait belt at all times so the therapist can hold onto you in case you fall."

I nod. "I want to earn better colors. What are they?"

"As you get more stable and learn your way around you can earn yellow, then white, and last green. While a green patient still has the responsibility of keeping track of their daily schedule and getting to their classes on time, technically they can go anywhere they want at any time, on their own."

That sounds almost too good to be true. I've got to earn a green piece of tape for myself.

Dad has to leave, but Mom decides to spend this first day at Pathways by my side. I'm both pleased and nervous to have her here. After all, I think I'm weaker in some areas than she realizes. I'd rather she thought of me as smart and strong.

Evonne leads us through the building. She points out rooms where a few patients stay overnight. I'm glad I'll be spending my evenings with my parents at the Marriott Hotel. The condo mom and dad had been staying in had only one bedroom and it's pretty far away, so the hotel is a better option.

The receptionist walks me through the community room and kitchen and lets us breathe in the fresh air on the large deck; then she points out the basketball court. Finally she shows me the various therapy rooms and the different exercise equipment. I like this place. It feels much more casual than the Shepherd Center.

Of course, that makes perfect sense because this isn't a critical-care facility at all. It's a place for healing people to learn how to return to society. We're going to practice shopping, balancing a checkbook, eating with manners at restaurants, and more. Therapy will be a big part of it too.

A gorgeous blonde woman steps away from helping another patient and extends her hand. "You must be Saul."

"Yes, and what's your name?"

She points to a tag pinned to her shirt. She has an infectious, bubbly enthusiasm about her. "I'm Megan. I'll be your physical therapist."

"Great. When can we start rehab?"

She smiles. "I'm not sure I've ever met anybody so anxious for this. Do you really enjoy therapy that much?"

"I like exercise, if that's what you're asking. I'm addicted to endorphins, but honestly, I dread rehab. It's such a struggle. The mental part, especially, is so hard. To me, an hour of problem solving feels like doing an eight hour all-out bike ride. That doesn't mean I don't want to attack it, though."

She looks at me with genuine interest. "So, I'm curious. How does what you've gone through so far compare to your training for bike racing?"

"It's insane. As a pro cyclist I've never experienced fatigue like therapy gives me.

Fifteen days straight of racing never even came close to touching the fatigue I felt at the Shepherd Center. A couple of times I fell asleep in the middle of conversations."

"It's only going to get harder from here on out. Did you know that?"

I didn't, but I'm not about to back down from her challenge, either. "I'm one tough S.O.B. and I'll keep giving this everything I've got. I plan on making a full recovery. Believe me, I know that's not going to be easy."

Megan pats me on the shoulder. "I can tell we're going to get along great. Sessions start at nine in the morning and last through three in the afternoon with a one hour lunch break. It will be similar to the ABI Ward you came from. You'll have time blocks devoted to speech therapy and occupational therapy as well as the physical stuff. This first day, though, will be devoted to testing. We need to understand what your strengths and weaknesses are?"

"Can I stay and watch?" Mom asks.

"We'd be happy to have you," Megan says.

"Since you're anxious to start, Saul, why don't we get to work right now? I need to take a good look at you to figure out what we need to work on. Please step onto this platform."

The platform has walls around it that extend higher than my head. It's sort of like a human sized box. I do as she says.

"This is a balance test, Saul." She fastens me into a harness.

"I have good balance now. I don't need a harness."

She smiles. Moments later the boards beneath my feet begin moving. I steady my posture but then a wall moves and it's almost as if my world turns upside down. I would have fallen flat on my face if not for the harness. "Did you buy that crazy thing from Disneyland?" I ask.

She chuckles. It measures the torque on your feet and determines how well your inner ear can compensate. Normal score is a sixty-one. You got a twenty. That shows me you're balancing almost entirely by sight."

Megan continues checking me out with her battery of exercises. She quickly recognizes what a problem my left arm is. I'm still not using it well, and attempting to lift the forearm any higher than my shoulder, even with help, remains impossible. I feel excruciating pain in the shoulder joint whenever the arm is raised. She also says we need to work on the way I walk. I have an uneven gait, and I veer to the left. She says there are a bunch of other skills we'll be working on, too.

After Megan finishes her test she introduces me to my speech therapist, Mary Ellen. She's a young, vivacious woman I instantly fall in love with. Happiness practically exudes from her pores. She hands me a book and asks me to sign my name on the front. In high school I used to practice this until it was effortless, and as a pro cyclist I always loved it when someone asked me for an autograph. Now I have to muster all my concentration just to create a semblance of the signature that used to be so easy.

Mary Ellen opens the book and shows me puzzles she calls Sudoko inside. She claims they're easy, but they make no sense to me. I can't even see the point of working on them, and thinking about the numbers hurts my brain.

Finally she takes the book away and puts a different book in front of me. Then she starts asking questions. "Look at these three pictures then circle the one that's different."

They are simple drawings of a cat, and all three look exactly the same to me. I concentrate as hard as I can, sure that there must be a difference because she said so, but I can't see any at all. "All three are the same," I finally say.

She points to the whiskers. One of the cats is missing some.

Why couldn't I see that before?

Mary Ellen turns the page. "Tell me the next number in this sequence."

There's a two, then a four, then a six. This one's not so tough. I write down the answer. Seven.

"If Sally has two apples and Martin gives her three more how many does she have now?"

I think about it hard, feeling sure there's a trick in here somewhere. Finally I answer. "Three."

I look at Mom. She's crying. It hurts me to see her feeling like this, especially because I can tell it has something to do with me. I put an arm around her. "Everything's going to be okay. Don't worry."

After a long, hard day we go to the Marriott. We have a suite with two bedrooms. I'm sitting alone in the living area when I'm surprised to hear my parents' voices close by. Then I notice the sounds are actually being transmitted out of the receiving end of a baby monitor that's sitting right beside me.

"It was so hard today," Mom says. "They gave him a neuropsychological test, and he really struggled."

"Did they tell you his score?" Dad asks.

"Yes. They told me was on about a third-grade level. He has limited reasoning skills, he can't read and comprehend, and he has very limited math skills," Mom says.

"Oh boy." Dad sounds upset. "I guess that means we're just going to have to work harder."

Soon, Dad comes in and walks me to bed. The moment I lie down I fall into a dead sleep.

The next morning I wake up remembering an incredibly vivid dream. There's a field surrounded by flowers, and I'm running through it with my arms spread wide. I run and run and run and run and run. The field never ends.

They push me hard all week. In physical therapy we do exercises for balancing, speed, coordination, and endurance. My speech therapist helps me practice voice inflection and expression recognition. We also study logic problems, math exercises, reading assignments, and handwriting tests. In occupational therapy they drill my fine motor skills, requiring me to do things like put puzzles together, color pictures, count money, wash dishes, turn the pages in a magazine, and play billiards. I used to play pool all the time while at the Olympic Training Center. Although I never got very good, I'm able to win here every time, not just against other patients but against interns and therapists as well.

Some days we come up with lunch menus and then go to a nearby grocery store to buy things. It feels weird to be out in the community. I'm like a stranger in a strange world, but I love being there and take in all I can see. Afterward we return to Pathways, and the other patients and I get to help with cooking the meals. It's lots of fun.

On Friday they have a new exercise in mind: swimming. I've always loved to swim.

"Okay, we're just going to wade in the shallow end for awhile," the therapist says.

As I walk down the steps I can feel every drop of water surrounding me. The sensation takes my breath away. It's like I'm bathing in jelly. "I can swim the whole length of this pool underwater," I say.

"No you can't," the therapist says.

I slip underwater and push off the wall with my feet. Remember how I said I react when people doubt me? The pool is fifty meters long, but I know I can make it. I've done this many times before.

I love the sensation of flying I get while underwater. I like to swoop along the bottom of the pool, staying as close to it as I can without touching. The water feels invigorating as it flows along my body, and then I reach the far wall and swim up toward the surface. It's a long way, and that's when I realize this pool is twelve feet deep and I was at the very bottom.

When I break through the surface the therapist is standing there, and he's not one bit happy. He grabs my arm. "Climb out of the pool, Saul. I told you not to do that."

I shake my head, "No. You said you didn't think I could."

He scowls. "I don't know how you got that out of what I said."

I know what I heard, and later I hear him telling some other therapists how amazed he was by my swimming.

After our adventure we return to Pathways. Hour by hour we're nearing the major reward that's driven me to give rehab everything I've got. I get to go home to Dalton for the weekend. I'm about to see my oldest friends. I'm going to travel the roads where I fell in love with cycling. But most of all, tonight I'll sleep in my childhood bed, though it won't be inside my childhood room. Dad's going to reassemble it in the study on the main level so I won't have to use stairs. They've also brought the baby monitor from the hotel so they can listen to me all night from their room.

"Can I ride my trainer at home over the weekend?" I ask Dr. Talbot who is supervising my care at Pathways.

"That's a great idea, Saul," she says. "But you're going to have to follow a few guidelines."

"What are they?"

"You've got to keep your heart rate low. Wear a monitor and don't exceed 140 beats per minute. I see from your medical chart that concerns remain about possible heart problems detected in France. Let's remain careful until we're sure there's nothing to that. If you can go for ten minutes that would be great. Also, I'm sure you realize you need to have supervision the entire time you're riding."

Of course, I agree to her rules. I haven't been able to get my heart rate over 120 so that restriction isn't going to be a problem. The bigger issue is that I can only walk short distances. How long will I be able to ride a bicycle?

I can't wipe the smile off my face the whole way home. Neither can my parents. There have been times during the last two months they didn't think this journey was ever going to be possible. If I'd had enough mental power to understand the situation I'm sure I would have agreed with them.

By the time Dad exits I-75 at the North Dalton Bypass my skin is tingling with excitement. Soon, we turn onto our street, and as we near our home I can't believe my eyes. There are ribbons and "Welcome Home" signs on every mailbox in the neighborhood. There's a hand-painted banner stretching the full length of our driveway, and there are balloons and streamers everywhere. The whole street looks like one big love letter.

Mom rolls down her window. "We are so blessed."

I can tell Dad's trying to hold back tears. "Saul, did you realize that friends and neighbors have been taking care of our yard and seeing to our other obligations for nearly two months now? They've been hurting nearly as badly as we have."

I wipe my eyes. Before my injury I might have tried to hold back the tears when experiencing an outpouring of love like this. That's changed now. As far as I'm concerned there's no good reason to hold back tears ever again. I won't stifle laughter or kisses or heartache or smiles either. I'm going to treasure sunrises and snowstorms and lazy summer days in ways I wasn't capable of before. I've been given a second chance at life, and I'll be damned if I'm not going to savor each moment with every fiber of my being.

Chapter Eleven

A friend who purchased the Litespeed Ghisallo bicycle I rode when I won "Best Young Rider" at Tour de Georgia has loaned it to me for rehab. What a gesture! Dad is setting it up on the stationary trainer in my old workout room above the garage. He removes the front wheel and locks the forks onto the trainer. Then he moves to the back wheel and engages the roller. Once I'm pedaling, the resistance will be created by pushing an air turbine.

I need Dad's help to lift my left leg over the top tube. My toe won't click into the left pedal. "I think my cleat is broken," I say.

Dad inspects it. "Nope. It's fine." He clicks my shoe in place by hand.

I don't even have the strength or coordination to clip into my own pedals? Wow. I have a long way to go.

The right shoe clips in easily and I rise onto the seat and begin pedaling. It's an incredible feeling to once again ride the bicycle that played such a major role in my early career.

I turn the pedals in choppy motions. My left leg just won't behave. It's trying to move in squares or triangles instead of circles. Maybe more resistance would help. I try to push the left gear lever to put the chain onto the big ring, but I don't have the strength. Dad works the click shifter for me.

The resistance helps a little, and my pedaling improves slightly. Soon, sweat streams down my face. Dad stands beside me in case I have a temporary loss of balance. I don't think that's going to happen. I'm feeling really good. Even my left arm, which has been by far the weakest part of my body, is gaining strength.

My thoughts drift to my girlfriend, as they so often do. Daniela will be visiting sometime soon. We're deeply in love and fully committed to each other. I can easily imagine spending the rest of my life with her. She and I have the same sort of supportive relationship I've always admired my parents for. I feel so fortunate to have found her.

With Daniela there are no pretenses. She never hides her feelings or opinions. I love that. She's also an extremely hard worker. She's trained with me as much as twenty-five hours in a week. I remember one day after a six-hour ride when she couldn't even walk without support. If I touched her leg she moaned, but the next morning after I helped her to her feet she insisted on going on another five-hour training ride with me. To some people I'm sure that sounds crazy, but it's the sort of toughness I really admire. Last night I sent her a text message that ended with, "You are the good in me." It's the truth.

The fact that Daniela was my parents' guardian angel through such a difficult time makes me love her even more. I wish she could have just skipped her summer semester of school and stayed with us through the rest of this recovery, but I know that's asking a lot. At least I get to speak with her daily by phone, and most important, we'll be together again soon.

After riding the bike, Mom helps me to the couch where I sit down. I'm not allowed to walk anywhere without someone at my side. Being accompanied to the bathroom is the part I hate most. While I was in the hospital that was one thing, but now that I'm with my parents it's quite another. I hate standing there next to my dad with my pants down, but if he isn't available, it's even worse. That's when the only choice is to have my mom standing next to me. It's definitely not a comfortable experience for either of us. Unfortunately, Dad has gone somewhere at the moment when I feel the urge. "Mom, I've got to go," I yell.

"Do you think you could do it yourself this time?" she asks. "I'm in the middle of cooking dinner."

"Yeah."

"Just be careful, okay?"

I'm thrilled with the idea and quite confident everything will be fine because I'm getting pretty stable, so I get up and walk to the toilet on my own. Inside the bathroom I look in the mirror. My hair has grown back in, and my coloring has really improved. I still have work to do, but I'm headed in the right direction. I think about my journey and start wondering why I came in here; then I look down and discover a puddle on the floor.

"Mom! Who peed all over the place in here?"

She comes running. "Is there a problem? What are you yelling about?"

I point to the floor. "Who do you think did this?"

She looks straight into my eyes and says, "You did, Saul."

"I did not."

She's already cleaning it up as she says, "Then please explain why your underwear is soaked."

I look down and discover she's right. I'm telling you, you have no idea what disorientation feels like until you go through a brain injury like mine.

In the afternoon we sit around the living room with cousins, aunts, uncles, and others to discuss what we've gone through so far. I'm tapping my foot against the coffee table because sitting around like this bores me.

"The most frustrating thing about a brain injury," my dad says, "is that while a lot is known about the brain, even more is unknown."

"How does Saul's recovery so far compare to what the doctors expected?" Grandma asks.

"They don't give those sorts of expectations," Dad says. "It's not like a broken bone where everybody has an understanding of what's required for it to heal. Even the most knowledgeable neurologists don't have answers to some seemingly basic questions about the brain."

Mom puts a hand on Dad's knee. "We're still very confused, even though we have full access to some of the best experts in Atlanta. Imagine how much worse it was in France. I believe Saul's doctors over there were extremely competent, but words can't express how frustrating it was not to be able to easily communicate with them."

Uncle Phil sets down his glass of soda. "What sorts of things are you still unclear about?"

"Almost everything," Mom says. "At our first medical meeting in the U.S. the head doctor said, 'We're sorry, but the answer to most of the questions you ask will probably be, *we don't know*.'"

I wish I could get up and leave the room, but I'm not allowed to walk without somebody holding my gait belt, and I know my parents aren't willing. I'm not being rude … or at least, I don't mean to be. It's just that I don't know how anybody can stand sitting around this long.

It's so nice to be home, but I hate that the weekend is going by so quickly. We'll have to return to Pathways for more therapy soon.

The next morning I log onto my web site to read my message book. The supportive notes always make me feel so good. As a thank you, I upload as many recent pictures as I can. When I finish I add a diary entry:

Riding the trainer
Contributed by Saul
Monday, 29 May 2006
I put some pictures up of me riding the trainer. I went swimming yesterday, and my left arm is getting better. I could swim freestyle ok, much better than the last time I went swimming. It feels like it is taking forever but I am getting well. Brain injuries are very difficult; every day is a surprise … Always wear your helmet while riding. I go back to the Rehab center today for the rest of the week. :(Saul

I return to Atlanta more determined than ever to defeat my deficiencies and put this injury behind me. I've never been through anything so difficult in my entire life. I desperately want to return to living a normal life once again. I ask God to please allow me to earn that gift every day. I dream of things like leaving my gait belt behind and taking a shower by myself.

At therapy I ask Dr. Talbot about a plan I've come up with. "I think I'm ready to start riding a trainer in the evenings in our hotel room. It would help me get my strength back." Dad is worried she'll feel like I'm pushing too hard. He thinks I might not be giving myself enough recovery time.

"That's not a bad idea," she answers. "From your progress over the weekend it's obvious the bike is working miracles for you. It seems to have strengthened your mind as well as your legs and arms."

I smile. "I know it has."

That evening my dad sets up the trainer in the hotel room for me. I ride it hard for more than half an hour. I'm working overtime to get well. What I do in therapy I plan to duplicate as much or more out of therapy. I've got to get my endurance back. Every night I plan to increase the length of time I spend on the trainer.

One day the staff takes us to a park for a picnic. When we reach our table the aide lets go of my gait belt and returns to the van to help someone else. I haven't sat down yet, though, and then I notice all the flowers. I know this place from my dreams. I spread my arms wide and start to run.

I haven't taken a lengthened stride like this in months, and I'm much clumsier than I dreamed of being, but I'm running nevertheless. I'm basking in the feeling of freedom until suddenly someone grabs my gait belt and stops me.

"What in the world are you doing, Saul?" It's Megan.

I smile at her. "I had to run."

She shakes her head and I can tell she's panicked. "Well, you shouldn't. You could hurt yourself."

I doubt she'd understand me even if I explained why I had no choice, so I don't.

By Thursday of my second week in Pathways, June first, Megan has great news. "I'm changing the tape on your notebook from red to yellow," she says. "Do you know what that means?"

"Not exactly," I say.

She grins wide. "No more gait belt. You've proven you have the strength and balance to walk on your own."

At this moment it feels like the single most significant accomplishment in my life. I know I've said that sort of thing a lot lately, but you have to realize, my accomplishments are building upon one another, and each one truly is bigger than the last because it becomes part of the same journey.

As soon as Megan removes the gait belt, I start walking around the room just for the sheer pleasure of it. I literally can't sit still. After being tended to for such a long time, it's hard to describe how liberating it feels not to have someone watching over my every move.

When Dad arrives I walk toward him all on my own. Of course he immediately notices the change. It would be impossible not to.

"Should you be doing that, Saul?" Dad asks.

"Uh huh," I answer. I show him the yellow tape on my notebook.

He smiles. "Congratulations. I'm proud of you. You're making slow but noticeable improvements."

I'm grinning from ear to ear. I throw my arms around him and give him a big kiss. It doesn't matter to me that he calls my improvements "slow but noticeable." I know in my heart they are actually "rapid and gigantic." I can understand why Dad doesn't want to get carried away. That's not his way, but I actually look forward to getting carried away every now and then.

The next morning I post a message to my blog:

Checking in
Contributed by Saul
Friday, 02 June 2006
Just checking in here ... I am doing well. I am getting stronger mentally and physically everyday and I can almost see my own progress. I am still going to therapy everyday during the week. On top of the rehab I am riding the trainer 30-40 mins, also not bad. It feels good to do some exercise. After lying in a hospital bed for over a month, you can imagine it is not easy. I want to thank everyone for continuing to support me. It really means a lot to me.

I'm not just spinning my freewheel when I say how grateful I am for the support. You wouldn't believe the massive amount of encouragement I've received. Mom used to put scrapbooks together with memorabilia from my career, but there's no way she could possibly keep up with this.

Entire elementary schools full of children have mailed me handmade get-well cards. Fans have sent everything from inspirational books, to signed jerseys, to photos of themselves on their favorite rides. Sponsors have shipped boxes full of gear to me. One of the Shepherd Center nurses looked at my web site before I arrived and noticed 'Raisin Hell' printed on the side of my shoes. She came up with the idea of selling green and white 'Raisin Hell' bracelets to raise money to cover my care. My parents liked the idea, but we decided to donate the profits to the Shepherd Center. The bracelets have been selling so fast we can't keep them in stock. When DeFeet saw the bracelet idea, they donated cartons packed with custom-woven 'Raisin Hell' socks. On top of all that, teammates and friends call daily.

These positive vibes do more for me than I can possibly explain. Just imagine how it feels to have thousands of people you don't even know sending you their prayers and encouragement. It makes me feel obligated to get better; and that's the sort of obligation I want to take on.

Most of the patients here at Pathways don't have the sort of external-support system I do. Some of them don't even have family members who regularly check on them. Their fight must be so much tougher than mine. I'm in awe of the people I've met here and the obstacles they've overcome. I'm humbled by their accomplishments. Sometimes when I watch other patients doing pottery or painting pictures, I feel so proud of them. I can see the progress in every single person here.

These days when I see a handicapped person, I feel a whole new kind of respect. Challenged people are the angels of the world, truly the best of mankind. There's a lot to be learned from them. I admire the way so many of them battle their disabilities to achieve simple victories, defeating the odds on a daily basis.

When you take away all of someone's freedom, the things they take for granted change completely. For some, all they have left to treasure are their cries and smiles … and their dreams, for dreams can come true. I know that for certain.

It changes a person at their core when simple freedoms are removed from their life. Enjoying a shower alone, standing up, putting food in your own mouth, going to the bathroom in private; most of us normally don't give a second thought to such small things, but for challenged people these small dignities might be nothing more than fond memories. Despite that, many people adapt and achieve the impossible. In the process, some of them come to truly understand the value of simple pleasures. They can be happy with fresh air, a sunny day, or the smile on a child's face. When you sit back and think about it, aren't those the sorts of things that really make life worthwhile?

Journalists visit me often. There have been lots of stories in the local media, a few stories in the national media, and even a couple of stories that have gone worldwide. Today there's a crew here from an Atlanta television station.

"Do you dream of riding the bike again?" the reporter asks me.

My dream is really much bigger than riding the bike. How can I explain this to him? "I dream of having a normal life."

"Are you saying that riding a bike will be only one piece of your full recovery?"

I nod. "True, true." I'm on the road to capturing that dream, and the momentum increases every day.

After a weekend in Dalton we return to Pathways for another excruciating week of therapy. They're making all the usual exercises tougher. It used to be that I just had to lift my arms, but now I have to do it holding five-pound weights. They used to be satisfied if I wrote down the answer to a math problem, but now they want the writing to be perfect. They used to give me a puzzle and just let me put it together at my own pace, but now they start a timer. They used to congratulate me for walking, but now they make me turn my head as I do it.

You can't imagine how many different exercises they've dreamed up for me. "Drum your fingers on the table faster and faster, Saul. Now turn this row of pennies over and then turn them back. Squeeze the water out of these sponges. Punch holes with this hole punch. Unscrew all these jar lids. Now, screw them back on. Wind these clocks and set the time. Please open this combination lock. Bounce that basketball. Kick that other ball. Make a peanut butter and jelly sandwich. Organize a grocery list. Now, make a list of all the exercises you can remember doing today."

Then, the next day, we do the same sorts of things again. It's amazing how busy they can keep all of us, while at the same time accomplishing almost nothing. I'm not really serious when I say that, though, because I realize we're actually accomplishing a lot.

"I'm really proud of you," Megan says. "From a physical standpoint you've always been ready to work hard and pursue your goals. You could see a direct correlation between where you were and where you wanted to be."

"If anything, you've had to hold me back, haven't you?" I ask.

She nods. "We don't want you to hurt yourself. Now you're catching onto the mental stuff and seeing how important it is, so I have a question for you."

"Ask," I say.

"If you were to measure the mental versus physical skills required to race a bike at the pro level what would the percentages be?"

I think for a moment. I hadn't expected a logic problem, but then an answer comes to me. "They are two separate pies, and you need ninety-eight percent of each, minimum, to race at that level. I have a big appetite so I'll take an extra slice of each."

Megan laughs. "Very good, Saul. That's quite an answer. You've earned a break for yourself."

I grin. When those rare moments for relaxation do come along, one of my favorite things to do is to sit talking with Zach Phillips. I met Zach at the Shepherd Center and now we are also at Pathway's together. My parents and his often talk for hours at a time. Talking to people is a very important step in getting well, not only for the victims of these accidents, but also for their loved ones.

Cars are responsible for so many of the injuries here. Very often it's somebody else paying a huge price for a driver's mistake. That's what happened to Zach. It embarrasses me to say that when I was young I used to drive recklessly, too. I just didn't understand the consequences.

Once, when I was sixteen years old, I was showing off how fast I could drive my pickup. I missed a corner and totaled the vehicle with two of my friends inside. The impact ripped the cab right off the truck, but somehow everybody walked away unharmed. I realize now how lucky I was. I'll never drive recklessly again, and I wish there was some way I could get the word out to other young drivers. Once someone truly understands what brain and spinal injury victims have to go through I'm certain they'd never put others at risk like that again.

Zach and I never discuss our injuries too much. The main thing we like to talk about is how gorgeous the women are around this place. We've decided it's unfair that we have to be surrounded by such beauty all day long, especially because we're never allowed to make the sorts of comments that come naturally. It's got to be some sort of test an evil doctor dreamed up.

The therapists are very creative. They think up new activities each day to keep things interesting. One day we go to the bookstore and have a scavenger hunt. I have to find books with pictures of cyclists on the covers. Zach has to find legal thrillers.

Another time they take us to Starbucks and give us each five dollars. We're supposed to make purchases and figure out the correct change. This is the first coffee I've had since my accident, so I'm very happy to be in this place, and I have extra money in my pocket they don't know about. Before we're done I've had four Double Red Eyes. That's a cup of coffee with two shots of espresso, so four of them are equal to twelve cups of coffee. I'm proud that I'm able to figure that out. It's proof that I'm getting better at math.

By the time Mom comes to get me I'm tripping out. I have tremors, I'm talking out of control, and I feel like I'm flying. Mom asks the therapists what's wrong with me. It didn't take them too long to figure it out. From now on, no more coffee for me.

At the end of the week I make another blog entry to keep my supporters updated on the most recent news:

> *Breaking out*
> Contributed by Saul
> Friday, 09 June 2006
> I am doing so well. I will be released from the rehabilitation center the 30th of this month. After I go home to Dalton GA, I will go to rehab there for awhile. Everything is going well and I am progressing every day. With rehab I am riding the trainer 30min each day and swimming some. Thank you for your thoughts and prayers. Also: I am sorry but because of the high demands for the bracelets we are running out quickly. We have a new batch on the way. Just a reminder: the bracelets are going to a good cause to help fight brain and spinal cord injury. Thank you again for all your support. Saul

After another wonderful weekend in Dalton we return to Atlanta. This week we're starting things off by visiting with Dr. Clare, one of the region's most respected neurosurgeons. He's going to give me some training limits that will dictate how high I can safely push my heart rate. I walk into his office, and he looks into my eyes. He sets his coffee mug down with a thud. "You're Saul Raisin?"

I nod as I take a seat alongside my parents.

He points to some x-ray films on a light wall frame. "Those are your brain scans?"

"You'd know better than I would." The truth is, I wouldn't know my brain scans from my house plans, but I've been told that the interior of my noggin has been a frequently-photographed subject over the last few months.

"Well, they have your name on them, but the reason I'm uncertain they're yours is that someone whose brain looks like that probably shouldn't be able to stand."

I shrug.

"Can you move your left hand?" he asks.

I lift it and wiggle the fingers.

"Very good. You're fortunate, you know. The brain tissue in the area they removed often plays a major role in motor skills. Often that sort of ability is irretrievable."

What is this doctor talking about? Is he saying that part of my brain has been removed? Would they do a thing like that?

Dad looks confused. "When we first got to France they told us they'd removed a piece of Saul's brain and that he'd never move his left side, but when he started moving it the doctors clarified things with the surgeon. He told them there'd been a misunderstanding and that nothing had been removed after all."

Dr. Clare stands up and walks over to the light frame to look at the image more closely. "They told you no brain matter had been removed?" He consults some notes and inspects the image again. "Well, I'm here to tell you that there's been another misunderstanding because in these films it appears to me that a portion of Saul's brain is no longer there."

"How much is missing," Dad asks.

"Between the size of a half-dollar and a lemon," Dr. Clare says.

"A lemon!" Mom looks like she's going to faint.

"Now we truly know how lucky and amazing Saul is," Dad says.

I'm still too far off balance as a result of the revelations coming out of this conversation to comment.

"You've got to understand," Dr. Clare says, "when the doctors got in there it would have been like tomato juice and pasta sauce. They had to remove the blood and clots, but differentiating one thing from another under ideal conditions is tough. Figuring out what's what when a life is on the line is another matter entirely. The bottom line is that the surgeon performed a miracle and saved Saul's life. Not only that, but he somehow preserved the pieces of the brain that were necessary for Saul to continue carrying on all normal functions. You ought to be thankful for the physician's skill."

"Oh, we are," Mom says. "We're just amazed and confused at the same time."

We look at one another uncomfortably for awhile and then finally I ask, "Weren't you going to give us some training limits?"

He smiles. "Yes, Saul, I was. And that's the good news. I don't see any reason to put any limits on you going forward. As far as I'm concerned, you can push your heart rate as high as you're able."

I'd been increasingly overwhelmed by the discussion, but I'm not anymore. Now I can't contain my smile. "You're serious? Does this mean I can go back racing?"

Dr. Clare looks at me like I've just spoken some incomprehensible foreign language; then he shakes his head and gets very serious. "I didn't say that, Saul. Not at all. Training on a stationary bike and racing on the road are two entirely different things. Another blow to your head could be fatal. If you were my son you'd never race again. No way."

Chapter Twelve

I don't feel like talking as we walk to the car. What had been a beautiful spring day has suddenly been ruined. Imagine first learning that a piece of your brain has been removed and then being told you should never again do the thing you love most.

"Saul, I'm not going to tell you what you can or can't do in your life, but I think Dr. Clare's opinions ought to carry some weight," Dad says.

I look him in the eyes. "Are you saying you don't want me to race again?"

He nods slightly. "If I got to choose for you, that's the choice I'd make. You're still young, and you can get a great education. A world of possibilities is open to you."

I look at my mom. "Do you agree with him?"

The love in her eyes is obvious. "Every time you race I cringe inside because I know you might be a millisecond away from disaster. Do you think I enjoy that?"

I shake my head. "Of course not."

"Of course not," she repeats. "And it would be worse now than ever before. You almost died, Saul. There were times we thought you were lost to us."

"So what's your answer?" I ask.

She looks at me fondly. "Does it really matter?"

I nod.

Her eyes have become sad. "I can't give you the answer you want to hear, but I'm not going to steal your dreams by giving you the answer in my heart."

I find myself looking at my hands, watching my thumbs nervously trying to find a place to rest. "The bike is what has saved me, too."

Dad is a cyclist himself. He knows the renewal I seek on the road. What would he think of a doctor who tried to take that away from him?

Sure, the dangers make Mom nervous, but she's lived through the joyous moments, too, and I know how much she loves them. They're addictive. When I win, nobody soaks in the experience more than she does. If I ever win again, I doubt any of us can imagine how happy we'd be. How can I possibly abandon my dreams, especially when I don't think living a safe life is for me? I'll admit that I'd be a little bit less likely to suffer a concussion if I worked as an accountant, but I'd also be a lot less likely to reach my full potential. Should I be willing to make that trade-off?

I once heard a quote by a Greek philosopher that said, "Let each man pass his days in that endeavor wherein his gift is greatest." It reminds me of the feelings I experienced from the time I entered my very first race. From that moment, I knew I'd been born to race a bicycle. As my career progressed it was becoming more obvious every day that pro cycling was the place for me. Within the last few days the trainer has brought back all those wonderful feelings.

So am I lacking in maturity if I'd rather spend my life riding a bike than doing anything else? Probably by some people's definitions. Is it self-centered to put my dreams ahead of my parent's peace of mind? Absolutely. Am I being arrogant in saying I believe I can make a positive impact on the world by riding a bike? I don't think so. I believe I can make a difference in this world by showing people it's possible to achieve the impossible. Isn't that worth trying?

Even if my dreams are arrogant, self-centered, or immature, I still believe to my core that racing bicycles is the thing I most need to do with my life, and I'm not about to let the air out of my inner tubes based on just one doctor's comment. "We should get a second opinion," I say.

Dad knows me too well to let this comment slip by. "Or a third, or a fourth, or a fifth, right? You're going to want exactly the number of opinions it takes to find a doctor who agrees with you."

I give him a kiss because there's no point trying to win that argument. We both know he's right.

*   *   *

The next morning the three of us head to the Shepherd Center. We're going there today because Outdoor Life Network has asked to film a segment about me to be aired during their upcoming coverage of the 2006 Tour de France. It's exciting to have OLN paying this sort of attention, and it increases my confidence that I will race again, despite yesterday's setback.

We enter Shepherd's through the main entrance and walk down the hall. I gaze at the walls. They're covered with photos of Shepherd graduates playing tennis in wheelchairs, winning Paralympic medals as a basketball team, crossing the finish line at an Ironman competition, working as scientists, raising children, and delivering inspirational speeches to packed theaters.

I've passed these photographs many times, but I never stopped to comprehend the triumphs they represent. If I hadn't regained the ability to walk, I wonder if I would have had the strength to embrace my new situation as completely as the people in these photographs.

My injury has given me the opportunity to meet all sorts of patients, and I've come across many people who will probably never walk again. In most cases their inability to stand isn't due to a lack of will, but to the nature of their injuries. But what really impresses me is how so many of them have accepted the hand that has been dealt them and decided to make the most of it. Some of them have accomplished things they might never have if they'd remained "able-bodied."

Can I make the most of the hand I've been dealt? Of course. What can I contribute to the world? Lauren flattered me that day with her high expectations. She believes I can motivate families to encourage their loved ones to fight harder. I've seen patients who've given up improving for one reason or another.

Sometimes patients reach a certain level and decide it's good enough. Other times they just decide the pain and hard work of therapy are no longer worth enduring. Can I somehow provide these people with the motivation to push their limits for one more day? And after that, can I convince them to push for another?

I know that part of my success in overcoming my injuries is due to my unwillingness to give up. If I'm able, not merely to return to the level I was at before my accident, but to exceed it, won't that be proof of the value of determination? Will it benefit the injured or sick if I can ride the Tour de France? I think so. Not only will it call attention to a critical cause, help raise money, and drive research, but it will also inspire those who are going through similar challenges to keep fighting with everything they have. That would probably be the most valuable contribution I could make.

I'm thinking more complex thoughts than I've been able to in months by the time we reach Dr. Bilsky's office. We're glad to have some time to talk with him because the film crew will be here any moment.

Dad clears his throat. "Yesterday Dr. Clare told us a piece of Saul's brain was removed."

Dr. Bilsky shakes his head. "Dr. Clare and I spoke after your meeting. We're not sure the current films are clear enough to determine whether or not any of Saul's brain tissue was removed. Part of the problem is that the French medical records are a bit confusing on this point. That might be due to translation difficulties. It's possible that they were simply talking about performing this sort of surgery but didn't actually do it."

"Yesterday Dr. Clare seemed pretty certain," Dad says.

"I'm ordering more tests, including an MRI and an MRA," Dr. Bilsky says. "Once we see those we should know for sure."

"This is one hell of a roller coaster ride," Dad says. "We never hear the same story twice.

Dr. Bilsky nods. "I understand. We'll get you a definitive answer soon."

"There's another question that came up yesterday," Mom says.

"Cycling?" Dr. Bilsky asks.

We all nod.

"Dr. Clare told me about your conversation. I don't agree with him on this issue. It's way too early to decide whether Saul can eventually race or not. In my view, the goal of returning to the pro ranks is one that Saul ought to keep pursuing. At worst, it will help him continue to get better. What can it hurt for him to try?"

His answer isn't exactly the one I'd been hoping for, but I doubt my smile could be any broader. What more can I ask than that judgment on my future as a pro cyclist be withheld until I've got my health back? I look at my dad. "I agree with Doctor Bilsky."

Dad punches me in the shoulder. "Of course you do … now."

Dr. Bilsky smiles. "I think everybody here knows I always speak as plainly as I can. I'm no pie-in-the-sky dreamer. I've seen too much harsh reality in my life for that. There are a huge number of unknowns in any brain recovery. Even if everything goes perfectly, there is only the slimmest chance that Saul will be able to perform at the elite pro level. Only a fraction of a fraction of people are capable of doing that sort of job under the best of conditions. It will be no disgrace if Saul is no longer one of them. At the same time, until I see something that tells me Saul can't race I'm not going to be the one who steals his dream away."

"So, how long will it be until I can start training on the road," I ask.

"Oh, good Lord," Mom says.

Dr. Bilsky chuckles. "He can never resist pushing for the next step, can he?"

"That's how he's always been," Mom says.

Dr. Bilsky looks me in the eye. "Okay, Saul. If you keep working as hard as you are right now, and if we don't encounter any setbacks, I think you can be on the road in six months."

The receptionist leans into the room. "The television crew is here."

We rise from our chairs and head into the lobby. I put my hand on Dad's shoulder. "Did you hear what he said? I can ride again soon."

"That's not what he said," Dad says. "Six months, and then only maybe. Besides, Dr. Bilsky specializes in physical medicine and rehabilitation. He's focused on different issues. To counter the opinion of a neurologist you need another neurologist."

It's almost as if Dad heard a different comment than I did. Dr. Bilsky said it would take six months if I keep working as hard as I have so far. What if I work twice that hard? Then we might be down to three months. The time frame isn't the important part, though. I'll gladly work toward that goal for twice as long if I have to because from the moment he said I could ride again I felt a refreshing new breeze in my face.

In the lobby we meet the OLN crew, and for the next nine hours the three of them go everywhere I go. They talk to therapists, doctors, and friends. They interview me and Mom. Then they set up to talk to Dad.

He's never enjoyed being the center of attention. The outgoing part of my personality definitely came from Mom. "Dad's not going to talk to your camera. He'd faint and it wouldn't be pretty," I say.

Dad nods. "Yep. Keep that contraption away from me."

The OLN crew sees everything about how I live these days. They are even with me when my Pathway's therapist changes the strip of tape on my notebook from yellow to white. I explain what an epic moment this is. I tell them I'll now be allowed to go into the bathroom on my own. Someone will be there for me, but they'll wait outside from now on.

The OLN guys are really nice, and they seem to understand what a big deal this is. I wonder if I could have comprehended how important these small milestones are before my injury. By the end of the day I'm absolutely exhausted, and I unfortunately prove it by bumping into things from time to time. I wish they hadn't gotten that on film.

Chapter Thirteen

Within a few days my team manager, Roger Legeay, arrives for a visit. "Saul! It is miracle to see you standing there."

I start jumping like a little kid. I can't control myself. We hug and trade a *bise*, first left then right. Roger doesn't let go. He squeezes me tight, as if trying to satisfy himself I'm not some sort of hallucination. Maybe he's just trying to convince me to stand still.

"I'm so happy to see you, Roger. I can never thank you enough for your support." I have tears in my eyes a lot these days, just like I do right now, but I don't mind them one bit. Blood, sweat, and tears remind me I'm fully alive.

Roger is looking me over again. I don't blame him for being stunned at how well I'm doing. I concentrate as hard as I can on my behavior. I want to walk in straight lines, not fade to the left as the therapists' videos and my parents' reminders show I'm prone to doing. I need to increase my attention span, even when the conversations get boring. I need to do everything I possibly can to prove to Roger that I'm well.

"I want you to know, Saul," Roger says, "the team remains behind you one hundred percent."

I've never doubted that, but hearing him state it so bluntly feels good. It's a reaffirmation of the reasons I ignored the offers from other teams after my breakthrough ride at the Tour of Germany. Several squads threw big cash my way, but I renewed with Crédit Agricole for a fraction of the price. I remember telling Roger, "I want to stay on your team. Draw me up a fair deal and I'll sign." He put something together within a couple of days. I flipped to the back page and signed it. That's how much I trust him.

I'd agreed to a long-term contract with a guaranteed base significantly less than rival squads were offering. The money in my new contract is mostly incentive based. I think that pay for performance is the best way to go, but after I signed some people told me I was crazy. They're entitled to their opinions, but I don't ride for the money, and the day I start thinking that way is the day I plan to quit. What do a few Euros matter? I ride for love, and I love riding for this team. I love the mechanics, the directeurs, the doctors, the soigneurs, and the fans of Crédit Agricole. Besides that, loyalty means something to me. In fact, it means everything. It's what binds us together in business and life. Crédit Agricole feels the same way, and their actions over the past several months have proven I made the right decision.

"How long since your accident, Saul?" Roger asks.

It takes my mind a moment to return to the present.

Before I can process the question and come up with an answer my dad says, "Seventy-four days."

Roger nods. "And just over one month and a half since I last saw you. Your improvement is remarkable. Do you think you will be well enough to come to France in October for team photos?"

"I know I will," I say.

"Saul thinks he knows lots of things he doesn't," Dad says. "I'll talk with his doctor about it."

"I know this. I'll be healthy enough to go to France by October." I grin. My parents and I sometimes have a feisty relationship, but it's good natured. We say what we mean and we stick to our guns. They never lie to me and, until recently, I've never lied to them. Since the injury I admit I find myself telling fibs now and then. For some reason I can't stop myself. Little lies just sneak out of my mouth, and even though I get busted every time, I soon find myself doing it again.

It's fun showing Roger around Georgia. He was here for the Tour de Georgia, but there's so much more to show him. We see the sights in Atlanta, Dalton, and a couple of places in between. He marvels, as he's done before, at the miles and miles of great cycling roads around here. He buys some mementos of his trip, and he leaves me with some good stuff too, including a fresh supply of Crédit Agricole clothing and the Look 585 bicycle I crashed on. It suffered only minor scratches.

He's also brought along a cool photo from last year's Tour l'Avenir. The name translates to Tour of the Future. Many people refer to it as the Mini Tour de France. The field always includes several top teams but also a number of developmental squads. The racing was insane from the starting gun because if a young cyclist wins a stage at Avenir he is virtually guaranteed a pro contract. Guys were putting everything on the line, and as a result, there were lots of crashes. That caused my morale to dip from the very first day. I just tried to stay safe.

Several days later when we finally hit the mountains I saw my chance to accomplish something. I attacked at the base of the first climb and eventually seven other men joined me. I spent 135 kilometers in the breakaway as we crossed seven mountain peaks. I was the first man over most of them. As we neared the finish line, only two members of the breakaway were left: me and my British teammate, Bradley Wiggins. We shook hands as we passed under the one-kilometer-to-go-banner; then he outsprinted me for the win. The remnants of the peloton finished three and a half minutes behind us, and men were still straggling across the line half an hour after we finished. It felt incredible to shatter the field so completely.

In the photograph Roger has brought I'm standing on the podium in the polka-dot jersey I won for being the best climber in the race. I'm shaking the hand of Jean Marie LeBlanc, the man who directs both Avenir and the Tour de France.

Jean Marie has signed the picture and written a note that says, "I look forward to the day I see you racing in the Tour." Those are motivating words.

By day's end I'm getting exhausted. I bump into a couple of doorways on my left side, and I stumble one time. Then I fall asleep in the car on the way home.

The weekend rushes by, and all too soon Roger's visit is coming to a close. It means so much to me that such a busy man would fly this far just to spend a weekend. He's a nice person, and he tells me again I have his complete support. He writes a check to cover my parents' expenses at Logis Ozanam and insists that they take it. He asks me to just continue focusing on getting healthy, no pressure to race. My salary will be paid. It would be impossible to overstate how much his kindness means to me.

"Do you know what amazes me?" Roger says as we near the airport. "Your French is better than before. Your accent has improved. I never expected that."

"Do you really think so?" I ask.

He nods. "Definitely."

"I'll bet your high school French teacher would be stunned," Mom says.

I think hard for a moment. "Is that the class I failed?"

"Yes. The only F you ever received," she says.

"Well, the French they teach in high-school is nothing like the French on the streets of France," I say. In fact, I consider the last three years in France to be a part of my education. I didn't go to college, but I doubt I could have learned as much on the world's best campus as I did on the roads of Europe.

Dad pulls up to the curb, and a skycap takes Roger's luggage. We hug and say our goodbyes all over again, and then he has to leave.

After he walks into the terminal I turn to Dad. "I did pretty well while Roger was here. Huh?"

"Yeah, Saul, you did well," Dad says.

I wonder if he knows how fantastic it makes me feel to hear him agree without qualification. I know that he could call my attention to the fact that I wasn't perfect in every respect, and he'd be justified in doing so. There were times I was impulsive, and impatient, and inappropriate. I often can't help "dancing on the walls" and I know I sometimes say things that would be better unsaid. But this time Dad doesn't bring any of that stuff up. He's the world's best dad. "I love you," I say, kissing him on the forehead.

"I love you too, Saul, and I'm proud of you. Prouder than words can express." He drapes an arm around my shoulder and pinches my cheek. It's a silly thing to do but it makes me feel loved.

Ever since Roger mentioned team photos I've been dreaming of all the things and people I miss in Europe. There's one person I care about more than any other. "Do you think Daniela will be excited to see me again?"

"Probably," Dad says.

"I told her the other night that if our relationship makes it through this it will soar. She agreed."

Dad pats me on the back. "I'm sure you're both right about that. It's the tough times that bond people. Anybody can stand by your side on a sunny day, but bring on some nasty weather and let's see who is willing to remain. Daniela stuck around when you needed her most. That speaks well of her."

I head to my blog to write down my thoughts:

LIVING LIFE
Contributed by Saul
Saturday, 24 June 2006
The last couple of months have been the hardest in my life mentally and physically. I have gone through almost every emotion and feeling possible. From learning how to eat and walk again it has felt like I have been reborn again. I feel like I have been given a second chance in life. I still get emotional when I think about how far I have come. I see the blue skies ahead and I want everyone to know "You can over come obstacles in life." I believe and feel you can achieve and accomplish anything you set your mind to in life. Life is a beautiful thing. "Living life is learning to love." My best Saul

In movies you see someone wake up from a coma and seem fine. That hasn't been the case for me, and looking at the other people at Pathways and at the Shepherd Center I can tell it doesn't match their experience either. Technically, you could say I woke up about two and a half months ago, but from my perspective I'm not fully awake even yet. Sometimes I wonder when I finally will be. Two days later, just before we leave for Atlanta again, I post another message to my blog:

Last week.
Contributed by Saul
Monday, 26 June 2006
This is my last week of Rehab in Atlanta. After I will be coming home for good going to rehab once or twice week in Chattanooga TN. Life is good. I hope to be getting back on the road in a month or two. I do miss my girl friend Daniela. ouch*** it hurts being away from her this long. I hope she can come in August. Saul

Our first stop is Dr. Bilsky's office. He wants to talk about my progress.

"What does he still need to work on?" Mom asks.

The doctor looks at his notes. "Saul needs to work on his attention span, impulsivity, and short-term memory problems. He still has some cognitive problems, too. Those are usually the last skills to come back. A better question might be, what do you think he still has to overcome?"

Mom doesn't even hesitate. "He's become egotistical. Saul never used to brag about himself or his accomplishments. Nowadays he's talking about that stuff all the time."

Dr. Bilsky writes something in his chart. "Do you agree, Saul?"

"Everybody's always talking about me. It's pretty hard not to respond," I say.

The doctor nods. "Your point is valid, but I agree with your mom you should work to overcome it. Think of it this way. A five-year-old child is developmentally very self-centered, but by definition a child doesn't have that much to brag about. How much can anybody accomplish in the first five years? Your brain, in many ways, was reset to your early years, but unlike your five-year-old counterparts you have a lot to brag about. When you look at it that way, you're just doing what comes naturally. As your mind continues to mature you should see significant improvements in this area. You're a conscientious kid who wants to get better, and I'll bet you will."

We talk about my lying, my left side neglect, my gait pattern, and my spatial awareness. I've heard some of this stuff many times but I can feel it sinking in. It's odd to feel like such a science project, but that's the nature of my life now. I have more work to do to return to my baseline than it ever took for me to get to that level in the first place. I look forward to it. More than that, I want to push my baseline to higher levels than it's ever been before.

I believe the human mind is so powerful it can actually change genetics. I'm certain that even the best among us has never tapped into more than a fraction of his or her mental or physical power. I realize some people would argue that point with me, but I've seen the proof in my own life. As far as I'm concerned, if I can dream it, I can do it. My mind is powerful enough to define my own reality, and that's the reality I prefer.

"Aren't you going to ask about the MRI and MRA results?" Dr. Bilsky asks.

Dad looks surprised. "You have them?"

Dr. Bilsky nods. "Dr. Clare called them in to me."

I swallow hard. "Do I have all my brain or not?"

He chuckles.

"Don't laugh. I'm sure there are people who believe I've always been missing some of it."

"Well," Dr. Bilsky says, "those people are right, now. There appears to be vacant space where we would expect the second and third giri to be. The good news is, you've already proven they aren't necessary for you to live a normal life."

"Is racing bikes normal to you?" I ask.

"Not to Dr. Clare. Simply stated, his opinion is that bicycle racing is too dangerous an activity for you."

I look away. "But you disagree."

"I don't necessarily disagree. I just think it's still too early to make that decision," Dr. Bilsky says.

I want to hug Dr. Bilsky and thank him for refusing to put a cap on my capabilities.

"Dr. Clare also came to more conclusions from your tests," Dr. Bilsky says.

"Like what?" I ask.

"Well, he sees no signs that your accident was caused by brain problems."

The cause of the accident hadn't crossed my mind in a long time, but I realize this is very good news. After the crash some people speculated that I was epileptic. If that had been true, it would have prevented me from racing again. This good news makes me happy. Now all I need is a neurologist who disagrees with Dr. Clare's opinion about bike racing.

At my first opportunity after leaving Dr. Bilsky's office I write an e-mail to Lance Armstrong. I tell him one of my doctors is saying I should never race again. Can he help me find a second opinion?

Lance's reply comes back in no time. "I'm on it."

I realize it sounds like hero worship to say this, but I can't fully explain how Lance has inspired me over the years. Since we're both pro cyclists, people sometimes assume I know him well. That's not correct. Lance's life is a whirlwind of events and obligations, and just as his cycling career has been winding down mine has been ramping up. I've had only one face-to-face conversation with him, after we raced in training up the Col de Braus. You can't imagine how cool it felt to go as hard as I could against him with our audience, Axel Merckx and Sheryl Crow, following in the car behind.

For these reasons it means a great deal to me that he'd take the time to respond at all. I see myself as the student and him as the teacher. It lifts me up, both morally and physically, each time he answers my calls or replies to my e-mail. And the fact that he took the time and initiative to call my mom while I was in the coma in France puts the exclamation point on our relationship. He'll never comprehend how much that call meant to us as a family.

At Pathways, Megan points me to the balance test again. I've taken this many times, and my performance has gradually improved. She straps me into the harness, and then the floor starts moving. Pretty soon the walls are shifting around, too, but I'm standing steady. Eventually the ride stops. I look back at Megan.

She's holding up a piece of green tape. To me it's as beautiful as an Olympic medal. This sticky piece of cloth is the credential that tells anybody who matters that I'm allowed to go where I want, when I want. Of course, it's my job to get to my therapy sessions on time, but in between I can now walk around the outside of the building without supervision if I want to, or I can go up and down stairs. If I want to go out on the basketball court and shoot hoops to destress for awhile I'm allowed to do it without permission. No one even needs to wait outside of the bathroom. It feels so good to be free.

For the remainder of the week in therapy I work as hard as I possibly can. I push my brain and my body to their maximum limit every day. Each evening I return to the hotel and ride my trainer until either Mom or Dad force me to get off. Every night I collapse into bed, exhausted. I'm improving so fast I can feel it.

Then a big day arrives. In fact, it's the biggest of all days at Pathways. It's graduation day.

Throughout this process at Shepherd's Center and Shepherd's Pathways I've met many people with brain injuries or spinal-cord injuries. Every person's story is fascinating. All of them can tell amazing tales of survival and perseverance. Two people that stand out are Amy Hawkins and my good, life-long friend, Zach Phillips.

I've mentioned Zach before. Amy was in a huge F4 tornado in Nashville, Tennessee. She threw her body on top of her two children while the storm picked up their house and left her in a heap of rubble on the foundation. Debris rained down on top of her. As a result she was paralyzed from the waist down, but she saved the lives of her children in the process. She's a true hero.

As the graduation ceremony begins I don't know what to expect, but I'm looking forward to this huge steppingstone in my recovery.

All the therapists and support staff enter the therapy room. Each one says something kind about me and the other graduates. Then they hand each of us a diploma. It's a simple ceremony, but already very emotional.

"Can I make my own speech?" I ask. The last three months have taught me how precious life is. I've made a vow never to leave anything important unsaid or undone.

"Of course," the counselor says.

"I'd like to thank each and every one of you for all your caring and love." Tears run down my face and my voice cracks. "We are the miracles, and you're our heroes. I'm sure I speak for everyone standing here when I say, we wouldn't be doing as well as we are now without your help. I would like to thank you all from the bottom of my heart. Thank you for being my heroes."

After the festivities I post another message to my blog:

My last day
Contributed by Saul
Friday, 30 June 2006
Today was my last day of Rehab at Shepherd's Pathways. I was a little emotional on
my big day. Graduating was personally one of my biggest achievements in my life.
All my fighting is paying off. I will still go to rehab once or twice a week in
Chattanooga TN. All I see is blue skies … "I am going to make it." Saul

Chapter Fourteen

It seems ironic that the 2006 Tour de France gets underway just as I make it home for good. I'm going to be able to pay closer attention to this year's race than any race of the past several years. For the next three weeks it will motivate me to train harder and to make it all the way back.

I have to address another issue that's big in the news right now: doping in cycling. I'm saddened that the most beautiful sport in the world is constantly being tarnished by this kind of stuff, but it makes me happy that illegal operations, like the one uncovered in Operation Puerto, are collapsing under their own weight.

One of the reasons I love my team is that we are under the strictest doping controls in the business. I can't imagine how anyone could cheat while riding for Crédit Agricole. Our reputation is backed up by such rigorous testing that some people have actually said things to me like, "You've got to get away from that team. There's no way you can take the steps necessary to win under their scrutiny." What they don't seem to understand is that as a clean athlete, that's music to my ears.

In addition to the regular urine and blood tests all pro cyclists are subject to throughout the year, the French Fédération requires every member of my team to submit to frequent and random blood tests, both in and out of competition. Our data is stored and compared longitudinally. If any variations to our blood chemistry show up we're required to explain them in writing and submit to another test or we will be suspended. This means that if my testosterone numbers aren't consistent from one test to another, even if the values aren't moving outside of established guidelines, I have to explain why. That happened to me last spring, in fact. It turned out the increase was just the result of the normal maturation process.

The testers also monitor my hematocrit and determine if the profile is consistent with my training and racing regimen. Am I dehydrated, or are other factors in play? If my blood count was to rise in the midst of a heavy racing schedule, I would have to explain why that happened. Such scrutiny makes the sorts of manipulations that characterize modern doping impossible.

I hope more teams sign on to do this sort of testing. Longitudinal testing is the way to go, and blood tests give much more reliable and detailed information than urine tests. All this will mean a rude awakening for those who might push athletes to use illegal substances. It will also shut down opportunities for athletes who are willing, or who have felt forced into turning their bodies into chemistry experiments to win races. Meanwhile, it's great news for upcoming young racers like me who are unwilling to allow drugs to be a part of their career. I think it's truly wonderful that the sport is going through these changes.

I know beyond a shadow of a doubt that it's possible to win while racing clean. I can point to my results and say without reservation that I accomplished them honestly. It can be done. Will power is better than drug power in every respect.

Dad sets up the television in front of my trainer and tunes it to OLN. I watch the Prologue in France while riding in place. The winner of this stage will become the race's first leader and will wear the yellow jersey.

The course is short but technical. It favors a rider with great handling skills, fearless aggression, and the physical strength to accelerate hard out of every corner. Although he's not being talked about as one of the favorites, I know a rider who fits that profile perfectly. He's my teammate, Thor Hushovd of Norway, and he's one of my best friends in the world.

When I first joined Crédit Agricole I didn't speak French. Thor, one of the few Crédit Agricole members who spoke fluent English, helped me a lot. He has chiseled features and a charismatic personality. He's a guy people just like to be around. I admire him both as a person and as a cyclist. He was there for me long before my crash, and he's called and written in support many times since the accident. Thor is our team's sprint specialist, so while he's not a threat to win the final yellow jersey in Paris, he just might capture the green sprinter's jersey like he did last year. I'll be cheering for him.

My palms sweat as I watch the Norwegian God of Thunder power through the turns, and cross the line. The clock stops, showing he holds a four-second lead. That's a big hunk of time on a stage like this, but the favorites are all still to come.

One by one, they fall short. As the final cyclists cross the line I'm cheering at the top of my lungs in support of Thor. I've long since quit riding my trainer as I watch my friend pull on the yellow jersey. I'm so happy for his accomplishment. I post a quick message to my blog:

Raisin HELL!!!!!!
Contributed by Saul
Saturday, 01 July 2006
THOR Raisin some hell all the way to the Podium in France … Feels good!!!!!!!!!!!!
I am with the team all the way!!!!!!!!!!!!!!!! Saul Raisin

Thor's success has me dreaming of returning to race by his side more than ever. I'm not a sprinter and I never will be, but I've proven I can ramp up the pace and keep it there for a long lead-out when I'm asked to. I can't wait to do that again for my teammates. I'm so excited about the day's stage, I can't calm down. I call Thor.

"The team drank a glass of champagne in your name before the race," he says. "We feel you here with us."

That means a lot to me, and it motivates me even more. "I dream of riding side by side with you again."

"You told me that before in your raspy voice from your hospital bed. Now it's my dream, too, and I know you're going to make it come true," Thor says.

The next morning I push myself for three hours on the trainer. I feel the fog encroaching, and that's just what I want. If I'm going to overcome my weaknesses I need to confront them head on. Every time I reach the fog it's another step in pushing it farther away. Racing a Grand Tour in Europe is going to put me into serious energy debt, and with that will come the fog. I need to deal with it now to prove to myself I can conquer it. I don't climb off the trainer until my legs are flimsy and my head is light. I recover quickly, though.

The fatigue I used to experience is almost gone now. Sometimes I take a midday nap, but it's not as if I absolutely can't stay awake like before. I can walk up and down stairs pretty well, and I hardly ever slip. I don't bump into stuff as much as I used to, either, and I'm using my left hand and arm more and more.

The energy around cycling in July has me wired. I spend my free time visiting Internet cycling boards and chat rooms like DailyPeloton.com, trading e-mails and instant messages, and just plain being a fan. I enjoy talking with other cycling enthusiasts about racing, and I start making all sorts of friends online.

I talk to a woman dealing with surgery after a broken collarbone and she asks me how I dealt with the pain.

"There was no pain," I say. "By the time I was coherent, my bones had mended."

"You're lucky," she says.

She's wrong. I choose not to tell her this, but I'm convinced that if you have your choice, it's far better to feel pain than to feel nothing at all.

*   *   *

Ever since my parents flew me home on the Learjet the issue we haven't had time to deal with is my heart. The doctors in France were concerned it had sustained some sort of damage during the crash. I think they were wrong, and so do my parents. In fact, the only muscle in my entire body that's felt fine through this whole process is my heart.

We visit a cardiologist named Dr. Ahmad. Dad has brought my bicycle and trainer because Dr. Ahmad normally runs his tests using a treadmill, and I simply don't have the balance to put in a hard workout on my feet.

The doctor starts by taking an ultrasound of my heart; then he instructs me as he hooks electrodes to my chest and a pressure cuff to my arm. "Begin by riding slowly in an easy gear."

I start pedaling.

Dr. Ahmad keeps glancing at a bank of monitors and back at me. "Okay, increase your heart rate."

I speed up my pedaling.

"Increase again."

I shift to a harder gear. Every few minutes he asks me to raise the effort level. Eventually he says, "I need a higher heart rate, Saul. Give me your maximum."

I shift into my highest gear.

"Still not enough. I need five more beats per minute!"

I stand on the pedals and push as hard as I can.

"Go Saul! Good Saul! A little more!" Dr. Ahmad yells.

I grit my teeth and push.

"Beautiful," the doctor says. "Now off the bike quickly and lie down for one more ultrasound."

Dad helps me hurry to the table.

Dr. Ahmad applies lubricant gel to my chest and finds an image of my heart using his transducer. "Incredible!" He moves the device around to create images from different angles. "I can't believe what I'm seeing."

"What is it, doctor?" Dad asks.

The doctor is scribbling notes. "One moment. One moment."

We wait while he finishes. Then he looks at me with a wide smile. "Even at your huge effort level your heart reached only 140 beats per minute. Then, once you laid down your pulse returned to its resting rate incredibly fast, faster than I've ever seen before. I almost didn't capture the images I needed."

"So, am I okay?" I ask.

"Oh, yes. You're okay. You've got a very, very healthy athlete's heart, Saul."

I already knew that, but I'm glad we've put the issue to rest.

"There's something else, Saul," Dr. Ahmad says. "I doubted your dad when he told me your heart was so large. Often we think of an enlarged heart as a problem, but that's obviously not the case with you."

"How big is Saul's heart?" Dad asks.

The doctor grins. "The average human heart is about the size of an orange. Saul's heart is the size of a grapefruit, but the left ventricle is the most impressive. This chamber pushes blood through the body. Saul's left ventricle measures 6.1 centimeters. Based on his age and size, the typical measurement would be 3.5 to 4 centimeters. This is a significant difference."

Dad puts an arm around my shoulders. "Nobody has a bigger heart than my boy."

"I think you may be right," Dr. Ahmad says.

Each day the Tour de France progresses I push myself further. By July seventh I'm swimming for forty-five minutes twice a week, lifting weights for long sessions with my left arm, and riding as much as five hours a day on the trainer. Sometimes I ride until nine or ten at night. By the time I get off I'm limping, drooling, and slurring my words. It scares the hell out of my mom and dad, but they can't make me stop because we all know it's helping me return to life. Every time I exert physical force I feel great, and the main thing I look forward to afterward is recovering so I can push harder the next time.

Even as a pro cyclist I've never before ridden the trainer for such long sessions, and I don't know of anybody else who has, either; but the strangest thing has happened. Before the accident I considered time on the trainer to be an unpleasant but necessary alternative to riding on the roads when circumstances didn't allow. Now my time on the trainer is sheer freedom. Today I rode for five hours, without a television or fan, while drinking only two bottles of water. I loved every moment. I wouldn't mind spending my entire day pedaling because, even though it might look like I'm going nowhere, I'm actually on the journey of a lifetime. The bike, even though it's just the stationary trainer for now, is my key to a healthy future.

The swimming is helping, too. It's a great total body workout and helps my left arm strength and coordination a lot. Swimming has always been one of my favorite sports. I went to national meets with my high-school swim team. When I was seventeen I thought triathlon would be the perfect sport for me because of the swimming and biking. I entered a race and won, even though I found the running part miserable. Running is the reason I never entered another triathlon.

I've learned it's possible to continue improving from a brain injury for your entire life, but eighty percent of the progress is usually made in the first six months. I'm three months in and doing well, but the way I see it I've got to get as much rehabilitation as possible into the next three months. The further along I am by that time, the greater my chances for a full recovery.

My left arm is still weak, but sixty days ago I couldn't even lift it. I still have mental problems, including short-term memory loss, poor problem-solving abilities, and diminished reasoning, but even my doctors say that none of these are very bad anymore. My parents often correct me for things like talking too much, standing too close to others, and being too restless. I appreciate their criticisms because only through awareness can I drive my deficits completely away.

I'm starting to believe it's possible I'll come out of this injury in better shape, both mentally and physically, than I went in. I know I'm better emotionally. It's not that I had head problems before the accident, but now I can see I took too much for granted. As crazy as it is to say this, I'm going to live a fuller life because of what I've been through.

I post another message to my blog to catch people up on some of the many things going on:

Saul Raisin Woods. New photos.
Contributed by Saul
Monday, 10 July 2006
Today is my first day of Rehab in Chattanooga TN. I am excited to get this show on the road and get well. Yesterday I went out to "Saul Raisin Woods," the mountain bike Park in my town named after me. I took several pictures. It is a real honor to have a Park named after me. Thank you to everyone who helped build it. I look forward to the day that I can ride it.
Saul Raisin

On July 11 we meet with Dr. Paré, a new neurosurgeon here in Dalton who just happens to be French-Canadian. Our family physician, Dr. Delay, told him about my case, and he translated all our French medical records to English at no charge. He has more than one hundred x-rays to show the progression of my brain damage. I'm interested in learning if he has more details than Dr. Clare mentioned.

He slaps my back and leads me over to the x-ray table along with my mom and dad.

"Here is your progression, Saul." He has several sheets of film, each with a dozen or more images on it. "The machine photographs slices of your brain, or cuts as I like to call them. This way we can see what's going on at different levels. So first let's look at the film taken right when you went into your coma."

He positions one of the x-ray sheets on the light table. The images look more like Rorschach Ink Blots than anything else.

"These are pictures of a brain in very bad shape. See the white areas on the right-forward edge in each of these cuts? That's clotting blood. We call that a hematoma, and this is a large one. It has both subdural and intracranial elements, which means it's not only on the surface of the brain, but within it. The potential for brain damage under these conditions is extremely high. The medical records show your right pupil was blown by this time, and the reason is obvious."

"What do you mean by blown," Dad asks.

"Fully dilated." He spreads his fingers to show that dilation went way beyond the normal range. "That happens when the brain becomes so swollen it squeezes the oculomotor nerve shut. Signals are no longer traveling to or from the eye. In Saul's case the pressure was so great that not only were the ventricles swollen shut," he points to some lines in the middle of the scan, "these should normally be visible spaces in the cranial cavity— but the entire brain rotated under the pressure."

"How can you see that?" I ask.

"See the midline on this image here?" A central axis has been superimposed to make the division between the brain hemispheres clearly visible, but it's not down the center of the skull at all. "The swelling has forced everything to rotate. It would also be pushing the brain down through the spinal column and potentially damaging nerves in that region as well." He taps his finger on the film. "This, my friend, is the photo of a brain on the verge of death."

There's not much I can think to say looking at an image like that, except, "I'm glad they fixed it."

"They had to do radical surgery, and in a big hurry." He puts a new sheet on the light table. "See this image here? This is the same cut we were looking at before, but the time stamp tells us that this was several weeks after your surgery. Can you tell what's different?"

"Yeah. Where the white hematoma used to be there's now a lot of black space," I say.

"Do you know what black space represents?" he asks.

"Nothing, I guess."

He nods his head. "Nothing is right. The surgeon evacuated quite a bit of material, including some brain tissue. It was probably damaged beyond repair."

He makes some measurements. "The missing piece appears to be about four centimeters by two centimeters."

"Lemon sized?" Dad asks.

The doctor shakes his head. "Maybe half that."

"Was it the right decision to take it out?" I ask.

"Your surgeon did what had to be done," Dr. Paré says. "He did a fine job."

"Saul was truly blessed to have been in that hospital," Mom says. "It just happened to be one of the leading centers for brain research in all of Europe. They saved his life."

Dad nods in agreement, but I can tell there's something on his mind. Finally he asks, "What does the missing portion normally do?"

Dr. Paré pulls out a model of the human skull. He removes the top and starts pointing to pieces underneath. "The brain is an incredibly complicated organ. Some portions define the personality, some control balance, some portions are concerned with major motor control, and other portions specialize in minor movement. Under ideal conditions, we can test to see what sort of information is stored at different locations in a healthy brain, but that kind of caution is impossible under emergency conditions.

"Several things might have been contained in the part of Saul's brain that was removed. Since he's left handed, there was an increased chance it would house his speech center, but fortunately it didn't. That was a stroke of good fortune. The removed part probably contained some of his motor function memory, which explains the hard work Saul has had to do to regain the use of his left side. We've already known, and he has proven again it's possible to find new storage sites for information like that. This explains why he's had to relearn so many simple skills as if he'd never done them before."

"So he can live normally without that part of his brain?" Dad asks.

Dr. Paré holds out his open palm toward me. "There's your proof."

"Am I at greater risk for another injury because of what I've gone through?" I ask.

Dr. Paré shakes his head. "After your brain fully heals, eighteen to twenty-four months post impact, a second hit would be like a first injury."

My mouth drops open as I look at my Dad.

"Not magnified?" he asks.

"I don't see any reason it would be," Dr. Paré answers.

My parents and I discuss this new opinion in detail on the way home. Honestly, none of us know what to make of it. We decide that it proves how little is actually known about the brain. It seems amazing that one doctor can conclude one thing and another can see exactly the opposite using the same evidence. Maybe it has more to do with their personal tolerance for risk than anything else. It can't be denied that racing a bike involves risk, no matter what precautions someone takes.

At home I log onto the computer to do some research of my own. I share an e-mail account with my parents, so I check for messages first. There's a note from Daniela that appears to be a response to a message from my dad. He asked her if she could come to America soon because I'm not yet ready to go to France. He told her how badly I want to see her.

Daniela's response is that she's planning to break up with me. It says she "will not be making a grand entrance to the USA." Grand entrance? How about just getting on a plane and coming for a visit? The message also says she's going to be calling to tell me, but how could she not know I'd be likely to see her message here first? It almost seems as if she wanted me to stumble across it this way. I read the words again and again, trying to make sense of them. I want to convince myself I'm misinterpreting the message. That can happen so easily by e-mail.

She's written that we weren't getting along well before the accident and our lives were headed in different directions. That's not true. The fact is that we were getting along spectacularly. She told me she felt as passionately about me as I did about her, and I'm certain she was telling the truth, at least at that time. I can't make any sense of the things she's written about breaking up, and I'm even more confused that she'd announce it to my parents instead of me.

For the next few days almost the only thing I can think about is my relationship with Daniela, but I resist calling her to ask. If she wants to break up then she's going to have to do it herself. I recall some statistics that one of the therapists told us in a meeting at Pathways. Seventy percent of Americans who survive catastrophic events are abandoned by their significant other as a result. At the time I couldn't have dreamed that statistic would become relevant in my life. I've always looked at the strength of my parents' marriage and assumed I'd have the same sort of relationship for myself. Until now, I was certain it would happen with Daniela. Surprise!

When Johnathan Vaughters, a former teammate of Lance's and current directeur of one of the top American cycling teams calls, it distracts me from thoughts of Daniela. He knows a specialist named Dr. Cooper he'd like me to talk to. I'm always interested in information on my injuries, so I give him a call.

I'm immediately glad I did. Dr. Cooper says he agrees with Dr. Paré's opinion that my brain won't be at greater risk than normal once it's fully healed. Then he adds something that I don't like so much. Because of the surgery and damage to the right temporal part of my brain I'm now at high risk for seizures. He thinks I should use a seizure monitor once I'm taken off the Keppra, the drug which is currently keeping some of my brain activity under control.

So I have to take the good news with the bad. As if we didn't already know it, we're continuing to see that there are no definite answers when it comes to brain injuries.

A couple of days later, as we're getting out of the car at Raisin Textiles, Daniela finally calls. "Hi, Saul."

"Hi Daniela."

Mom gives me a knowing, compassionate nod. "We'll be inside. Take your time."

I wave to her and Dad. They're hurting as badly as I am about this. They would have given Daniela the world if she'd stuck around.

"There's something we need to talk about," Daniela says. Her voice quavers, and then she starts to cry.

In a way, I'm glad I've been prepared. "Then talk."

"You always say love grows, but my love does not grow with you any more. It has gone away. I simply do not love you any more. I cannot say those words and mean them." Her voice is as sweet as it's always been, but her words have such a bitter taste.

"Is this because of my brain injury?" I ask.

By now she's crying really hard. "No. That only makes it harder. I truly don't want to hurt you. I want to be your friend, just not your girlfriend."

What's happened to the woman I love? What happened to the beautiful person who stood by my side and brought me back to life while I lay in a French hospital? Where is the girl who made my parents' lives bearable for those first terrible weeks? Even though I knew this was coming I simply can't believe what she's just told me.

A part of my mind I've never been aware of before takes over my mouth. "How can you be so cold-hearted? Does love mean something different to you than it does to me?"

"Don't talk that way, Saul," she cries.

"I'll talk how I want. You breaking up with me is nothing more than a bee sting. You cannot break my heart. I broke my own heart when I crashed and hit my head." Even as the words pass my lips I know they don't contain a shred of truth. She can break my heart, and she has. I lost so much in my accident, but I'd come to terms with all that because I thought I'd survived with several important things intact. The most valuable of those was Daniela's love. Now that's been stolen away from me, too.

I'm feeling a type of misery I've never experienced before. I hear myself moaning, but it's really more of a disembodied defense mechanism. It's no use trying to explain my discomfort, because each time I think I understand what's going on inside my head the pain only gets worse. And now I realize something: whenever I used to tell her I loved her in her native tongue she never responded, "*Ich liebe Dich.*" I should have recognized the signs.

"Saul. Let's talk about this. I want to be friends," she says.

"I can't be friends with you, Daniela. That's not possible." I disconnect the call and drop to a seated position on the concrete steps, sobbing.

Chapter Fifteen

Over the next few days I call and write Daniela several more times. Even though I want to speak sanely, that mean part of my mind keeps taking over our conversations. Harsh words flow from my lips, and I'm sure I scare her to death in the process. I'm just not in the mental state to understand what's happened or to deal with it maturely.

When I'm thinking clearly I know that Daniela helped my parents beyond her duty, something I can never thank her enough for. She will always be someone I think of as special in my life. I wish her the best, but when I speak to her I can't make those sorts of words come out.

Something else is also bothering me. A strange tingling sensation has been traveling down my back and into my left leg. It's especially strong when I lower my chin to my chest. We head to Dr. Paré's office for an opinion. He doubts it's anything to worry about but schedules an MRI just in case. I recall what Dad said about this experience being a roller coaster ride, and I agree. I get good news one day and bad news the next.

My thoughts turn to Daniela again. They won't stay away from her. I'm not mad. I understand. I'm sure she thinks she's lost her boyfriend. She's young and has a full life in front of her. I've already died to her, maybe more than once as a result of the vicious things I've said. I want to apologize, but I don't trust myself to get through it with dignity. I doubt she'll listen to me anyway.

Dad wants me to take my mind off her by doing Sudoku puzzles. Forget that. To feel better I ride my trainer instead. Then I post a message about it on my blog:

Afterward I try to keep myself distracted from my relationship troubles by reading some of the thousands of supportive messages on my web site. Most of them are wishing me well, telling me to never give up. Not many people have support like this to fall back on. It makes me realize, day by day, the debt I owe. I need to write a book so people can understand the experience of going through something like this. Maybe it could help others recover strongly as well. I want to inspire people who have brain and spinal-cord injuries to fight as hard as I've tried to, no matter how bleak things sometimes look.

Then I come across a message that says, "I have a request to ask of you. On Saturday June 17th I had a very good friend, Bret Neylon that was involved in a racing accident 100 meter from the finish line. He will be moving to the Shepard Center for rehab. I was wondering if you could stop in and give him some encouraging words." As I scroll down the page I see another ten similar messages. I'm glad people believe a visit from me might be helpful to a fellow cyclist, and since we're headed to Atlanta to pick up a friend from the airport, I visit Bret. I learn that he checked in just a week after I left. His accident resulted in a fracture of the C4 vertebrae in his neck, and he's currently quadriplegic.

When I enter the spinal-injury ward, a girl in a wheelchair beckons me over. "You're new here, aren't you?"

"I've been around," I say.

She motions me to come close and whispers, "Don't go near the brain-injury ward. It's a freak show."

I pat her on the shoulder. "I've already been there."

"You've heard the way they moan?" she asks.

I nod. "Things do get better." Thinking back to my time in this hospital I realize my moaning was probably as freakish as anything she's referring to. I didn't realize that's how I sounded at the time. Now it's a language that I understand.

I check in at the nurses' station and a woman points me toward Bret Neylon's room. I walk in carrying a Crédit Agricole cycling hat and jersey, and a Raisin Hell bracelet. The moment Bret sees me he looks down at his wrist, which is his only way of pointing, and I notice he's already wearing one of my bracelets. Seeing this almost makes me cry. He's touched my heart instantly.

"You have a lot of friends, Bret. They're overwhelming my guestbook," I say.

"I'm lucky." He's just come off the ventilator and his scratchy voice reminds me of how painful my throat felt at that time in my recovery.

I put a hand on his shoulder. "Just stay strong. Okay?"

He nods.

"Never give up, Bret. Things do get better." I squeeze his hand gently and have a vision that one day he's going to be able to squeeze mine back.

It's hard to explain, but there's a sort of energy surrounding this guy I've never experienced before. He has an incredible smile that never stops. To an outsider it might appear the odds are stacked against him, but he won't accept that. Although he has no use of his arms or legs he's still full of fight. I can tell that he'll never give up. I leave knowing he's going to be fine, no matter what hand life deals him. I came here thinking I'd give him courage, but instead I'm the one leaving with renewed strength. I'm very happy to have made this new friend.

Afterward in the hall my parents and I run into Dr. Bilsky.

"How long until I can ride my bike on the road again?" I ask.

He smiles. "Saul, you never give up, do you."

I laugh. Of course I don't.

"Let me watch you walk," he says.

I know I've made big improvements, and I love seeing his surprised expression as I do better on each test than he expects.

Finally he says, "You've made incredible progress. If you keep this up you'll be riding on the road in three months."

I'm so excited that I pump my left arm and clinch my left fist. The moment I do it, I realize I probably haven't made that gesture since sometime in March, maybe even since back when I won at Langkawi. It's a nice reminder of my returning strength.

After our visit to Shepherd's we head to the airport to pick up my friend, who also happens to be my cycling coach. His name is Jim Lehman, and he's based out of Colorado Springs. He's come all this way just to show his support and to ride his trainer beside me. Only a true friend would cross the country for the pleasure of sweating in my attic. At times like these I realize how lucky I am. It's great to see him and show him my progress.

We watch the Tour de France together while riding our trainers. Jim has brought me a Power Tap. It's a complex device that transforms a bike into a rolling laboratory. A high tech rear-wheel hub transmits data wirelessly to a handlebar-mounted computer. The computer also gathers data on heart rate, cadence, speed, distance, and more. It converts the collected input into valuable training data. The coolest thing is that I can see instantly how my power output varies with small changes like body position, cleat orientation, and cadence changes. Not only can I use the real-time data to perfect my technique, but I can download all the information to the computer for Jim to study and dissect. He can create complex graphs which compare performances over time. It will help me plan peak fitness levels to coincide with my targeted races. Power meters are rapidly taking bicycle racing to the next level.

I push the readout to 350 watts. I can sustain it for several minutes, but I can't go higher. It's as if I have a governor attached to my engine. Still, 350 watts isn't bad. I'll bet an awful lot of people never dreamed I'd hit numbers like that again. I plan on going a whole lot higher.

Jim has been watching me closely. "You're motivated, aren't you, Saul?"

"Yeah," I say.

"More than ever, I mean," Jim says. "You've always been very hard working and coachable, but now you've taken it to a new level."

I nod. "I've taken a lot of things to a new level. Relationships are more important to me. Maximizing my gifts is more important to me. The bicycle is more important to me, too."

"You see a higher purpose to racing, don't you?" Jim asks.

"Yes. I love racing my bike, and I think I can do something good just by crossing the starting line, let alone the finish line."

In France Floyd Landis has been quietly dominating the race, but on this day, Stage Sixteen, he's in trouble. His only teammate still barely hanging on to the lead pack is my good friend Axel Merckx. That's bad news because, while Axel is an amazing climber for his size, he's no mountain specialist. He doesn't have the strength to offer Landis much support. Worse, Floyd's rivals know it. They're pressing the pace and denying him the opportunity to get more food and water.

After a fast descent, they reach the final climb. The attacks are relentless. The other cyclists remind me of jackals harassing an injured antelope. Then suddenly Landis cracks. He doesn't merely hiccough. His body practically shuts down. He looks like he's hardly moving as the race roars past him up the hill.

"This is brutal. What a tough day," Jim says.

I nod. "Yeah, it must hurt. It's all over for him. What a Tour de France, though."

My parents and Jim Lehman agree. There are still a handful of potential winners with only one mountain stage and a long time-trial to go.

The next morning by the time television coverage begins in the United States, Floyd has already launched a suicide attack. He's tearing up the road, but the peloton should easily bring him back if they play it right. People unfamiliar with cycling usually vastly underestimate the sport. At first glance it looks like a simple game, but in reality it's extremely strategic, political, and complex. It takes a lot more than physical strength to win. Today the top contenders will probably let their teammates do the work of chasing Floyd down while they stay out of the wind and preserve their strength for the final climb. I like that Landis has the guts to go for this all-or-nothing gambit, even though he's far more likely to get nothing. No man, no matter how strong, can outrun a motivated peloton for an entire day. It will take some serious misjudgments on his rivals' parts for Floyd's strategy to succeed.

We watch in awe as he holds onto his margin throughout the day. He dumps bottle after bottle of water over his head, and at the point where his margin over the pack ought to be crumbling it actually starts increasing.

"The other teams are underestimating him," I say. "They're playing cat and mouse, trying to get their rivals to chase. Meanwhile Floyd's running away with the race."

That's exactly what happens. Landis is amazing on the final climb and even better on the dangerous winding descent to the finish. He crosses the line, punching the air with an emphatic fist. Then he hops from his bike like a delivery boy running late.

"Wow!" Jim says. "That's racing!"

"It's the sort of performance that made me fall in love with the sport," I say. "It doesn't get any better."

I'm also excited because the OLN special they shot about me will be airing during tomorrow morning's coverage. Floyd's triumph will mean a lot more people are likely to tune in and learn about my fight. That can only be a good thing.

But the next day when I watch the vignette on my recovery, I see something I hadn't expected. I don't look like a promising pro cyclist at all. I look like a gangly boy, lost in the fog. It breaks my heart to see myself looking so bad, especially when I realize that what they captured was nothing close to my worst day. In fact, at the time I thought I was doing great. It makes me wonder, am I doing great now or am I only fooling myself?

A sour mood overtakes me, and I can't seem to shake it. I post a new message to my blog:

Life
Contributed by Saul
Saturday, 22 July 2006
My life has truly been turned upside down. If becoming a champion means coming close to the brink of death it is not worth it. Imagine one minute you're racing a bicycle in France and the next you're lying in a hospital bed in Atlanta, Georgia, not being able to move an inch. I have had highs and lows. Some of the highs are walking again, swimming, and riding a bike for the first time. The lows are not being able to do simple math and being stuck in a fog where everything around me was in slow motion. If you were able to watch the OLN special you could see some of the fog I used to have in my eyes. As of now the fog is almost gone, and I am so much better than I was in the interview. I just about lost my life and I did lose my girl friend. Did you know 70% of people that have something catastrophic happen to them have their loved one leave them? As of now I am riding the trainer every day while watching the Tour. It is so exciting this year!!!!! I would like to thank everyone for their support and answered prayers. You don't know how much it means to me. I will be at the USA Professional championships to watch the race.
Saul

Everything I said in the message I posted is deeply meaningful to me. The part about Daniela is there because I think about her constantly. I can't get her out of my mind, and I can't understand what went wrong. The part about my injury not being worth it comes straight from the heart. Even though I know I'll be a stronger competitor because of it, I would go back and change things in a heartbeat if I could. The anguish I've put my parents through weighs heavily on me. I would never have put them through this if I could have avoided it.

Yet even as I think those thoughts I realize I'm devoting every bit of energy to returning to my old life and pro cycling. I certainly don't plan on crashing next time, but I never did before, either. I'll be riding in the world's toughest races where mishaps are always a possibility; therefore, my parents will always have frazzled nerves. How come I can't stop myself from chasing goals like these? Why can't I be satisfied with compiling the world's greatest butterfly collection or something like that?

The answer is easy. I was born to ride a bike. I feel an obligation not only to make the most of my abilities, but to prove I can accomplish positive things and inspire others. Now, more than ever, people are counting on me. Brain and spinal-cord injured patients need proof that the highest levels of accomplishment are still attainable for them. I'm in the position to provide that proof. They are my angels, and I owe them the best I can deliver.

It's a strange irony that many of the best athletes in the world have gone through major trauma of some kind, and that seems particularly true for American Tour de France champions. Lance Armstrong won the biggest of all races seven times and changed the way millions view cancer in the process. Greg LeMond survived a near fatal shotgun wound and rebounded to win the final two of his three Tour de France titles. Floyd Landis looks like he'll win this year's Tour with a hip most people wouldn't consider fit for walking.

But even if I win the Tour after my major trauma, it would only be a big added bonus. Living is more important. Enjoying a sunny afternoon surrounded by family beats pulling on a yellow shirt any day of the week. There are times I think just plain living a regular-size life with regular-size dreams is what I ought to do.

And then I think again about how and why I survived this injury that experts thought might be unsurvivable. Why have I thrived in its aftermath when those same people claimed some basic functions would be impossible for me? I think it's all because of the bike, so turning my back on the bike now wouldn't make much sense. I went into this experience in good shape both mentally and physically. Because of cycling I'd already proven to myself how hard I can fight when the chips are down, so it wasn't as tough as it might have been for me to do battle again. I attacked my problems in the same way I'd been taught to attack a race. I wouldn't give up until I got to the finish, where I wanted to be. Living by myself, racing bikes again, has been the driving goal since this journey started. Only when I'm on the start line again will I finally be able to say this battle is won. I can't quit chasing my goals now.

Chapter Sixteen

My thoughts are on Daniela again. It's like she's at the bottom of a valley with steep roads climbing out of either side. If I ever quit pedaling away from her, if I relax for only a second, I roll right back down the hill, and she dominates my thoughts once again.

I can't blame her for her decision. She helped my parents so much when I was in the hospital. Without her assistance translating everything, from basic communication to medical prognosis, their challenges in Angers would have been even bigger. She is also still young, just twenty-two. She can't be expected to put her life on hold for me, can she?

I turn on the television. The 2006 Tour de France has exceeded every expectation, and today Floyd Landis will ride into Paris victorious. If ever there was a strategic win, this is it. While Floyd's physical strength was certainly a key factor in the victory, he sealed the deal with mental strength and brilliant tactics. On certain key stages he gave rival teams just enough incentive that they were willing to work hard, allowing him to preserve not only his strength but the strength of his teammates. On other stages he artfully tricked his foes into slitting one another's throats. He played everything to perfection and is soon to be a deserving winner.

Thor had some bad luck and won't be able to defend his green jersey, but he's also ridden a valiant race. I hop onto my trainer and begin watching the final stage roll toward the famed Champs-Elysées. I'm dreaming of the day I'll get to race on that most famous of avenues.

The final stage of the Tour, as usual, is essentially a victory parade with champagne toasts, publicity stunts, and lots of smiles. Predictably, all that changes once the race reaches the finishing circuits. There the final sixty kilometers are played out on eight twisting laps at breakneck speeds. One attack after another is launched, but Crédit Agricole cooperates with the other major sprinter's teams to shut any and all escapists down. It puts a smile on my face every time I see a Crédit Agricole cyclist riding near the front, and I become especially happy when I notice Thor is wearing one of my Raisin Hell bracelets.

With half a lap to go, a handful of men, each dreaming to etch his name in the history books, launch themselves toward the line. None of the cyclists in this breakaway are capable of the forty-five mile an hour explosion of the sprint specialists, but there are a few who can hold thirty-eight miles an hour for an amazingly long time. Will it be long enough?

As the final few hundred meters whiz beneath the cyclists' wheels it looks certain the breakaway will win the day. Suddenly, with all cylinders firing, the big guns overwhelm the opportunists. From out of the pack, Thor hurls a thunderbolt. He flies down the finishing stretch, crushing all rivals in his path. Then he crosses the line with both arms stretched to the sky, my Raisin Hell bracelet spinning on his wrist.

"Wooooohooooooo!!!" I yell.

"Way to go, Thor!" Mom screams.

"Incredible! What a race!" Dad has a huge smile on his face.

Our house has erupted into mass chaos. My friend has just captured the most prestigious single stage in the world of professional road cycling. I'm so happy for Thor that the tears won't stop.

Within minutes my cell phone rings.

"Saul, my friend, the team is drinking champagne in our honor right now," Thor says. "We won the stage together! Your fight inspires me. I carried you across the line on my wrist!"

This recharges my tears. "Oh, Thor, I dream of the day we can ride side by side again. I'm going to make it all the way back."

"I know you will, Saul," he says. "I know you will."

I log onto my blog and post a message:

Thor RaisinHELL
Contributed by Saul
Sunday, 23 July 2006
Thor was Raisin Hell on the Champs-Elysées. Raising my bracelet high … he gives me so much motivation to get back so I can race side by side with him again.

A couple of days later Dr. Paré calls us into his office to review the MRI results. It turns out the tingling isn't the result of anything related to my brain injury at all. It's probably just a stressed muscle. I let out a sigh of relief upon learning no new problem has cropped up after all.

In celebration I talk Dad into letting me ride on the rollers. They are similar to the trainer, except full balance is required. The bike isn't held upright by anything. The rear wheel rides atop two stainless steel drums, and the front wheel rolls on another drum that's powered by a belt hooked to one of the rear drums. It's the closest thing there is to riding a bike outdoors on the road without going outside. In fact, in some ways riding the rollers is actually harder than riding on a regular road. I've known people who were never able to get the hang of it.

Dad stabilizes me. "Careful now, Saul."

I'm sure I'd be able to get started just fine without the support, but I appreciate his concern. "Of course." I begin pedaling and dad stands back.

"You're looking good," Mom says.

My parents are probably a lot more surprised that I can ride than I am. This is easy for me, something I could never forget how to do. It's just like … well … riding a bike.

Then again, there was a time not so long ago when I didn't even remember how to lift a fork to my mouth.

I ride the rollers for more than an hour, and as the wheels turn, gradually my parents' tension is pushed behind us as well. I'm getting better. It feels good.

*　　*　　*

A couple of days later Mom and Dad have to head out on separate errands, and I'm alone. Nobody is going to be with me for at least an hour. It's my first time in months to be unsupervised for so long. I can't explain how good it feels to finally be in charge of myself after so long under watchful eyes.

I keep bumping around the house, looking for something exciting to do. Eventually I walk out to the garage and see Dad's bicycle hanging from its hook. It looks so beautiful. I love the angles and lines of these magical machines. I'd like to take it down and feel it roll along the ground. In fact, I need to do that. I know I probably shouldn't, but I can't resist.

Soon I'm walking the bike in circles around the garage, the way a breeder might take his prized dog through the paces. But this still isn't enough for me. Dr. Bilsky said I can't ride my bike for three more months, but riding the rollers proved to me I had the balance, and inside my head I keep dreaming about how it would feel to have pavement beneath my wheels again. I know I shouldn't try it, but the temptation is too strong.

I clip on a helmet; then I swing my left leg over the top tube and put it onto the pedal. My right foot is still on stable ground. I work the handlebars back and forth and squeeze the brakes a time or two. It feels like riding would be easy, but I can't be sure.

And then suddenly I know. I'm riding in small circles inside our two-car garage. Each time I pass the kitchen door I think I ought to get off. I should quit pedaling before somebody discovers my sin or before some bizarre accident occurs … but I can't. Riding feels so fantastic. I've got to do just a little bit more of it. For five minutes I go round and round, and then finally I stop.

I lift the bicycle back onto its hook, put my helmet back on the workbench, and go into the kitchen. I sit down at the table with a snack. The garage door opener whirrs, and a moment later Mom walks in carrying an armload of groceries.

She looks at me. "Hi, Saul. Did everything go all right while I was gone?"

I grin. "I rode my bike."

Her mouth drops open. "You what?"

"I rode my bike in the garage where it's safe. It was great."

She drops the groceries with a thud. "Saul! Can't we trust you?"

"What do you mean? I have my balance. You saw me ride the rollers."

She shakes her head. "And what if you something had gone wrong? Would I have come home to find my son collapsed in the garage? Sometimes I wonder if you have any common sense at all inside that head of yours."

I look down at the floor. "Sorry, Mom."

"I'm just glad nothing bad happened. From now on, ride the trainer only, okay?"

"Okay."

"Supervised!"

I'm sure her rules are for the best, but it's hard to agree to them. She keeps staring at me until finally I do. "Okay."

*   *   *

By the beginning of the second week of August we're heading back to the Shepherd Center for a visit. Of course I stop by Bret's room. He's improving rapidly. We talk about all sorts of things, not just our injuries. I like spending time with him. It's easy to understand why this guy has so many friends. His motto is, 'Fight to the finish.' You can learn so much from a man like him. He has an easy confidence which makes him the most natural of leaders.

Afterward, my parents and I have an appointment with Dr. Bilsky. He tests me in all the usual ways as we talk. Eventually I say, "I'm doing well, huh?"

"Yes," he says. "Really well."

We talk about all sorts of things before I try to sneak in the question I've wanted to ask most. I try to do it as gently as I can, so it doesn't call too much attention to itself. "So, Dr. Bilsky, there's something I was wondering."

"What is it?" he asks.

"How long until I can ride again?" I try to sound like I don't particularly care what answer he gives me.

Dr. Bilsky smiles. "I wondered how long you'd take to ask that. I must say, I'm impressed by your patience."

I'm getting better at these social niceties, but I'm not feeling nearly as patient as he seems to think I am. I want an answer. It takes all my concentration to resist demanding one for a moment longer.

Finally, he breaks the silence. "I can't believe I'm saying this, Saul …"

He looks me in the eye, and for awhile I can't believe it either, because he isn't saying anything at all. He seems trapped between words. I wait.

Dr. Bilsky takes a deep breath. "… but I think you're ready to ride."

"I knew it!" I go around to his side of the desk and throw my arms around his neck. I let go and dance around the room, and then I return to hug him again. My parents look incredulous. They may be contemplating killing Dr. Bilsky.

"What are we waiting for, Dad?" I say. "If we head back to Dalton right now we'll have time to go riding this afternoon."

"All right, Saul. Just take it easy," Dad says in a stressed voice. "You're sure about this, Dr. Bilsky?"

Dr. Bilsky nods. "I do have some rules."

"What are they," Mom asks hopefully. I think she's praying that one of them involves riding only tricycles.

It doesn't.

All the way home in the car we discuss the rules the doctor has dictated. He wants us riding only over level ground or up hills. He wants us on preferably vacant roads with mom following close behind in the car, just in case. If we go up a mountain I have to ride back down in a car. He wants me off the bike if I start feeling tired or sweating or experiencing discomfort of any kind. I'm not allowed to ride within an arms length of any object: another cyclist, an automobile, a mailbox. And I have to promise to quit riding if Dad doesn't think I'm operating my bike safely or for any other reason that might come up. These rules are all completely fine with me. I just want to start turning the pedals.

We get home, dress in our cycling clothes, load the bikes onto the car, and head out toward the stretch of road we've selected. I keep kissing my mom and dad the whole way. What a triumphant journey this is. There are no two people I'd rather have at my side for my maiden voyage.

We park the car. The afternoon is still and peaceful. Four deer graze silently in a nearby field. A soft breeze blows from the north causing little yellow flowers at the roadside to dance in anticipation of what they're about to see. Dad has removed the bikes from the car. Mom wants a picture of us posing with our bicycles. Dad checks the bicycles again for any mechanical defects. Eventually, neither of them can think of anything else to delay the inevitable. It's time to ride.

I step over my top tube and clip my right toe in. The last time I rode a bike outdoors, summer was just starting. Now it's just ending. I can hardly wait to resume my passion.

Dad clips in as well and nods at me. We start pedaling. The gentle wind on my face brings memories of a million other bicycle rides rushing back. The touch of the breeze and the feel of my bicycle transforming circular leg motion into smooth forward energy ignites sensations I couldn't possibly re-create in any other way. I'm riding my bike!

The road meanders past orchards, picket fences, homesteads, and forests. These byways of northern Georgia provide the best road cycling I've ever experienced anywhere in the world, and I've ridden in a lot of places. The tarmac is as smooth as a baby's bottom. There isn't a pothole in sight, and traffic is nearly as rare. Sometimes you'll travel for miles and miles without encountering a single stop sign or automobile. From my home in Dalton, a cyclist can experience any sort of terrain they like, from pancake flats to rolling hills to brutal mountains, just by pointing their handlebars in the right direction.

"This is the life, isn't it, Saul?" Dad says.

I grin. "Oh yeah."

"A few months ago I couldn't even have dreamed of this moment," Dad says.

"For a long time it's almost the only thing I've dreamed of," I say. "If I never have another victory on the bike, this will be enough. I almost can't believe I'm experiencing it. It's as if I've pedaled right into my dreams."

"Yeah," Dad says. "This is the greatest day of my life."

I knew he'd come around. With his full support the day feels even better than it already did. I'm doing what the doctors said I would never do again. I've proven to myself I can achieve the impossible. How will I ever surpass this moment? To the moon I go!

We ride for an hour and a half, soaking in the joy of living. Mom drives up the road to take pictures while Dad and I approach. She pumps her fist in victory as we pass. "You're doing it, Saul! You're doing it!"

"I love you, Mom! You're the best!" Tears stream down my face. Some things are worth crying about no matter how tough you are, and this is one of them.

There are no two people in the world I'd rather be with right now than my parents. They are my best friends. They are the reasons this dream has come true. In the car on the way home I collapse in the back seat, overwhelmed by emotions and thoughts I can't explain.

The 2006 Tour de France is now over, but the victory has been made hollow by drug accusations. It's a sad development. I really don't know what to think about it, but the combination of events has caused me to see the Tour in a new perspective. Winning the most prestigious bicycle race in the world doesn't compare to the ride I took today. It's not even close. The Tour de France is just a race. I've returned to life. All the mental and physical work I've done to get back onto the bike has to be ten times harder than winning a grand tour. I know the pain and suffering in those events is enormous, but it can't compare to what I've gone through. With death as the competition, I just won my own personal Tour de Life.

Chapter Seventeen

I've got to get back to racing to show other injury victims they can achieve the impossible. I don't necessarily need to win, but I do need to compete. I know it's possible to accomplish impossible dreams, especially because I've just done it. I don't merely think that I can inspire other injury victims. I know it. More than that, I have an obligation to do it. God has tested me with this injury for a reason, and I intend to pass the exam.

As soon as we get home, I log onto my web site and post a blog entry. This moment wouldn't have been possible without the support of thousands of people. They deserve to share my joy:

> *Raisin Hell Again Soulevant l'enfer encore*
> Contributed by Saul
> Tuesday, 08 August 2006
> Today was the best day I have ever had on a bike. I feel like I won a huge race. Today I rode on the road for an hour and a half with my Dad. It has been a little over four months since I crashed and was in a coma. Today was nothing short of a miracle. Today I also visited my friend Bret Neylon. He is doing well and looking better than ever. I have put up some new pictures of everything. I think this song off this site best describes my ride. It is a free download. Click "YES" under Open to download. "God Moves Through You."

It's a simple ballad accompanied only by a clear acoustical guitar. I can't catch all the lyrics, but the title line is repeated many times and it resonates to my core. It must have been written and performed by someone who loves their guitar in the same way I love my bicycle. We've each found the inventions we were meant to master. The music describes my ride because I had such a great feeling it can't be explained other than as God moving through me. I'm experiencing so many intense emotions I can't possibly describe them all.

Mom often says I've become more religious since my accident. That's not exactly true because religion isn't what I'm responding to. It's a higher power that some call God. I can feel a positive universal energy, and I know it helped me in my recovery. Prayers were answered, and that means somebody did the answering. That's what I mean to show gratitude for.

It seems strange to say, but riding the bike on the road ignites all sorts of new emotions and feelings within me. I suddenly remember how good I once was at this sport. As optimistic as I've been, the goal of riding somehow didn't feel real until I captured it. It seems like so long ago I raced my bike. In reality, it's only been a few days more than four months.

My progress in the sport to that point had surprised even me. It's an incredible feeling to find yourself beside the icons of the sport you've devoted your life to and then to prove to the world that you belong there. It took a huge amount of work to achieve that level. At the time I thought nothing could be harder. Now I know differently … man, do I ever know differently.

One of the main things that drove my progress in cycling was a belief that I've been given unique physical gifts. I figured out I could become really good at this sport, and I became driven by an obligation not to beat any particular rival but to prove just how good I really could be. It didn't seem acceptable to waste my talent. Partially due to my large lungs and heart, my VO2 Max is in the high eighties. The average for a man my age is in the mid forties. Anything over sixty is considered excellent. This all means I can process far more oxygen than most people. Just as a bonfire needs fresh air for carbon combustion, muscles need lots of oxygen to convert fuels like glucose into raw energy. A body like mine that can deliver massive amounts of fresh air to its muscles is a gift.

Because my lungs are so large, I don't breathe the same way most people do. It takes me two contractions of my diaphragm to push all the air out. As a result I can't put anything near the force behind my breath that most healthy men can. Blowing up a tight new balloon is impossible for me. I can't expel air with any more force than a teenage girl, but I've learned to do it efficiently.

We now know a big part of these differences from the average are an indirect result of my back. The curvature in my spine combined with my very upright posture has resulted in a huge chest cavity while still maintaining an aerodynamic profile.

Once, when I rode for the Crédit Agricole Espoir Team, we raced in a time-trial. Cyclists were allowed to carry only to two water bottles in the cages on the bike frame. When I rolled into the start house, a race official said, "You're going to have to take off that Camelbak."

He was referring to the brand name of a soft canteen designed to be worn as a backpack. "I'm not wearing a Camelbak," I said.

He looked at me skeptically. "What's under your shirt, then?"

I removed my jersey to display my bare back and a strange expression crossed his face. "Okay. Get dressed. Your start time is almost here."

Last year something even funnier happened. On the toughest stage of the Tour of Germany which ended atop the massive Sölden, the hardest climb I've ever done, I came in seventh. The performance surprised a lot of people because I was by far the youngest cyclist to climb the mountain that quickly.

As we were waiting for the gun to go off to start the next stage Jens Voigt, one of Germany's greatest cyclists and a former wearer of the yellow jersey in the Tour de France, moved alongside me. He congratulated me on the previous day's ride, and then he rested his hand on the hump of my back and asked, "So, what is this?"

"It's my third lung," I say.

His eyes practically popped out of his skull. "No! No! No! You cannot do that! It is illegal!"

He'd bought it, chain, cable, and gearshift. Everybody laughed so hard. Thinking back on those days puts such a smile on my face. I want to return so badly.

*　　*　　*

Since that wonderful day returning to the road with my dad, I ride outdoors every day possible. Now that I have the asphalt under my wheels, my recovery shifts to the big chain ring. Within days I'm riding my favorite training ride again, the treacherous Fort Mountain climb. Halfway up, I roll over the top of my own name painted in large block letters on the asphalt. It's obviously a remnant from the Tour de Georgia. Cycling fans often paint these sorts of encouraging messages for their favorite riders. Whoever painted this tribute to me on my favorite training ride will probably never fully understand how much their gesture means to me today. I wish I could thank them for their faith.

I love everything about the Fort Mountain climb. The Blue Ridge peak gets its name from a mysterious 855 foot long rock wall that stretches along its highest point. Some believe Indians built it as fortification against other hostile tribes. Others say the wall played a part in ancient ceremonies. Either way, it takes eight miles and 2000 feet of tough climbing to reach the 2875 foot summit. The road averages about a seven percent gradient, and spectacular views across hardwood forests are visible all the way up.

Once I reach the top I'm required to ride back down the mountain in the car, but I don't care. Going up is the only thing that matters to me.

The improvements are coming so rapidly I can practically feel the synapses firing off in my brain, making millions of new connections per day. I beg Dad to go riding with me in any spare moments he has. I bug him all day long, every day. He loves cycling, but he has other obligations so he says no a lot. The way I see it, not only do I love this sport, but Crédit Agricole is still paying me to ride, so I owe it to them. Once in a while Dad gives in. Other times he allows me to go riding with people he considers responsible.

One guy he'll almost always let me ride with is our family friend, Ron Swopes. While riding together Ron tells me about the day he and his wife Jennifer came to visit me at the Shepherd Center.

"You were so absent. We cried all the way home," Ron says. "At that time it was hard to imagine you could ever make a full recovery. I'm so thrilled about how well you're doing."

I'd like to stop the bikes and share a hug. I'm so fortunate to have such great friends. I'm learning that nearly everybody who saw me back in those dark days had a good cry afterward. I feel badly to have done that to them.

Riding like this is so good for me. People underestimate the power of bicycles. Cycling has forced me to fight all my major problems: left neglect, impulsivity, reasoning problems, slow processing speed. Riding a bicycle fights every one of those deficits. I know the drive to get back on a bike has really helped my recovery.

Not too long ago things were so bleak my parents were contemplating donating my organs. I can't imagine how low they must have been feeling to discuss such a subject, but I also now understand something they'd been trying to convince me of even before the accident. Becoming an organ donor is the right thing to do. I'm going to sign up. Doctors aren't going to harvest anything early as I'd once feared. If they take organs, it will only be because they're no longer of use to their current owner and could be the key to saving another person's life. That's a wonderful use of science. If I ever needed organs I'd certainly accept them, and that means I'd better be willing to give them as well.

*   *   *

One evening Jim Birrell, the man who directs every one of America's most prestigious bike races, calls and invites me and my parents as VIP guests to the U.S. Pro Road Cycling Championships in Greenville, South Carolina, over Labor Day Weekend. When we accept, he asks if it would be possible for me to lead out the Palmetto Peloton Project charity ride which will be raising money to fight cancer. Dr. Bilsky gives his okay as long as I'm careful. I'm not allowed to go down hills quickly, and I have to ride with my dad.

The day before we leave town I learn of a tragedy so similar to mine it shakes me to my core. Christophe Brandt of the Davitamon Lotto cycling team has gone down hard in the Sels to Merxem Cup race and fallen into a coma. I call his wife and encourage her to stay strong, keep her morale up, and call me and my family if there is any support we can offer. I assure her he can hear her when she talks and feel her when she touches him. She needs to stay at his side and let him soak in her strength and support. She's both shaken and grateful on the phone.

I log onto my web site and leave a message there as well:

Christophe Brandt
Contributed by Saul
Tuesday, 29 August 2006
I would like for everyone to send their thoughts and prayers to Christophe Brandt. He needs them. I wish him the best. I want him and his family to stay strong. God speed, Chris.
My Best,
Saul Raisin

As we drive to the championships in Greenville, my thoughts turn to Chris over and over again. His situation reminds me yet again of the journey I've made, as well as all my good fortune along the way. It's such a miracle to be alive. I'm so excited for this opportunity to be among my racing friends again. I can't wait to give them hugs and laugh at their jokes.

The first day of the event is the time trial championships. My friend Dave Zabriskie holds on by a fingernail to beat Chris Baldwin who crashes when he overcooks the final corner.

The second day is the charity ride. I roll up to the starting line and am overwhelmed by the kind words and positive vibrations so many people send my way. This is the sort of place I love spending time. I'm facing 700 cyclists who have chosen to donate their time and money for the benefit of people they'll probably never even meet. I'm grateful to them for including me in the event. This will be the first group ride I've participated in since my accident.

My mom says, "Saul, you look like you're slipping into a fog. Maybe you shouldn't ride."

I wave her off. "Leave me alone."

"No Saul!" she says. "It could be dangerous for you to ride."

"Mom, it won't be dangerous. I'm just feeling emotional. It's a big day. Please don't worry about me."

Somebody hands me a microphone and asks me to say a few words. Mom walks away, and I can see she's upset. I hold off speaking to the crowd for a moment and go to her. "I'll be all right, Mom. I promise you."

"Okay, Saul. You'd better talk to the crowd now. I just worry about you."

I understand and appreciate what she's saying. I nod and turn to the crowd.

What should I tell these people? I clear my throat. "I want to thank everyone for coming out today. You don't know how much the opportunity to ride with you means to me. Don't forget why we're here today. We're here to fight, to fight cancer and all illness and injuries. Never give up and always reach for the stars." The dam breaks and tears fill my eyes. "Today we are reaching out and putting the stars in our pockets. Thank you for joining me. Let's have an enjoyable and safe ride, and I'll see you at the top of Paris Mountain."

I notice many people in the audience crying, too, and I wonder how many of them know what I've overcome. I'm not wondering this because I think anybody ought to feel sorry for me. It's just that I believe my story might be inspiring to them or someone they love. I look back on how far I've come, and I can't believe it myself. You never know what sort of difference the right piece of information will make if it gets into the right person's hands at the right time. I know my story can help others, and that makes me happy.

The charity peloton rolls through the streets of Greenville and then toward the slopes of Paris Mountain. Dad stays behind me, protecting my rear wheel. A constant stream of well-wishers rolls alongside. Dad warns everyone to stay an arm's length away from me.

Everybody is very accommodating to the rules. Some cry when they talk to me. Others congratulate me on coming back. Many tell me my speech or my recovery inspired them. I won't try to downplay my feelings. It feels so cool to hear people say things like that.

As the ride continues, my strength seems to increase, so when we're invited to join the pros for a lap of the course I can't resist. George Hincapie, Levi Leipheimer, Dave Zabriskie, and others are there. I look back and see Dad panting to keep up. He's a horse, but he isn't nearly as strong as I am.

As we climb Paris Mountain side by side, Levi says, "I'm impressed, Saul. You're strong."

It makes me feel good to hear that from a top pro. "Considering I almost died a few months ago I think I'm doing great. I've been putting in twenty-five hour weeks on the trainer."

George Hincapie looks incredulous. "Twenty-five hour weeks on the trainer? You're sick!"

"Yeah, I'm sick, and I love it."

By the time we crest Paris Mountain my dad is no longer in sight, but he's instructed Kevin Livingston about how to watch after me so everything should be okay.

"Should you wait for your dad?" George asks.

I shake my head. "I just have to go slow downhill. Until I'm fully healed I have to avoid an accident at all costs."

George nods, and rides alongside as Kevin leads me down the slope at a controlled pace. I'll bet neither of these guys has gone downhill this slowly in several decades. It's very kind they'd do it for me.

I love my dad, but I can't explain how good it feels to be with my friends for awhile instead of my parents. Before the accident, I'd been living on my own in Europe for two years. Now I have to answer to Mom and Dad for everything. It's exhausting for all of us. I'll bet Dad is glad to have a break from me.

Just then Jim Birrell pulls alongside in his race director's pickup. "Hey, Saul. Your parents aren't too happy with you. They asked me to track you down and put you in the truck."

That's when I allow myself to admit I was fooling myself concerning how Dad would feel about getting a break from me. He's going to be pissed.

Back in Greenville at the race festival area, I'm signing autographs and waiting for my parents when a woman I met on the ride comes up to me. "Check out this photo I took of you climbing Paris Mountain," she says.

Just then Dad arrives. "Let me see that shot."

She shows him the digital display on the back of her camera.

"Saul," he says. "Do you see me in this photo?"

I look at it and shake my head.

"Didn't Dr. Bilsky say you were supposed to stay with me? Good 'ole Dad's not there, is he? How come?" he asks.

"I don't know," I say. "You couldn't keep up?"

"You're damn right I couldn't. You dropped me like a hot potato. You weren't supposed to do that, were you?"

I hug him and give him a kiss. "I could have ridden harder, and I didn't go downhill. Dr. Bilsky would have been okay with the way I rode."

Dad doesn't hug me back. "No he wouldn't, Saul. You broke his rules. You're not going to be allowed to ride if you can't do it the way you've been told to."

I'm sorry to have made my dad so mad, but there are people lining up who want photos and autographs. It's hard to discuss these sorts of things in an environment like this. Recovering from this injury seems to have new complications at every turn.

That evening at a preview for tomorrow's main event, race announcers Dave Towle and Jeff Roake invite me onstage to talk about my accident and recovery. I wonder how many brain-injured patients get to experience the massive sensory input of talking to a crowd of thousands over a multimegawatt sound system. I'll bet if they did a study, they'd discover that answering questions in front of an audience who's roaring their approval is good therapy for the brain, even if it is a bit exhausting.

Eventually all the race favorites are invited onstage, too. Jeff Roake asks each one who they think tomorrow's victor will be. I'm the last in line. When he reaches me I say, "I don't know about tomorrow, but in 2007 it will be me."

The crowd lets out a roar louder than any crowd I've ever heard in my life. I'm telling you, this weekend is making me feel like a rock star.

After I step off the stage, Mom tells me I need to get my feet back on the ground. Of course, she's right, but I can't resist chiding her. "Nope. A cyclist's feet float above the ground at all times. Haven't you noticed that?"

The next morning we check out of the hotel before heading to the race venue.

"Did you rent a movie while we were here, Saul?" Mom asks.

"No."

She shows the room bill to Dad and asks again. "Are you sure you didn't rent a movie?"

"I didn't," I say.

"All right, I believe you. I know you wouldn't lie to me." She sounds upset. "I'll have to talk to the manager and get the charge removed."

Panic strikes me and I cry. "Wait a second. I'm lying. I don't know why I'm doing it. I did rent that movie. I'm sorry."

"Saul! What's gotten into you?" Mom's tone is scolding, but her arms are open wide and I step into them for a hug.

I don't know what's gotten into me. There are times like this when it's as if I can't differentiate right from wrong, and it scares me. It hurts that I'd lie to anybody, much less my mom. I'm not that sort of person, and I can't imagine what's causing me to lose control of my actions.

We head to the race venue. I spend a big hunk of the day on the grandstand commentating on the action and talking about my recovery with announcers Dave and Jeff. Each time George Hincapie passes in front of us the crowd cheers wildly. After all, this is his home town. I'm flattered that he's wearing one of my green and white bracelets.

As the hours wear on, my brain is turning into cold oatmeal, but I doubt anybody else can sense it. I might be able to subject myself to hours and hours of physical effort, but the mental strain of talking to an audience, plus the stress of sitting still in a chair for an extended period of time are much tougher for me. I'm starting to get tremors in my left hand, but I'm still talking well. I've been drinking a lot of coffee to keep my energy up, and I think that's helping.

As the race heats up for the final few laps they excuse me from the stage. I don't want to go, but Dad takes my hand and walks me down the stairs.

"I did pretty well, huh?" I ask.

Dad shakes his head. "Saul, you got off topic every time they asked you a question, and you kept repeating yourself."

I spot Mom waiting for us.

"I didn't do so badly, did I?" I ask her.

"You started out well, but you're talking so slowly right now."

"I'm talking slow?" I accidentally bump into her as we walk.

"Saul, you're exhausted, and for some reason you just can't see it," Mom says.

In truth I could see it, but I didn't realize others could. I let my parents escort me to the car like a little child.

The moment I sit down the fog rolls in like no other in recent memory. I'm asleep before we're even moving, and the next time I wake we've gotten all the way back to Dalton. That's a four-hour drive and I don't recall a single detail.

The next day I write about the amazing weekend in my blog:

Raisin Hell at USPRO Championships
Contributed by Saul
Monday, 04 September 2006
I was at the U.S. Pro Championships this weekend. I had a great time. I saw a lot of old friends and I made several new ones. I did the Palmetto Peloton Project charity ride on Saturday with hundreds of people. It felt so good words cannot express. I was very emotional. I would like to congratulate George Hincapie for RaisinHell this weekend. Thank you for the support. You do not know how much it means … That goes for everyone. All the sales of the RaisinHell Bracelets go towards a great cause.
Love,
Saul

There are other recent developments I haven't mentioned yet. Not only did my parents and I make final arrangements to travel to France for team photos, and not only have I gone on long rides nearly every day since the championships, but we also put the final pieces of the puzzle together to make a book happen. A couple of days later I post the details to my blog:

6-Hour Rides and Writing a Book
Contributed by Saul
Thursday, 14 September 2006
I did a 6-hour training ride over 2 mountains today 4000kcal with my PowerTap. I am getting strong!! Feels Good!! I have cool news. I have decided to write a book with author Dave Shields. I have read and I loved Dave's books. I feel he can tell and express my story very well. I think he can put my pain and triumph into words. My whole motivation behind the book is to help other people and families who are going through and have been through the same things my family and I have experienced. I want the world to know to never give up. Always keep fighting. It always gets better no matter how bad it seems.
Saul

I'm excited to get my story on paper, but there is less and less time in my life to make these sorts of things happen. Before the month is out, it's time for another of my dreams to come true:

Going to France
Contributed by Saul
Monday, 24 September 2006
I am going to France tomorrow for my 2007 team pictures. Crédit Agricole has been wonderful supporting me 110%. Everyone is great. I am looking forward to see my team and all my friends. I think I am going to cry.
Saul

Chapter Eighteen

I press my face against the window as our plane descends into Nice. The azure Mediterranean laps against the soothing hearthstone shores of the Côte d'Azur. How I love France. This is the heart of the old world and the place where Western society emerged. The moment I set foot on French soil, this land spoke to me. Returning is like a dream come true. Beyond a dream, in fact. For awhile I couldn't have imagined ever returning.

Inside the airport I spot Lionel waiting for us. "*Bonjour, mon ami!*" I yell.

He laughs. "Saul, our American Dreamer! You look so good. The last time I saw you, you were dead."

"Don't remind me," I say. "Death sucks."

We embrace, crying. They are tears of joy and tears of shared misery at the same time. "I love you, Lionel. I'm so happy to be back with you again."

He's still hugging me, and I realize we're starting to make a scene. People are looking at us. I don't care. I doubt these strangers have any concept of the wars we've been through together. I cry some more.

Lionel steps back and I finally have a chance to take a good look at him. He's wearing my USA Cycling team uniform. This is no small deal. Lionel is a patriot, intensely proud of France and suspicious for a lifetime of American intentions. Wearing the symbols of a rival country, France's biggest nemesis in some ways, cannot be easy. It's a gesture I don't take lightly.

Our countries have an unfortunate recent history of misunderstandings. It makes me sad when I hear Americans disparage the French. So often their insults are ill informed. I know from experience the vast majority of French people bear no resemblance to the characterizations in stereotypical jokes. By wearing this jersey Lionel is telling me he's come to understand that America is also a land mostly filled with good, hard-working people, despite the jokes and biases he's grown up hearing.

I can't help thinking that if more people were willing to question their suppositions, not only in America and France, but worldwide, this planet would almost instantly find itself in better shape. How could we possibly send our sons and daughters to war if all factions spent some time to learn a little bit about the dreams and fears of their so-called enemies?

Lionel turns his attention to my parents. "You both look so much better than last time we saw one another. Back then you were zombies. Now your faces hold smiles."

Mom trades a *bise* with Lionel. "Those were the worst of times. You look much better now, too."

Dad and Lionel share a greeting and we head for the car. From the airport we go to my condominium in Beausoleil, France. The name means Beautiful Sun, a perfect description. The address of the building I live in is Number One. The location is unique because if you step out the back door, you're in France, and if you put a foot out the front entrance, you're in Monaco.

The apartment is in need of some repair. The toilet is leaking, a couple of pictures have fallen off the wall, and I need more furniture.

"Can you call a plumber, Saul? Ask him to be here when we return," Dad says.

It's a good plan because we're going on a bike ride and will want to take showers afterwards. Even though Mom will be here while we ride, she'd be lost if the plumber showed up and started speaking French to her.

I down a couple of Zippy Zoos as I dial the number. I've been addicted to these chewable vitamins since I was in elementary school, and now I'm well known for them in the peloton. One day an Italian rider on another squad even came up to me and whispered, "Can you get me some of these Zippy Zoos I have heard about?" He acts like they're illegal. Does he think I'm some sort of dealer?

We quickly reassemble our bikes and get dressed in all our gear. Moments later Lionel, Dad, and I are pedaling up my favorite training ride in all Europe, the Col de la Madone.

Remember when I said this trip felt like a dream come true? Well that description doesn't do it justice anymore. If I found a genie's lamp and rubbed it for a wish, he couldn't possibly deliver a gift to me any greater than this day. When I was lying in hospitals, unable to move half my body, unable to sense my own bodily functions, unable to put food in my mouth, I may have talked about the dream of riding my favorite French roads in the company of my friends, but it wasn't real. Anybody in their right mind could have told you so. What I mean is that everybody who witnessed that event except for me knew there was no way it could eventually lead to a moment like this.

The ride is a tough one, winding higher and higher on the semi-arid face of the Madone where it erupts from the Mediterranean. Below us, Monaco glistens like an emerald. The city is built on steep, rocky cliffs, and the treacherous real estate is some of the most expensive in the world. The high price explains the hundreds of beautiful skyscrapers. Once somebody buys land there's no extra charge for using as much of the sky above them as possible, so in this tiny country virtually everybody builds tall. Monaco sky is high-quality stuff.

I'm carrying 179 pounds of body weight up the climb. This is by far the most I've ever weighed while riding this hill. On the lower slopes Lionel and I ride shoulder to shoulder talking.

"You're the man who discovered me as far as elite pro cycling is concerned,"

I say, "so watching me ride now, do you think I can come all the way back?"

Lionel grins. "You are the same optimistic Saul. Let us not forget that six months ago you were in a coma. The doctor told me you would probably be *un légume.*"

"He said I'd be a vegetable?" Nobody has ever told me this before.

Lionel nods. "It will take time to recover fully."

"Yes," I say, "but do you think I can compete again at the highest level?"

He thinks for a moment. "From the first time I watch you race I know you have the strength to win, and then as we become friends I learn you are very hard worker. Soon you get even stronger. Since the accident it seems that quality has increased. I don't know if I ever meet a guy who works so hard as you do now. This tells me you can be good."

"Thank you," I say, "but I want to be better than good. I want to be great."

"Ahhh, there is my American Dreamer." He smiles wide. "Great is not easy. It takes more than strength to win big races. In the beginning you had a lot to learn about tactics and our way of life. The tactical mastery was coming along well before the crash, but it's too early to know whether that part is going to return. Will you be able to think clearly enough when the pressure is on? I do not know yet."

I laugh. "Remember the Circuit des Ardennes? You were pretty unhappy with my tactics that day."

Lionel smiles. "Yes. How could I forget? Our strategy works perfectly to launch you onto the final slope in the lead; then at the critical moment you slow down to answer nature's call. And this was before your brain injury. What hope is there now?"

"Probably not much," I answer with a grin.

"At least you are still the same good person," Lionel says. "You want to help people. You want to make your dreams come true. I like that."

"Today is a dream that came true," I say.

Lionel nods in agreement.

"Arm's length, Saul," Dad reminds me. He's taking that one too far. Lionel is an extremely competent bike handler, and so am I.

The climb is fifteen kilometers long and quite steep, rising directly from sea level to over 3000 feet. On the upper slopes the road is little more than a paved cart path clinging to the steep slope. There are lots of switchbacks and small tunnels along the way, and many more bikes than cars traverse it. By the time I gain the summit, I'm in a full sweat. I get off my bike and step over to touch the altitude sign. It seems a shame I've passed this marker so many times in my life and never paid it this simple respect before. The Col de la Madone is one of the locations on earth's face that means the most to me, and I'm so grateful I have the opportunity to experience it again.

Lionel walks over and punches me in the shoulder, hard.

It hurts. "Why did you do that?"

"That's for what you put me through. Do you realize that while you lay in bed we were talking about the solution to your pain?"

"No. What was it?" I ask.

"Pulling the plug. Now, don't ever put us through that again. Understood?"

"Understood." Then I punch him in his shoulder.

"Why do you do that?" he asks.

"Because I can."

He smiles. "Aha. That is a very good reason. I'm so happy about it that I'd like for you to punch me anytime you want."

"We need to get back before the plumber arrives," Dad says.

"I'll bet he charges us a hundred Euros," I say.

Dad's jaw drops. "Are you kidding? That would be nearly $120 to fix a small leak? It would be overpriced at fifty Euros."

He's not used to prices around here. My parents have never understood Europe too well. Dad will be in for a surprise when he sees this bill.

We descend the mountain. I've never used the brakes on a bicycle the way I do these days. Usually I fly down hills at top speed, but now I've got to be very cautious. Even when I'm going really slow Dad keeps asking me to go slower.

When we finally reach home Mom is standing on the deck looking out at the Palace of Monaco. "It's like another world over here, isn't it? Life moves at its own tempo. Daily concerns are just plain different."

I nod.

The doorbell rings. "There's the plumber," Dad says.

I answer it. While I show the man the problem Dad keeps hounding me to ask for a price before the work starts. I'm pretty sure that will offend the plumber, but I have to do it anyway or my parents won't be able to relax. "How much?" I ask.

"Thirty Euros," the plumber says.

Wow, what a bargain. I can't believe my ears. "Are you sure you don't need more?"

He looks at me like he thinks I'm crazy as he opens his tool chest and takes out a wrench.

I explain the situation to my parents and say, "He's such a good guy. We ought to give him a fifty euro tip."

"Are you crazy, Saul?" Mom says. "It's a good thing we're here with you. The doctor's warned us you might have judgment issues. Emptying your wallet over a leaky toilet is too much."

"Your mom's right," Dad says. "People with injuries like yours have to relearn how to watch out for themselves. You'd be a perfect target for a snake oil salesman."

Snake oil? What would I want with snake oil? Do they think I'm some sort of fool? It makes me mad they're double-teaming me on a nonissue like this. "I'm going to pay him the tip."

"Listen to me, Saul," Dad says. "No tip."

"It's embarrassing you'd force us to argue about this in front of the plumber," Mom says.

"I doubt he understands English," I say.

Dad shakes his head. "Not a good assumption, Saul. If you're going to be living on your own again you're going to have to start showing me a whole lot better judgment than you're doing right now."

*   *   *

The next morning we head to the port of Monaco. I'm sitting at a café drinking a cup of coffee when a family passes pushing their son in a wheelchair. They stop at a table near us. The boy is using an oxygen mask and he's belted into a seated position exactly the way I used to be.

Instantly, my heart falls to him. That was me such a short time ago. I know how he's feeling right now and I have a good idea what the family is going through, too. I walk up to them and ask the father if he speaks French.

"*Oui*. We are French," he says.

I swallow hard. "I have to tell you something. I do not know if it is my place but I feel it must be told."

"Please," the father says. They are all listening intently, the mother, father, and the younger brother. I think the boy in the wheelchair is paying attention as well.

"This year in April I crashed in a bicycle race. I hit my head very hard and slipped into a coma. I had surgery to reduce the pressure in my skull, and the doctors actually even removed a small part of my brain. This left me paralyzed on my left side. Now, six months later, I'm doing everything the doctors said I'd never do again in my life. Yesterday I rode my bike for six hours on the road, something that half a year ago was less than a dream."

Tears are running down the mother's cheeks.

"What I want to say," I continue, "is, never give up. Fight. Fight. Fight. It always gets better. Never give up!"

The father takes off his hat and holds it over his heart. He bows slightly.

The younger brother stands and takes my hand. He shakes it saying, "Thank you. Thank you."

The moment feels so good, even though I haven't actually done anything for them. I can tell my words have made an impression. I bid them adieu, knowing we'll probably never see each other again. I wish I could do more for them.

Have I helped them at all? I hope so. What I do know is that they've helped me at a level I can't even explain.

Along those same lines another nice thing happened recently. Christophe Brandt's wife called and told me that while Chris was still in a coma she told him about my call and he smiled. That makes me feel so good. He's doing well now and is back home. She passed the phone to him and he thanked me as well. We're hoping that next year we get to race against each other. How cool would that be?

Over the next few days one friend after another shows up to ride my old routes with me. One day I climb the Col de Braus with a group of friends including my dad. Last time I ascended this hill the only guy who could keep up with me was Lance Armstrong. I attacked him, but he held onto my wheel and then came around me at the end.

When I reach the top I pull out my cell phone and dial Lance's number. I get his message machine. "Lance," I say. "Guess where I am right now. The top of the Col de Braus. I wish you were here. I would have attacked you again."

"Who are you talking to?" Dad asks.

I disconnect the call. "I was just leaving a message for Lance."

Dad shakes his head disgustedly. "You've got to leave that poor guy alone. He's going to be completely fed up with you if you don't quit bugging him. You have some serious manners to relearn."

I don't see what the problem is. Lance is a big boy who can take care of himself. Sure, I call him a lot and write e-mails too, but if I was bugging him I have no doubt he'd let me know, loud and clear.

Mom and Dad are increasingly stressed. I need some space from them, for their sake and mine. When friends from Normandy drop in I tell my parents, "I'll be okay for the day. Why don't you two go sightseeing?"

"Saul, the doctors made us promise we'd watch you the whole time," Mom says. "Don't make it impossible. I'll just follow in the car. You can still be with your friends."

There's not much I can do to stop her. It's not like we can outrun an automobile on bicycles, so she follows us all day long. Just as I suspected, it turns out to be a total waste of her time. Nothing dangerous happens all day. My parents can't seem to accept how quickly I'm getting better, and the tension is really starting to wear on all three of us.

One morning my parents and I head out for breakfast. Mom and Dad want to stop at the first café they see, but I'd rather take them to a special little place I know. They make the best coffee I've ever tasted and the owner and I are great friends. He'll be amazed to see me.

"Let's go visit your friend later, Saul," Mom says looking at the steep street that leads to his shop. "I don't want to walk up that hill. I want to eat here."

"Just follow me," I say. Sometimes an executive decision has to be made, and that's what I'm doing now.

"You can't get your way all the durn time, Saul," Mom says.

I don't even look back as I walk up the hill. I know they'll eventually follow.

I reach the café. The owner gives me a big hug and pours my coffee for free. I drink it straight down and he fills another cup for me. I buy some pastries to go with it.

My parents are just arriving as I walk from the checkout stand. I hand them their food. "See. Free coffee. Great food. Aren't you glad we came here."

"Where do we sit?" Mom asks.

I look around. The few chairs along the sidewalk are already taken, but we ought to be able to find some place. I walk to the curb and sit down. I pat the spot next to me to signal my mom.

"You made your mother trudge all the way up that hill so she could sit in a gutter?" Dad asks.

"You're making it sound worse than it is. Just sit down and don't complain," I say.

Suddenly Mom is in my face. "Saul!" She's whispering so passers-by can't hear, but it's the maddest whisper I've ever heard. "It's time you shut up and quit being a horse's ass."

Dad is standing beside her and looks satisfied with her actions. Neither one of them has ever talked to me that way before, not in my entire life. It's simply not us.

"Why are you getting so mad?" I ask.

"Because you're being so self-centered, Saul," Dad says. "I don't think you realize that for years we've designed our entire lives around you and your cycling. Now I'm thinking we may not have done you a favor. You don't seem to recognize that other people have feelings too and your parents don't exactly enjoy being carted around like luggage you wish you could get rid of."

"Remember the statistic about the percentage of loved ones who leave after massive trauma?" Mom asks.

"Yeah," I say. "Seventy percent."

"That's right," she says, "and now I think I understand why."

It breaks my heart to hear her say that. I love my parents deeply, but I'm not sure they understand how stressful it is for me to have them watching over my shoulder every single second. I think if you followed anybody around all day long you could see problems in their behavior. It's tough because my parents are always looking for me to make a minor error, and then when I do, they always attribute it to my brain injury. I think it actually scares them how well I'm doing.

Everybody needs a little bit of space. Besides, these are the streets where I used to live a life of carefree independence. Being here again brings back so many memories, and it fuels my desire to return things to the way they were.

As spectacular as the days and nights in France are, it's exhausting to be butting up against my parents like this. We always used to tease, but never fight. Are our relationships ever going to be the way they were before the accident?

Chapter Nineteen

We fly into Paris for team camp and photos. I won't even try to describe the emotions of seeing these men again after such a long absence, except to say that the moment I stepped among them again, I knew with more certainty than ever before, that the Crédit Agricole Cycling Team is where I belong. There are twenty-seven cyclists on the team, and if you include all the directeurs, managers, mechanics, and soigneurs, almost an equivalent number of support personnel. There are a few I haven't met since the organization is in constant flux, but I love all the people I know here. I look forward to meeting the new members.

We stay at a beautiful château. Every detail is taken care of by the support staff. Stress is practically a foreign emotion.

"Don't you agree this is the greatest team in the history of the world?" I ask a security guard.

He looks at me like he thinks I've had a piece of my brain removed. Is it that obvious?

Mom and Dad seem to be enjoying themselves, too, though more than once I overhear my dad telling various teammates about the arm's length rule. I wish he'd give that a rest, but I can't worry about it.

My good friend and teammate Madds Kaggestad puts an arm around my shoulder. I place my arm around his. Madds has a wonderful smile and the most genuine demeanor imaginable. Like Thor, he's Norwegian, and he was also one of the few English speakers when I first joined the team. He helped me acclimate and has been a great friend ever since.

"When we spoke on the phone in May or June, you made me very sad, Saul," Madds says in a serious tone.

"I did?"

He nods. "I tried to joke with you like we did in the old days, but your mind was too slow. You sounded like a heroin addict."

Our arms are still draped across one another, and now I squeeze his shoulder. "I'm sorry."

"You don't need to be sorry," Madds says. "Going through this with you, even from far away, has made me a better person. I'm more grateful for blessings and more forgiving of others. Other members of the team feel that way too."

"Thank you, Madds."

He smiles his broad smile. "You know, Saul, the old saying is true."

"Which saying?" I ask.

"'That which doesn't kill me makes me stronger.' I'm a little bit stronger because of what you went through, and I'll bet you're a lot stronger."

I think he might be right. I'm so glad I got to return to France to visit my friends. I don't even mind the time it takes to pose for shots. The photographer wants so many individual pictures and then he wants tons of group photos. Normally when I have to stand in a lineup like that, waiting for everybody to get their clothes on straight and the right expressions on their faces, I want to slash my wrists by the time the shutter clicks. Not this time. Being with my teammates is sheer joy. I'll never take moments like these for granted again.

After photos it's time to ride. As we shove off, the twing-twang of four dozen cycling shoes locking into pedals in a matter of seconds dances in my brain. It's a musical experience that every cyclist knows well, and that noncyclists could probably never understand. To me it's both the sound of anticipation and the herald of great things to come. The damage to my brain destroyed many linkages, but not this one. The tone of cleats clicking in will always be music to my ears.

Not long after we're underway Thor Hushovd rolls alongside me. He makes a clicking sound with his cheek, and when I look over he says, "So, dreams really do come true."

My mind isn't on the same page. "Huh?"

"You told me in a raspy voice from your hospital bed you dreamed of us riding side by side again. You repeated it in nearly every conversation we've had since. Now it's happening."

"Yes. This is like a dream." At this moment you couldn't scrub the grin off my face with industrial-strength solvent. No way. I'm happier than a master mechanic in a grease pit.

Toward the end of the ride the pace gets hot, and soon guys are attacking off the front. I ride tempo and try to glue everybody back together. As much as it's a part of cycling, I don't want anybody to be dropped today. I bring the group back together with over three-quarters of the team in my wind shadow.

After I've neutralized the attack, Sebastian Hinault pulls along side me. "This is unbelievable, Saul, that you can ride like this, not only keeping up but pulling a big chunk of the team. I can't believe how well you're doing."

At a predinner reception that night the conversation turns to my accident. "I've heard some witnesses believe I fainted on the bike at the Circuit de la Sarthe. They said I had a funny expression before the accident and I didn't try to protect myself when I fell. That's supposedly why I hit my head so hard."

Roger Legeay frowns. "Didn't try to protect yourself? Ridiculous. Then why was your left hand black and blue for two weeks?"

Angelo Furlan, a new member of Crédit Agricole who rode the Circuit de la Sarthe for Selle Italia says, "I was three positions behind you when the accident occurred, Saul. We were going all out. There's no way anybody was paying attention to your expression at that moment. The entire finish was a mess. There was gravel everywhere, and it caused lots of crashes, not just yours. I know that's why you went down. I too almost crashed."

A female reporter from *L'Équipe* who is here as a special guest overhears us. "I visited the site of your accident. Angelo is right. There was gravel and sand too. I'm sure that's what caused the fall."

A narrow bicycle tire pumped to 220 pounds going at full speed is no match for a messy road. To think, a couple of rocks the size of gumballs or smaller are probably to blame for six months of pure hell. If I could get my hands on those little pebbles I'd grind them into powder so fine it would disappear in the next breeze.

At the same time, it's a huge relief to learn the disaster probably wasn't caused by an undiagnosed glitch in my brain the way some people had speculated.

*   *   *

Team camp is over all too quickly. There is only time for two rides, and they're both under three hours. After each of them, I return to the hotel and ride the trainer for another hour on my own. If I'm going to return to my previous fitness level, I'll need to consistently put in more work than anybody else. There's a lot of catching up to do.

After camp ends, my parents and I head to Paris for two days before returning to my condo in the south of France. I want to treat them to a good vacation in an awesome hotel with great meals.

While walking down the Champs-Elysées my foot starts to hurt. "These shoes have never fit well. Let's step into this shop and get a new pair," I say.

After I make my purchase, the clerk asks if I want to leave my old shoes behind.

"No. I'd like to give them to a poor person," I say.

"That's a nice idea," Mom says, "maybe one of the hard-working trinket salesmen beneath the Eiffel Tower."

Yes, that's a perfect idea. We leave the store and start walking down the avenue. Mom and Dad are deep in conversation when I notice a man who reminds me of the trinket salesmen. I want to make my parents proud by handling this on my own. He's sitting on a bus bench.

I approach him. "Would you like these shoes?"

He looks up, distracted. "Why would I want your shoes?"

"They're my old shoes and I'm giving them away."

"I don't want your damn shoes. Get those smelly things out of my face."

It's sad, but not surprising. People who live on the streets are often mistrustful and disoriented. "Really, you can have them," I say.

A hand grabs my shoulder from behind and spins me around. It's Dad. He speaks through clenched teeth. "What in the world are you doing, Saul?"

"I was just trying to give this poor man my shoes." Why is everybody so angry this evening?

He hurries me down the street, talking in an urgent whisper. "That's not a poor man. Did you check out the diamond stud earring he's wearing? Or the Rolex? Did you completely overlook the beautiful woman he's with?"

I look back. I hadn't noticed any of that before. The woman is gorgeous.

"Saul," Mom says. "That man has all the money he needs, and you're lucky you still have all your teeth. Do you realize what you've done? You really insulted him."

Slowly it dawns on me. Why had I totally misread this man? I had a picture of who I believed he was in my mind, and I ignored all the clues that could have showed me otherwise. I know better than that. "Yeah. I made a mistake. I guess my brain still isn't working exactly right."

"I guess not," Dad says. "Now, can you understand why your mom and I are still so concerned about you?"

"I guess so." I think about the experience all the way to the Eiffel Tower. When we get there I give my shoes to a man who's clearly thrilled to have them. I'm glad I can do something nice, but I'm a little bit worried about the holes in my reasoning this experience has exposed.

The next day we fly back to Monaco:

Blog From France
Contributed by Saul
Wednesday, 11 October 2006
Here I am in France … I am sorry I have not been writing my blog but my Internet is not working. While I was in the USA the Internet company was charging me 1,600 Euros a month. About 2000 dollars. My good friend/ banker saw this and canceled the payments right away. I never paid my normal 30 Euros a month so they cut off my service. Everything is going well. It is a dream to be back. I was very emotional to see my friends and even more emotional when I rode the big mountains in the area (Col de la Madone). I told my Dad to pinch me to make sure all was real. Last week I flew to team pictures with my Mom and Dad. It was great to see my team; it was like old times again. I got to go ride with the team twice. When I was Riding next to Thor I told him "it was like a dream." I now dream of the day I can race by his side again. To sum up my trip is easy. It has truly been awesome. I do not want to leave my French home, but I know I will be coming back. I guess patience is a virtue, but sometimes I feel like I am pushing patience limits. Thor was Racing Paris-Tours in my Raisin Hell Socks- Go Go Go Dreams Come True, Never quit fighting.
Saul

My parents and I are standing on the deck of my apartment watching the hustle and bustle below. "It really has been a wonderful trip, hasn't it, Mom?" I ask.

She shakes her head. "Are you kidding? This has been the trip from hell. The only worse one I ever took was when we went to Angers this April."

I have to look at her really closely before I'm certain she isn't kidding. "You haven't enjoyed yourself? I admit, everything hasn't been perfect, but it's been wonderful for me. You two aren't much for traveling, though, are you?"

She shakes her head. "That's a load of horse hockey, and you know it. I love to travel, Saul, but you're in your own little world and it's exhausting to me and your dad. You've been self-centered, tough to be around, and easily offended."

"Your brain has you thinking you're ready to live an independent life, but it's just not true," Dad says. "If your mom and I hadn't been running around behind you cleaning up messes and helping you avert disasters for the last several weeks, you'd have yourself killed by now. I'm certain of it. I can't even count the times you've broken the arm's length rule."

I can't believe my ears. I take another sip of my coffee. It's a triple espresso, and it's giving me just the jolt I need.

"And that's another thing," Dad says, pulling the cup from my hand. "Your caffeine consumption is totally out of control. It's got to stop."

"So does the nagging," I whisper.

"What?" Dad's tone is threatening.

"Never mind." I take my cup from him, head to my room, and slam the door.

*   *   *

As much as I want to remain in Europe, we eventually have to return home. I'm only able to tear myself away because I've been invited to the team camp in January and my parents have already agreed I can go. I might even be allowed to stay on my own for a week or so. That would be so fantastic. We're going to see what Dr. Bilsky thinks about that idea. Last time we talked he introduced me to someone and told them, "Everything's easy for Saul now." Maybe that means he'll soon be ready to give me more freedom.

Once we're in the air Mom tells me how worried she and dad had been that it would take a fight to get me on the plane. I don't like arguing with them, and I'm as happy as they are we didn't get all heated up about that. My parents truly are my best friends in the world. I wish we could get back to our old ways of not fighting.

A funny thing happens next. We land in Atlanta but our bikes don't. Apparently they love Europe as much as I do and they didn't want to return. Finally, after two hours of searching, I see them slide in through the oversized luggage doors.

I can't control my joy. "Mom! Mom!" I'm jumping up and down. "I found the bikes!"

She walks over looking exhausted. "Oh, Saul, what am I going to do with you? You're acting like a three-year-old. Calm down and let's go home."

Chapter Twenty

As fall turns to winter I continue to improve. We celebrate Mom's fiftieth birthday, Lionel and his family come to visit, reporters call several times a week, and a constant stream of friends uses our guest rooms. Life is busy, and good.

Every month I think to myself, I'm almost all the way back, and then I look at the previous month and I'm amazed I had the same thought when I was in so much worse of a condition.

I have the OLN special on tape, and I watch it again. My eyes look vacant, like I'm not all there. For me, I would say, it easily took four months for the fog to start lifting and seven months for it to go away. It still comes back now and then, but only when I'm extremely tired. Now the spark has returned to my eyes, and the happiness is coming back too. I look like the guy I used to be. I try to explain it in my blog:

The next day on a ride Lionel tells me something I find very interesting. "You know," he says, "your recovery is remarkable. I can still see you improving every day. Maybe I know why this is."

"Why?" I ask.

"I think that doctors in general don't understand athletes so well. They must think different about the possibilities for recovery because the athlete's mind and body is not the same as ordinary person. To me, you have proven that."

I think about his comment for a moment. "I don't know whether my career before the accident helped me or not, but I will say this. Many doctors I've met underestimate the power of exercise and especially the power of the bike. God made our bodies for moving, not for sitting on the couch. Exercise heals."

"You're right about that," Lionel says. After a moment he speaks again. "There's something else I've been meaning to say to you."

His tone tells me this will be important. "What is it?"

He looks me in the eye. "Keep dreaming."

A smile spreads over my face. We both know that all these years Lionel meant "American Dreamer" as a friendly criticism. I know he's not going to apologize for doubting me, and he doesn't need to. It's enough to know that now he can see dreams do pay off. We each shape our future through our own imaginations.

*   *   *

A few days later I'm honored to play a role in a wonderful event. An anonymous citizen has donated twenty-five bikes to the Boys & Girls Clubs of Dalton/Whitfield Counties. They've asked me to be the presenter at Saul Raisin Woods Mountain Bike Park.

I'm standing there as the school bus pulls in. The kids tumble out and run to their bikes with smiles on their faces that touch my heart. They ride with unbridled freedom and joy. One little boy says to me, "I feel like I'm flying."

"I know the feeling," I say. "Fly away!"

Thank you to whoever donated the bikes. You touched the lives of many children and made a difference. We need more gestures like that to help kids. Bicycles are a great way for children in tough situations to escape the hardships of their lives and ride free.

A week later I receive a similar honor. I'm invited to take part in the Spin for Kids Ride to raise money that will send children with special needs or serious illnesses to Camp Twin Lakes. It's a wonderful place with a fantastic mission. Organizations like Camp Twin Lakes make the world a better place. One day I plan to set up a foundation that will help accomplish goals like these.

The beginning of that organization just might be the Raisin Hope ride to benefit victims of brain and spinal-cord injuries. With the help of the people who turned the Tour de Georgia into one of the world's best bicycle races, we've decided to put on this event to commemorate the one-year anniversary of my crash. We see it as an opportunity to make chain lube out of axle grease, so to speak.

In keeping with my usual massive flurry of activity, I head to Atlanta again, this time for an eight-hour neuropsychological exam. It's a battery of tests that will determine where I stand in the thinking department.

In case you didn't know, I've never been much of a fan of tests, so this isn't exactly my cup of cappuccino. By the time the test is over, though, I'm feeling very good. It was easy. I think that means I'm going to be okay. I only hope my answers don't somehow prove I'm psycho. I sure don't want anybody sticking me back in some hospital to try to cure my personality.

Meanwhile my rides are getting longer and tougher. On November 20 I put in 110 miles, crossing Fort Mountain and back. Most days I spend at least four hours on the road, but some days I spend as many as six. The only days I don't ride are when my parents forbid it. They feel I'm too obsessed with my bike so they throw in mandatory breaks now and then.

A couple of days later, I return to Atlanta for the results of my neuropsych exam. Dr. Smalls conducted the test and will analyze the results for me. I can sense her happiness bubbling beneath the surface as she delivers the good news. "It's a pleasure to report results like yours, Saul. I don't get to tell people these sorts of things often enough."

I smile. "I knew I'd done well."

Dr. Smalls has a round face and a porcelain complexion. She uses precise words as she shows me the many categories and where I ranked on a chart based on my age and education level. "You're average or above average on every category except two. In those you remain mildly to moderately below average. That's to be expected at this point. In fact, I've never seen anybody with the amount of damage you had do as well as you've done so soon after their accident."

What can I say? "I've been blessed." Even as I speak I feel intensely determined to get those two lagging categories back up where they belong.

The areas of concern are impulsivity and processing speed. The impulsivity issues are evident in my attention span. It's challenging for me to focus on things I find boring for long periods of time. I think that might have been one of my weaknesses before the accident, but now I need to overcome it. Maybe I'll have to start forcing myself to watch political debates on television or something.

Processing speed has to do with things like my ability to find the right word in the midst of a heated argument. It could also suggest my ability to make quick decisions on a bike isn't what it should be, though I would be very surprised if that's the case. I can feel the delays in thinking when I argue. On a bicycle, decisions flow instinctually.

"Knowing exactly what my weaknesses are really helps because now I can devote my energy to solving them," I say.

Dr. Smalls nods. "I'm glad you're thinking that way, but don't overlook the good news. If you were a normal business person or a college student I would release you to go back to work or school."

I squeeze my chin between a thumb and forefinger. "But I'm a pro cyclist, and a problem in either attention span or decision making could have serious repercussions, right?"

"Right. That's why I'm not yet releasing you."

If you ask me, some of the most important remaining problems I have are things the test didn't even pick up. For instance, I used to have a doodle book where I drew pictures and wrote poems whenever I needed to distract myself. I have a very difficult time doing that anymore. It's as if I lost my imagination in my crash. That's something I'd sure like to get back.

Other things have changed too, but they aren't necessarily bad. I'm more talkative than before, and that's saying a lot because I was already a talker. I'm quicker to connect with people, no matter who they are. I love getting to know others, and I'm especially attracted to children. They have so many wonderful things to say about the world. Also, I'm an open book now. There's information within this story I might have protected with my life before my accident. Now it's become stuff I want others to know. No secrets.

But imagination and any other deficits I might believe I have don't matter much as far as satisfying the doctors is concerned. The important thing is passing the tests. That's how the rules are set up, and I realize I have to play by them. First I have to satisfy the doctors here in America that I'm well enough to be released. Then I have to satisfy the Crédit Agricole doctors that I'm in good enough shape, physically and mentally, to race a bike. As competent as I feel on a bicycle, I need to use the tests as they are designed to prove there's no reason for concern, even though the tests have nothing to do with bikes. I'm not complaining, but I sure would love to take an on-the-bike test. I'd score way above average on that.

I'll bet my training companions would agree. On November 27 I complete my toughest ride since the accident. It's an eight-hour epic, crossing eight mountain passes totaling 20,000 feet of climbing. My power meter registers 120 miles covered by the time we conquer the final brutally steep peak of Brasstown Bald. I burn over 5000 calories in the process, but my legs are never even in pain. Ever since my accident, no matter how hard I go, I'm unable to hurt myself on a bike.

Off the bike I'm practically an expert at hurting myself, though. One morning I take a seat at the Stone Cup Coffee Shop in Chattanooga. A gorgeous girl walks in, opens her laptop and starts working.

"I like your pink computer," I say.

She looks up. Her green eyes sparkle. "Thanks."

I play a hunch. "I'll bet you're French."

She laughs. "No. I'm from Chattanooga."

For reasons I can't explain, I felt sure she was European.

Then she adds, "I'm going to college in a European city called Angers. I'll bet you've never heard of it."

My jaw drops open. I fall into the chair beside her. What are the chances? This meeting feels like destiny. In French I say, "No way. I spent a month in Angers this summer."

"Isn't it beautiful," she answers, also in French.

I shrug. "I wouldn't know."

By the time we leave the coffee shop she knows a bit of my story, and I know some of hers. More important, her number is programmed into my cell phone. Her name is Liz, and I'm so excited to get to know her I call and ask her out the very next day.

She accepts. I'm so nervous I can't calm down. My palms are damp with sweat and I'm jittery all over. It's as if I've never gone out on a date before. Every new experience is like being reborn.

The moment I'm with Liz though, she calms me down. We spend a wonderful evening in downtown Chattanooga, but as soon as our date is over I want to be with her again. The next day I call her ten times or more. We chat a couple of times but mostly I talk to her answering service.

Finally my phone beeps with an incoming text message. It's from Liz. "Saul, you are making me extremely nervous. Please leave me alone."

Damn. The words really hurt, but it's all my fault. I blew it. I was worried I'd forgotten how to date, and now I have proof. I stalked this poor girl, and I feel terrible about it. I've been so anxious to rebuild a normal life, sometimes I forget that certain things can't be done at full speed. Man, do I ever have a lot of things to relearn.

That thought is déjà vu. I remember the exact same idea crossing my mind while at the Shepherd Center. A woman had been on my mind that time, too. Thinking it again is like unexpectedly passing a unique landmark for the second time on a country road. There's only one possible explanation. I'm lost. I need someone to lead me out of this place. I turn to my family yet again.

As the holidays arrive, I'm feeling gratitude as I never have before. This is a season I easily could have missed. I all but checked out of my room on this beautiful blue planet back in April of this year. Now I'm seizing life every day and sucking out all the sweet nectar I can get.

I'm thrilled as the relatives gather at Gram Cracker's home for a turkey dinner. Our family is big, loud, and happy. I love the chaos that rolls in the door along with my little cousins. I pretend to be a monster, and they run away in mock fear. The game ends as usual with lots of smiles and hugs.

Sitting at the dinner table I scold my aunts and uncles for waiting until disaster struck to finally visit me in Europe. "Next time you have to come to France when I'm healthy," I say. "Not when I'm lying in bed dying. I'll show you the beauty of the country and the people instead of the ugliness of a hospital room, plus you won't have to pay ridiculous amounts for last-minute airline tickets."

I act like I'm mad at them, but they know the truth. I'm so grateful, I wouldn't be able to control my tears if we started talking about the sacrifices they made to support my parents and help me get well. After the evening ends I'm making mental notes of all my blessings.

I'm thankful to Crédit Agricole, the greatest cycling team in the world, and to all my sponsors who've stood by me and made my recovery possible. I'm grateful for my friends and supporters for helping me see deeper inside myself than I ever could have on my own, and for pushing me to recognize my true capabilities. There are no limits to my gratitude.

At various holiday parties I get to hug many of the wonderful people who've made my life so rich. At one gathering, my sweet Aunt Teresa, who I vividly recall seeing in one of those brief flashes of consciousness while lying in the Angers hospital bed, looks me in the eye and says, "In my life I had never seen a miracle … until now. It's you." How can I possibly dream small dreams when people like that inhabit my world?

But more than anybody else, I'm thankful for my Mom and Dad. We're still butting heads, but it's done with love. I put them through a horrible nightmare this year. In some ways their experiences were worse than mine. I was benefited, in a bizarre way, by not being able to comprehend how bad things were when they were at their worst.

I've come to realize their sometimes suffocating concern for me is an absolutely natural reaction to the trauma I've put them through. In fact, it's a very real symptom of my injury in its own right, just like impulsivity and slowed processing speed. I see it as a side-effect of the accident, and I'm now responsible for attacking it head on and conquering it. It will take a million little demonstrations of the return of my competence for their comfort level to return to normal. One slight glitch could reset the process again. That's just the way it is, and I'm prepared to deal with it.

Mom and Dad have talked to me a lot about their experiences in Angers. Whenever they mention the first time they saw me in that ICU bed, their eyes fill with tears. While talking about how I looked and the fear they felt for me, they say they can't express the emotions that overwhelmed their hearts, but I understand. They've both told me they would gladly have traded me places, and I know it's the truth. They are the best friends I could ever possibly have.

These are the reasons my parents might never again be able to calmly watch me race a bike. There is no way to cure their fear that I might one day have another serious fall. While staying upright on a bike is mostly within my control, it's totally out of theirs. Together, on an ongoing basis, we'll have to decide whether the risks are worth the rewards. They've earned the right to have a voice in the decision process, and their input is valuable to me. I don't think they'll ever ask me to quit riding or racing my bike forever, but if they do I'm sure their reasons will be legitimate, and I'll abide by their decision.

I can make them another promise: If I can't get back to the level I was at before the accident by the end of the 2007 season, it will be time to turn the page. If it happens, I'll learn to be okay with that.

I've been granted such an inconceivably wonderful life. I know I'm among the luckiest people to ever walk the face of the earth. I often wonder what God has in store for me next.

Chapter Twenty-One

Team camp and France
Contributed by Saul
Wednesday, 10 January 2007
I leave today for 3 weeks for team camp and France. I am so excited. I do not have
Internet in my apartment but I will try to keep everyone up to date. Look forward to
some pictures from France and Team camp.

My parents and I fly into Nice again. It's amazing to think back upon how much has happened since I was last here in October. At that time I thought I had almost returned to normal. Now, when I look back, I can see how far I still had to go. Today I feel like I'm very close to being a new, improved version of the old Saul, but in three months will I look back on today and see shortcomings? Probably.

It's incredible to think back even farther, to the Crédit Agricole January team camp one year ago. I remember how excited I was to begin competing, and I vividly recall how thrilled I was about my victorious start to the season. Then came April and my world went blank. How could so much fit into a single year? When I was a little kid years used to seem so long, but nothing like this. 2006 lasted beyond forever for me.

At the airport Lionel is waiting for us. "No crying this time, my friend," I say. He chuckles. "Yes. We made a scene last time, didn't we?"

We hug and walk to his car. My parents are smiling. I ride my bike all five days until team camp, often with Axel Merckx, sometimes with Dad. Life is starting to feel normal. I can go riding whenever I want without permission, but I always choose to tell somebody my plans. My parents' trust in me is increasing every day. At the condo on the border of Monaco we are always really relaxed. Once again we feel like the family we used to be.

During one ride I get to talk with my former teammate, Geoffroy LeQuatre. He tells me a chilling story. One day, after I fell into the coma, a rumor that I was brain dead swept the cycling world. It frightens me to think about.

I almost wish I could scratch the year 2006 from the history books and go on without it. Mom and Dad would not know Angers from Albany. I wouldn't have my victory in Malaysia, but who cares. The pain of losing Daniela would be an unknown sensation. I don't love her anymore, but the loss hurts now more than ever. Is that because my mind is finally maturing to the point where it can deal with what happened but still can't make sense of our breakup, or is this just the nature of lost love?

Then I think about the good things I would have missed this last year. I might never have been aware of the wonderful people and mission behind the

Shepherd Center and other places like it. Some of the biggest heroes in my world today would still be unknown to me. And I wouldn't know our disabled friends and neighbors are actually angels on earth.

I guess the only part of last year I really want to delete is the misery others experienced at my expense. Pain is the thing nearly everyone would want to remove from their lives, though, and it obviously can't be done. It comes with positives, anyway. I know I'll live a better life because of what I've gone through. My experiences have taught me to value things in a new way. I'll never forget the lessons that have recently been pounded into my head.

On January 15, I travel to La Londe Les Maures for team camp. It's two hours west on the Mediterranean coast. We aren't technically racing, but each time we climb a mountain we ride hard because everyone wants to test themselves and get to the top as quickly as they can. I surprise myself and my teammates when I spend the entire first day near the front of the group and reach the top of the toughest climb with only one other teammate.

That night we have a meeting to discuss objectives. At the end of the meeting the team directeur gives me the opportunity to say a few words. "Guys, it's so great to be back. Being at camp is going to be my best therapy yet. It's very important that if you see me do anything out of the ordinary whether on or off the bike, socially or physically please tell me. I need to know. I won't take it as an insult. You'll be helping me become aware of things I might not yet be able to see. I want to become better than I was before, and this is the only way to do it."

We ride long and hard every day. For the first time since my injury my legs hurt. It's all good.

After one brutal ride Thor Hushovd says to me, "Wow, Saul. You're amazing!" I can't explain how good a statement like that makes me feel coming from a guy like him.

That evening *VeloNews* calls for an interview. "How are you feeling?" the reporter asks.

"To get back to the training camp is like walking on the moon. That's how far out of reach riding a bike seemed after my accident," I say. "To think I could be at the team camp right now would be just like saying 'I'm going to go for a walk on the moon.'"

It's not an exaggeration. Being where I am now was an inconceivable dream nine months ago.

Next I have an interview with *L'Équipe Magazine*, the major sports daily in France. "Would you like me to set up a meeting with the doctors in Angers?" the reporter asks.

"Are you kidding? I can't wait to meet the people who saved me and to see where I spent the missing month of my life."

"Then I'll arrange it," she says. "I'll call you with the details in a few days."

Team camp feels almost like being in a tough stage race, with the same military routine. Every morning we wake at 7:30. Breakfast is at 8:00, and the ride starts at 9:30. Anytime we need food, water, clothing, or mechanical assistance we drop back to the team cars. After around 200 kilometers on the bike we return to the hotel for another meal, a massage, and dinner. By the end of each day I have little energy left. Getting to bed is my main priority, but one evening I find the time to post a message to my blog:

Team Camp
Contributed by Saul
Saturday, 20 January 2007
Ok, here I am team at camp Londe here in the South of France. You should see the eyes on my teammates when I attack them up the climbs. Not only do I surprise them but I surprise my self. It is a more than a dream being here. It is proof that dreams come true. We are riding 5 to 6 hours a day. This is the first time my legs have been sore since the accident. Look forward to team camp pictures I hope to have them posted soon. My Raisin Hope ride should be posted soon so that you can register online. My Best, Saul

They save the toughest ride for the last day of camp. It's another 200-kilometer haul over a stretch of brutal road. At the base of the final mountain, where the grade kicks up to about eight percent, Patrice Halgand goes to the front and starts riding tempo, trying to put everybody in pain. He's a former Tour de France stage winner and a strong mountain climber. His move ignites something in me. I want him to know his pace isn't hurting me. I come around him and take over the pace-making. The gradient kicks up another increment, but I don't slow my cadence or shift to an easier gear. I don't look back, either. I figure if anybody is strong enough to follow me they will. Otherwise I'll ride alone.

The road gradually ascends the canyon wall. It becomes steeper until the gradient is around twelve percent. Eventually the route starts traversing a treeless slope, and that gives me the chance to glance over my shoulder and see the carnage behind. I'm alone. The remainder of the Crédit Agricole Cycling Team has apparently decided they don't want to go this hard. They must be back there somewhere, struggling to overcome the hill as a group. The pressure I've put them under motivates me even further. I stand on my pedals and dance up the mountain. My stroke is smooth and efficient. I inhale air in long, rhythmic breaths. My heart pounds mightily as it rushes fresh oxygen to my burning muscles. I feel plenty of pain now, and I love it. In fact, I love it so much I click to a more difficult gear and enjoy even more. I'm flying.

The last kilometer of the climb wends its way through the artificial canyons created by the builders of a quaint medieval town. On the summit ridge, a stone fortress commands the valley below. That's my objective. I bear down on the pedals, hardly noticing the village I'm passing through, and finally gain the summit with no teammates in sight. In this moment I finally know with total certainty I'm going to reach the elite levels of this sport again.

I unclip from my left pedal, set my foot on the ground, and wait for the others to arrive. A beautiful phrase crosses my mind: *Profite de la vie*: profit from life. There've been dark hours along the way, but in the end, I've learned invaluable lessons.

Nothing can stop me now. Three minutes later when my team arrives as a group, mouths agape, I can tell they know it too.

*   *   *

Mom and Dad arrive to take me home, but before we leave the directeurs, Serge and Denis, sit us down for a quick meeting.

"How did Saul do?" Mom asks.

Denis does the talking because his English is good. "Physically he is ready to race. I asked around team and everybody agrees. Saul is doing great."

"Were there any problems?" Dad asks.

Denis nods. "The only one that concerns me is concentration. Sometimes Saul's mind wanders, and he cannot get it back. He must work on that. He needs to prove he can stay focused before we can allow him to race."

It's true that my mind wanders when I get bored. I never get bored on the bike, though. Nevertheless, I'm going to put all my effort into improving my concentration. Any upgrade I make can only help me.

"Anything else?" Mom asks Denis.

He smiles. "Saul is more affectionate, but this is not a bad thing. We think he is doing fantastic, but there is no need for him to rush back. He should take his time."

Statements like that remind me what a great team I'm on. They pay me well, but they continue to be more concerned with my health than their investment. That sort of philosophy is rare.

Before we leave I get the call from *L'Équipe Magazine*. "Our meeting at the hospital in Angers is set for Tuesday afternoon. I've booked a Tuesday morning flight for you and your parents."

"I can't wait."

"Would you like to hear what the doctor said when I called to schedule this meeting?" the reporter asks.

"Sure," I say.

"I told him you were in France at a team camp. He said, 'It's miraculous he can be back here watching his old team ride. I bet he is enjoying that.' I explained to him you weren't watching, you were riding, and you were one of the strongest men there."

"What did he say?"

The reporter chuckles. "He said, 'Who are you and why do you tell me these lies?' It took me a long time to convince him that it was the truth."

*   *   *

On Tuesday we arrive in Angers. As we walk the cobbled lanes and see the sights, it's surreal how familiar everything feels. Other than the time after my accident, I once spent a night here while racing in the Tour de l'Avenir, but I've never walked these streets before. It feels like I know the place, though. I guess I've talked with my parents about Angers so much it has become familiar in my mind.

Part way up a narrow, winding alley I notice a sign that says Logis Ozanam. "This is where you stayed?"

Mom and Dad nod.

When we enter the front door, the volunteer tending the front desk immediately recognizes my parents. "*Vous êtes revenus!*" she says.

"She's happy you've returned," I translate.

They nod and point to me. "With our son."

"*Avec notre fils,*" I tell the woman.

She nods politely, and then suddenly she comprehends the meaning. Her eyes light up. "You? You are they boy they were praying for?"

I nod.

"I prayed too," she says.

"Thank you." I smile. "Your prayers were answered."

She looks at me incredulously and says, "Well, of course they were. I was praying to God."

I now know what pure faith looks like, and it's embodied in this woman. I give her a hug. "Can they show me around?"

"Yes, of course," the woman says.

Mom points out the door to the room where they stayed. I wish I could look inside, but there's a new resident. Eventually I walk upstairs to see the room Daniela used. I look into the simple shared bathroom at the end of the hall. I inspect the books in the sitting room and walk out to experience the lovely little garden. If ever a place came directly from heaven, this is it.

As time for our meeting with the doctors nears we walk down the route my parents took so many times to the hospital. We enter through the domed cathedral which served as a major navigational landmark while my parents walked endlessly around the town to relieve their stress.

Strolling through the corridors I can already feel the love. This is a special building.

"It's cleaner than when we were here," Dad says.

Mom nods. "They've repainted, too."

When we reach the prearranged meeting place we check in with the secretary. Soon a gray haired man wearing hospital greens leads a group of nurses from the ICU. They all have huge smiles on their faces. The man extends a hand. "Je m'appele Docteur Chapillon," he says.

"This is the heart specialist, but he doesn't speak English so we never got to know him well," Mom says.

Dr. Chapillon touches my cheek with his hand. He speaks in French. "You are looking well, Saul. Very well." His eyes dart around my face and body, inspecting me the way a concerned mother would study her injured child. He touches my arms and hands, my forehead and chest. He keeps inspecting my back. I'm overwhelmed by his compassion.

The nurses are looking at me in the same way, their eyes jumping left and right, taking in every detail. I feel like I'm their child … their work of art … their miracle.

"You are my heroes," I tell them. "Thank you for bringing me back to life. Thank you for taking such good care of my parents. They needed you so badly."

"Can I have your autograph?" a nurse asks. "I want to prove to those who couldn't be here today that you really came."

"Of course." I sign a piece of paper for her and include a short note. "I wish they could have made it."

Dr. Chapillon has to leave, but first he gives me a huge hug. He holds tight, as if he doesn't want to let me go. The nurses are shaking my parents' hands warmly, and everybody is smiling. We're practically drowning in love.

Other medical personnel come by to say hello. I'm taking in all the faces. Finally I see one I remember. "You were the man who kept pushing that terrible tube down my nose and into my lungs," I say. "It hurt so damn bad."

He smiles sheepishly. "I'm sorry."

I put my arm around him. "Don't be sorry. You did your job, and that's why I'm here today. Thank you."

His smile becomes happier. "You're welcome."

Another doctor arrives and immediately greets my parents in English. They're thrilled to see him.

"This is Doctor Fesard," Mom says. "He speaks the best English of any doctor here. He spent so much time trying to explain your situation to us."

I take his hand. "I can never thank you enough, not just for how you helped me, but for the way you treated my parents."

He puts a hand on my shoulder. He's looking at me the same wonderful way the others have. "We're very proud of you, Saul. I check your web site often."

"Don't we live in an amazing world?" I ask. "The Internet is fabulous. I'm so honored you read my site."

We talk for a long time, and I soon learn the man is both a brain specialist and a heart specialist.

"Have you had your heart checked?" he asks.

I nod. "Yes. It's big, and it's in perfect condition."

"I believe you do have a big heart." He grins wide and taps me on the chest. "But it's also a little bit to the left."

A studious looking man approaches. He reminds me of Dexter, the boy genius, from the cartoon called Dexter's Laboratory. Dr. Fesard puts a hand on each of our shoulders. "Saul, meet the surgeon who saved your life, Professor Philippe Mercier."

I love this man instantly. It's amazing to think he opened my skull, fixed what had gone wrong, and put me back together. With his open palm he directs us to a vacant conference room. He takes a seat at the table, and I sit down next to him.

"There are so many questions I want to ask you," I say.

He smiles. "Ask."

I decide to start with the one that's uppermost on my mind. "Do you think I'll be able to race a bike again?"

"You're already proving it," he says.

"But will it be more dangerous for him?" Mom asks.

Professor Mercier shakes his head. "It's always dangerous to crash, especially if he hits his head, but it's no more dangerous for Saul than for anybody else."

A wave of relief flows through my body. Who would know the answer to this question better than the man who touched my brain with his own two hands? "After team camp the directeurs told my parents I had the physical strength to race, but they want me to improve my concentration. How can I do that?"

He thinks for a moment. "Have you tried Sudoku puzzles? I think they would be good for you."

Dad kicks me under the table. I glance his way and he gives me an 'I told you so' look.

"I've been trying Sudoku. I'll try harder," I say.

"Any more questions?" he asks.

"We're still confused about how much of my brain was removed," I say.

His eyes widen in surprise. "None. You are whole."

Mom's brow furrows. "But an American neurosurgeon told us the scans show a hole in one spot. Not only that, we were told some of Saul's brain had been removed in our very first briefing at this hospital."

Professor Mercier touches my skull where the incision was made. "The hematoma put extreme pressure on Saul's brain. Some of the material may have become compressed. I didn't extract any brain matter, though. We only removed blood and clots."

My smile probably covers most of my face. What a relief to finally know for certain that none of my brain was removed. What an honor to sit next to a man like this. "I'm in the room with greatness. I look up to you the way some people look up to me."

He laughs. "Thank you. I'm surrounded by greatness, too, and not just you." His sweeping motion indicates the hospital and its staff.

How right he is.

"I want to thank you from the bottom of my heart for coming here today, Saul," Professor Mercier says. "Your visit gives strength and inspiration to all my colleagues. It shows them they did their jobs well, and it boosts their morale."

He's thanking me? "From now on, whenever I climb a hill on a bicycle, I'll feel every member of your staff lifting me. The things you've done for me will push me to ride harder and faster every day than I did the day before. The thanks go to the wonderful people in this hospital."

Professor Mercier shakes his head. "The staff here does not seek credit for saving lives. This is what they do, and no praise is wanted or needed. We are just doing our jobs."

"You do your jobs well," I say.

He smiles. "Thank you, Saul. Now, I would like to suggest just one objective for you."

"What is it?"

He speaks in flowing French. "*Allez Saul. Vas-y et gagne le Tour de France!*"

I almost jump out of my seat. I have permission from the man who saved my life, one of the greatest surgeons in the world, to chase my dream. It's go time! "Thank you! I will!"

Mom looks confused by my sudden enthusiasm. "What did he say?"

I translate the doctor's words. "He said, 'Go Saul. You go and win the Tour de France!'"

The End

Acknowledgments

This story would have been impossible to write without the tireless help of Jim and Yvonne Raisin and the access to records they provided. It was extremely difficult for them to live through these experiences once. Going over things again and again to perfect the book was a lot to ask, but they did it willingly.

We're grateful to Dr. Michael Paré for translating the French medical records and granting use of his documentation. Dr. Gary Shields, Dr. Charles Rich, and Dr. Jack Sanders provided invaluable help with medical research.

The experts at NovelPro, especially Jamie Lankford, Erik Giles, Pat Brown, and Rashmi Shankar took the manuscript to a new level. Anne Lemmon provided her usual expert line-editing advice.

Many thanks to those who allowed us to include their pictures in the book, and also to Fran Platt for the great job of laying out the photo pages. We're indebted to Bob Swingle and Shannon Bodie at Lightbourne for going above and beyond the call of duty to produce the best cover possible.

Thanks go to Dianne Hale for her enthusiastic assistance with the wide variety of tasks necessary to get this book to the marketplace. Eleanor Divver, Lynda Terry, and Marie Kayser all worked tirelessly on our behalf. We're also grateful to Cynthia Murphy, Mark Voigt, Mary Rowles and the other professionals at Independent Publishers Group for their critical assistance in creating and distributing this book.

Finally, we'd like to thank our families and friends for putting up with the challenges that resulted from a project of this scale under tight deadlines. We've asked far more of them than we have a right to. We're extremely grateful for their incredible support.

Sincerely,

Saul Raisin & Dave Shields

For updates on Saul, please visit www.SaulRaisin.com.

For a resource list, please visit www.TourdeLife.com

Other cycling books by Dave Shields:

For more information, please visit www.DaveShields.com.